Rethinking Urban Sprawl

MOVING TOWARDS SUSTAINABLE CITIES

OECD
BETTER POLICIES FOR BETTER LIVES

Please cite this publication as:
OECD (2018), *Rethinking Urban Sprawl: Moving Towards Sustainable Cities*, OECD Publishing, Paris.
http://dx.doi.org/10.1787/9789264189881-en

ISBN 978-92-64-18982-9 (print)
ISBN 978-92-64-18988-1 (PDF)
ISBN 978-92-64-29795-1 (e-pub)

Photo credits: Cover © hfzimages/Shutterstock.com.

Corrigenda to OECD publications may be found on line at: *www.oecd.org/about/publishing/corrigenda.htm*.

Foreword

Home to more than half of the world's population, cities are the engines of economic growth and employment. The 200 largest urban areas generate more than 60% of jobs and growth in the OECD. With the share of world population living in urban areas projected to reach 70% by 2050 (86% in OECD countries), the importance of cities will only increase.

Cities are increasingly interconnected, global arenas and face a range of environmental, economic and social challenges. They are responsible for over two-thirds of energy consumption and more than 70% of CO_2 emissions globally. The OECD has estimated that outdoor air pollution could cause 6 to 9 million premature deaths a year by 2060, with cities particularly hard hit. Cities face a wide range of interconnected challenges, such as road congestion, lack of housing affordability, and social exclusion. Urban sprawl, a particular form of urban development, is often cited as a driver of these challenges.

Rethinking Urban Sprawl: Moving Towards Sustainable Cities *offers a new perspective on urban sprawl, contributing to a better understanding of its evolution, causes and consequences. It provides new insights on the design, delivery and implementation of policies to shift urban development patterns towards more sustainable trajectories. This will be crucial to achieve the Sustainable Development Goals and meet the objectives of the Paris Agreement.*

In particular, the report looks at past and current urban development patterns of OECD cities and establishes a new set of indicators that quantify the multiple dimensions of urban sprawl. It shows that cities in most of the examined OECD countries have become more fragmented, and the share of low-density areas in population and urban land coverage has increased. While there are differences between and within countries, urban form is generally evolving in a way that induces higher car dependency and longer commuting distances. Such a development pattern also substantially increases the per capita costs of providing public services. Water, sanitation, electricity, public transport, waste management, policing and other services that are key for well-being are much more expensive to provide in fragmented areas of low-density.

Therefore, coherent and targeted policy action is urgently needed from different levels of government to steer urban development towards more sustainable pathways. Policy instruments for greener and more cost-effective urban transport, such as appropriate pricing of car travel and parking, can be particularly effective in addressing the environmental consequences of urban sprawl in the short run. Land-use policy reforms promoting socially desirable levels of population density, such as relaxing maximum density restrictions and incentivising developers to provide public infrastructure for new constructions, can bear fruit in the longer run.

How cities develop over the next years will determine progress on addressing key environmental, economic and social challenges, including climate change and access to affordable housing. This report provides an important step towards assessing the state and implications of urban growth patterns, and identifies policies to steer cities towards inclusive and green growth.

Angel Gurría
OECD Secretary-General

Acknowledgements

This report is an output of the OECD Environment Policy Committee and its Working Party on Integrating Environmental and Economic Policies. The report was carried out under the overall responsibility of Shardul Agrawala, Head of the Environment and Economy Integration Division.

The report was authored by Ioannis Tikoudis, Walid Oueslati, Alexandros Dimitropoulos and Lara Engelfriet of the OECD Environment Directorate. Walid Oueslati co-ordinated and oversaw work on the report. The authors of the individual chapters were:

Chapter 1	Alexandros Dimitropoulos, Ioannis Tikoudis, Walid Oueslati.
Chapter 2	Ioannis Tikoudis, Walid Oueslati, Alexandros Dimitropoulos.
Chapter 3	Ioannis Tikoudis, Lara Engelfriet, Walid Oueslati, Alexandros Dimitropoulos.
Chapter 4	Ioannis Tikoudis, Alexandros Dimitropoulos, Walid Oueslati.
Chapter 5	Alexandros Dimitropoulos, Ioannis Tikoudis, Walid Oueslati.

Tobias Udsholt provided valuable inputs and suggestions and improved the dissemination of the work. Elizabeth Del Bourgo, Gabriella Scaduto-Mendola, Stéphanie Simonin-Edwards and Janine Treves provided guidance throughout the editorial process. Katjusha Boffa, Soojin Jeong, Jacqueline Maher and Aziza Perriére provided administrative support.

The authors are grateful to the delegates to the Working Party on Integrating Environmental and Economic Policies and the Environment Policy Committee who provided valuable comments and feedback during the preparation of the report. The authors would like to thank the following OECD colleagues for providing insightful comments on earlier drafts of the report: Shardul Agrawala, Rudiger Ahrend, Ivan Haščič, Kurt van Dender and Paolo Veneri. Feedback and comments from Simon Upton (former OECD Environment Director) are gratefully acknowledged. The authors also greatly appreciate inputs and comments from Jan Brueckner (University of California at Irvine), Elena Irwin (Ohio State University), Eric Koomen (VU University Amsterdam), Colin Price (Colin Price Free-lance Academic Services), and JunJie Wu (Oregon State University).

This report is part of a broader project undertaken by the OECD Environment Directorate on Spatial Planning Instruments and the Environment (SPINE).

Table of contents

Executive summary ... 11

Chapter 1. **The policy challenge of urban sprawl** ... 15
1.1. Urban sprawl is different from urbanisation ... 16
1.2. Why is a new perspective on urban sprawl needed? ... 17
1.3. How does the new perspective presented in this report help address the policy challenge of urban sprawl? ... 18
1.4. Navigation through the report ... 22
References ... 23

Part I

Urban Sprawl – Definition and measurement

Chapter 2. **Urban sprawl as a multidimensional phenomenon** ... 27
2.1. Introduction ... 28
2.2. The multiple dimensions of urban sprawl ... 28
2.3. Summary ... 35
Notes ... 36
References ... 36

Chapter 3. **Sprawl in OECD urban areas** ... 37
3.1. Introduction ... 38
3.2. Background literature ... 38
3.3. Data ... 41
3.4. Cross-country analyses of urban sprawl indicators ... 48
3.5. Country-level analysis ... 65
3.6. Summary ... 66
Notes ... 67
References ... 68

Appendix 3.A. Mathematical exposition of urban sprawl indicators ... 70

Appendix 3.B. Country sheets ... 79

Part II

Consequences of urban sprawl and implications for policy makers

Chapter 4. **Causes and consequences of urban sprawl** ... 113
4.1. Introduction ... 114
4.2. Urban sprawl drivers ... 114

4.3. Effects of urban sprawl 122
4.4. Concluding remarks 137
Notes.... 137
References 137

Chapter 5. **Steering urban development to more sustainable pathways** 143
5.1. Introduction 144
5.2. Taking steps to reverse unsustainable urban development patterns 145
5.3. Following an integrated approach to make urban development more sustainable 160
5.4. Conclusions 162
Notes.... 163
References 163

Boxes

3.1. Densification and suburbanisation in Santiago, Chile (1990-2014).... 56
4.1. The determinants of urban sprawl in monocentric cities: some empirical evidence.... 115
5.1. Greenbelts and urban growth boundaries 147
5.2. Land value taxes 150

Tables

2.1. Characterisation of urban sprawl 30
3.1. Indicators of urban sprawl 48
4.1. Summary of studies on transport mode choice and urban form 124
4.2. Summary of the relevant literature on urban form and cost of providing public services 127
4.3. Residential and commercial primary energy consumption, decomposed by end-use.... 128

Figures

2.1. Geographic distribution of population in two monocentric cities with different total land uptake.... 30
2.2. Geographic distribution of population in two monocentric cities with identical population and land uptake 31
2.3. Derivation of the land-allocation function from the geographic distribution of population in two cities with identical land uptake and population 32
2.4. Derivation of the population-allocation function from the geographic distribution of population in two cities with identical land uptake and total population 33
2.5. Polycentric versus monocentric cities of identical population.... 34
2.6. Urban areas of low and high fragmentation 35
2.7. Centralised and decentralised urban areas 35
3.1. Obtaining municipal urban cores from municipal delimitations and population density data 42
3.2. Obtaining functional urban areas from municipal urban cores 43

3.3. The decisive role of cross commuting flows in delimiting functional urban areas 44
3.4. From satellite images to land cover and settlement data 45
3.5. Constructing a population raster out of a built-up area raster and census population data 46
3.6. Raster cells of built areas and population density of a given functional urban area 47
3.7. Average population density in urban areas of 29 OECD countries, 2014 49
3.8. Evolution of average urban population density at the country level, 1990-2014 50
3.9. Percentage of urban population living in areas with a density of 150-1 500 people per km2 in 29 OECD countries, 2014 52
3.10. Evolution of country-specific percentages of urban population living in areas of density 150-1 500 people/km2, 1990-2014 53
3.11. Percentage of urban footprint with a density of 150-1 500 people per km2 in 29 OECD countries, 2014 54
3.12. Evolution of country-specific percentages of urban footprint with density of 150-1 500 people/km2, 1990-2014 55
3.13. Coefficient of variation of population density across OECD urban areas and countries, 2014 58
3.14. Evolution of the coefficient of variation of urban population density, 1990-2014 59
3.15. Number of urban fabric fragments per km2 across OECD countries, 2014 60
3.16. Evolution of fragmentation in OECD countries, 1990-2014 61
3.17. Number of high-density peaks in the urban areas of OECD countries, 2014 62
3.18. Evolution of polycentricity in OECD countries, 1990-2014 63
3.19. Share of urban population residing outside urban centres in OECD countries, 2014 64
3.20. Evolution of decentralisation in OECD countries, 1990-2014 65
3.A.1. Population and land cover raster cells 71
3.A.2. Share of population and urban surface below different density thresholds 72
3.A.3. Obtaining the total artificial area and fragments from land cover data 74
3.A.4. Obtaining the 3-km moving average filtered density from population density 75
3.A.5. Obtaining the number of centres (peak-density points) from population density data 76
3.B.1. Sprawl indicators Australia 81
3.B.2. Sprawl indicators Austria 82
3.B.3. Sprawl indicators Belgium 83
3.B.4. Sprawl indicators Canada 84
3.B.5. Sprawl indicators Chile 85
3.B.6. Sprawl indicators Czech Republic 86
3.B.7. Sprawl indicators Denmark 87
3.B.8. Sprawl indicators Finland 88
3.B.9. Sprawl indicators France 89
3.B.10. Sprawl indicators Germany 90
3.B.11. Sprawl indicators Greece 91
3.B.12. Sprawl indicators Hungary 92

3.B.13. Sprawl indicators Ireland 93
3.B.14. Sprawl indicators Italy........ 94
3.B.15. Sprawl indicators Japan 95
3.B.16. Sprawl indicators Korea 96
3.B.17. Sprawl indicators Luxembourg 97
3.B.18. Sprawl indicators Mexico 98
3.B.19. Sprawl indicators Netherlands 99
3.B.20. Sprawl indicators Norway........ 100
3.B.21. Sprawl indicators Poland 101
3.B.22. Sprawl indicators Portugal 102
3.B.23. Sprawl indicators Slovak Republic........ 103
3.B.24. Sprawl indicators Slovenia 104
3.B.25. Sprawl indicators Spain 105
3.B.26. Sprawl indicators Sweden 106
3.B.27. Sprawl indicators Switzerland........ 107
3.B.28. Sprawl indicators United Kingdom 108
3.B.29. Sprawl indicators United States........ 109
4.1. Alternative development options for a land parcel 117
4.2. The long-run effect of a uniform building height restriction on city shape and population density........ 119
4.3. The short- and long-run effect of a 10-km-wide buffer zone acting as an urban growth boundary 120
4.4. Different long-term effects of a property tax on city size 121
4.5. Population and job density in compact and polycentric cities 123
4.6. Commuting distances and car dependency in two monocentric cities........ 125
4.7. Changes in urban footprint and arable land under two mutually exclusive scenarios 130
4.8. Free-market and socially optimal allocation of periurban land 131
4.9. Urban fabric versus habitat fragmentation 135

Rethinking Urban Sprawl
Moving Towards Sustainable Cities

Executive summary

Cities are a major driver of economic growth and employment, but they are also the loci where many environmental, economic and social challenges will have to be tackled. In many urban areas, development patterns have increased emissions of greenhouse gases and air pollutants, caused congestion, increased the number of road traffic accidents, led to significant costs of providing public services, and contributed to social exclusion. A particular form of urban development, *urban sprawl*, is often blamed as an important cause of these problems. However, urban sprawl remains an elusive concept that is often defined simplistically (e.g. as low average population density in an urban area) or in terms of its causes or effects (e.g. in terms of car dependency).

This report provides a new perspective on the nature of urban sprawl, its causes and its consequences. This perspective, which is based on the multi-dimensionality of the phenomenon, also sets the foundations for the construction of new indicators of the concept. New datasets are then used to compute these indicators for more than 1 100 urban areas in 29 OECD countries in 1990, 2000 and 2014. The report relies on cross-city, cross-country and country-level analyses of these indicators to provide insights into the current situation and evolution of urban sprawl in OECD cities. Following this assessment, the report outlines policy options to steer urban development towards more sustainable paths.

What is urban sprawl? What are its causes and consequences?

This report defines urban sprawl as an urban development pattern characterised by low population density that can be manifested in multiple ways. Urban sprawl may exist even in urban areas where *average* population density is relatively high, if those areas contain large amounts of land where density is very low. The phenomenon is also manifested in development that is discontinuous, scattered and decentralised, for instance in cities where a substantial part of the population lives in a large number of unconnected pieces of urban land.

The concept of urban sprawl spans multiple dimensions reflecting how population density is distributed across the urban area and how fragmented urban land is. These different dimensions of sprawl are measured by different indicators in this report. Average urban population density, perhaps the most widely used indicator of sprawl, is a useful metric, but not sufficient to describe this complex phenomenon. In addition to it, this report characterises urban sprawl by: i) the variation of population density across an urban area; ii) the share of urban population living in areas where population density lies below specific thresholds (1 500, 2 500 and 3 500 inhabitants per km^2); iii) the share of urban land occupying areas where population density lies below these thresholds; iv) the degree of urban land fragmentation; v) the number of peak-density areas within a city (polycentricity); and vi) the percentage of population residing outside these areas of peak density (decentralisation).

Urban sprawl is caused by various demographic, economic, geographic, social and technological factors. These include rising real incomes, individual preferences favouring low-density development, natural barriers to contiguous urban development (e.g. mountains, rivers), and the technological progress in car manufacturing. Certain policies have also implicitly encouraged urban sprawl. Maximum density (e.g. building height) restrictions, persistent underpricing of the externalities of car use (due to e.g. the absence of road pricing and too low on-street parking prices) and massive investments in road infrastructure are only a few examples of such policies.

Urban sprawl has been shown to have significant environmental consequences manifested in higher emissions from road transport and loss of environmental amenities within and at the borders of urban areas. Its effects on biodiversity are very context-specific; discontinuous development patterns may be harmful to biodiversity if they are accompanied by a fragmentation of the natural habitats surrounding urban areas. Sprawl's economic consequences include significant pressures on local public finance, as it is more expensive to provide public services to more remote, low-density areas, as well as notable time losses due to congestion. Urban sprawl is also associated with social inequality and segregation, as the regulatory mechanisms that maintain low density may severely affect housing affordability.

Have OECD cities been sprawling?

The analysis reveals that cities in the OECD have developed along very different paths since 1990. While average urban population density has increased in slightly more than half of the 29 countries examined, the share of urban land containing areas of very low density levels has grown in 20 countries, and fragmentation of urban land has increased in 18. Urban areas in most OECD countries have become more fragmented, but also more centralised as a larger share of their population now live in peak-density areas. The variation of urban population density has also increased in the majority of countries. Differences between and within countries are significant, but some notable patterns of urban development at the country level can be summarised as follows:

Sprawling urban development

Urban areas in some countries, such as Austria, Canada, Slovenia, and the United States, rank relatively high in multiple dimensions of sprawl. This implies that it may be worth monitoring urban development patterns more closely in these countries. Closer monitoring may also be justified in cities in Denmark, France, and several Central European countries, such as Czech Republic, Hungary, Poland and Slovak Republic, as in the period 1990-2014 they have sprawled along most of the dimensions examined in the report.

Suburbanisation hiding behind densification

In some OECD countries, including Hungary, the Netherlands and Poland, average urban population density has substantially decreased since 1990, driven primarily by suburbanisation (a shift of population growth away from urban centres). In contrast, a process of densification is observed in the urban areas of other OECD countries, which is, however, far from homogeneous. In some, urban low-density areas have grown faster than high-density ones, implying that suburbanisation has co-evolved with densification. This is witnessed, for example, in Greece, Ireland, Spain, Sweden and the United Kingdom, where increases in average urban population density have been accompanied by a growth in the percentage of urban footprint occupied by areas of very low density (150-1 500 inhabitants per km^2).

Controlling urban development

Cities in a small group of countries consisting of Greece, Japan, Korea and the United Kingdom, are at the bottom of the ranking of multiple indicators of sprawl. This implies a dense and relatively contiguous form of urban development, which entails a more efficient use of land and can contribute to the reduction of emissions from road transport. However, this form of development may also entail a higher exposure of urban population to air pollution and natural disaster risks. Looking at the evolution of urban sprawl since 1990, it has declined in Australia, Spain and Switzerland, where urban areas have become much denser and less fragmented.

How to steer urban development to more sustainable pathways?

Sprawling urban development patterns imply multiple *private* benefits, which should, however, be weighed against their *social* (i.e. private and external) costs, including greenhouse gas emissions, air pollution, and loss of open space and environmental amenities. Market forces fail to take external costs into account and, thus, policy intervention is in many cases necessary to direct urban development to more sustainable patterns. At the same time, the effectiveness of local policy makers' action to address the negative effects of sprawl, e.g. at the municipality or county level, can be undermined by neighbouring local authorities which may engage in policies favouring sprawl or refrain from policy action. To overcome these challenges and curb the consequences of urban sprawl, national and local governments need to coordinate policies. Recognising that developing policies to this end is difficult and highly context-specific, the report proposes a number of land-use, transport and fiscal policy changes that could be relevant in certain urban settings. Further specification of such policy changes requires a case-study approach.

Policy changes should promote socially desirable levels of population density, minimise urban fragmentation harming biodiversity, and mitigate the environmental and economic consequences of car use. Specific policy actions that could be considered to encourage densification and reduce fragmentation include: reforming urban containment policies; relaxing maximum density restrictions; leveraging property taxation to encourage more sustainable development patterns; and incentivising developers to provide public infrastructure for new constructions. Policy changes to tackle the externalities of car use could focus on introducing road pricing mechanisms, reforming parking policy, increasing motor fuel taxes, and shifting investments to more sustainable forms of transport infrastructure.

Overall, the design of future urban development would benefit from the adoption of an integrated approach that considers the interactions between policy interventions in land use and transport, and the wider policy framework. That framework includes policy instruments that shape urban development and influence the environment, but are usually set by national or local government bodies pursuing other objectives. It also includes land-use and transport instruments under the jurisdiction of local authorities in neighbouring urban areas that may give rise to policy competition. Collective, coordinated and targeted action by different government levels can control sprawling patterns and steer urban development towards more environmentally sustainable, cost-effective and socially inclusive pathways.

Rethinking Urban Sprawl
Moving Towards Sustainable Cities

Chapter 1

The policy challenge of urban sprawl

This chapter discusses the policy challenges associated with urban sprawl. It distinguishes urban sprawl from other forms of urbanisation and explains why a new perspective on the phenomenon is needed. It then describes how the new perspective on urban sprawl developed in this report can help policy makers address the challenges associated with it. To this end, the report's contributions on the definition and measurement of sprawl, the analysis of its causes and consequences, and the identification of policy actions to address the latter are highlighted. Last, the chapter navigates the reader through the different sections of the report.

1.1. Urban sprawl is different from urbanisation

The impact of cities extends well beyond their administrative and physical boundaries. Economic activities taking place within cities play a critical role for economic growth and employment, but they are also responsible for an important part of environmental and health problems facing the world today. Taking policy action at the urban level is not only pivotal for tackling major environmental issues, such as climate change and exposure to outdoor air pollution, but also for addressing social exclusion and pressures on public finance.

Cities are hubs for knowledge and innovation, and the loci where the cross-fertilization of ideas is crystallised into massive job creation. Only during the past fifteen years, the two hundred largest metropolitan areas of the OECD countries have generated more than 60% of jobs and economic growth in these countries (OECD, 2016). OECD (2006) identifies several mechanisms through which city size may translate into higher output per capita and productivity. First, it stresses the importance of agglomeration economies, i.e. advantages generated by the spatial clustering of firms. Second, it highlights the role of specialisation advantages and more efficient matching, which emerge due to larger and more diverse labour markets. The spatial concentration of firms and people also facilitates knowledge spill-overs, innovation and economies of scale.

The role of cities for economic growth, employment and the environment is expected to become even more important in the future. Current trends show that urbanisation is a global and momentous process that is unlikely to decelerate in the decades to come (United Nations, 2008; United Nations, Department of Economic and Social Affairs, Population Division, 2014). Recent forecasts estimate that 70% of the world population – a number that rises to 86% for OECD countries – will be living in urban areas by 2050. In the same time horizon, global urban land area is projected to increase from 603 000 km^2 in 2000 to over 3 million km^2 in 2050, hosting 6.5 billion people (Angel et al., 2011). It is, thus, of primary importance that urban development occurs in a way that stimulates growth and employment on the one hand, and has the minimum possible environmental impact on the other.

Many of the environmental, economic and social challenges faced by cities can be attributed to some extent to certain characteristics of urban development patterns. For instance, low population density and dispersion of key points of economic activity tend to promote car dependency. In turn, this translates into higher levels of car use and more emissions of air pollutants and greenhouse gases. Providing sparsely populated areas with public services is also more costly, which makes them more prone to the generation of public budget deficits. In addition, low-density development can negatively impact housing affordability and facilitate income-based residential segregation, thereby discouraging social inclusion. Fragmentation (i.e. discontinuity) of urban development can also have similar consequences, as it increases the need for travelling and the costs of providing public infrastructure.

Fragmentation of urban fabric and different manifestations of low population density are features of a specific pattern of urban development: *urban sprawl*. The phenomenon has been fuelled by the growth of population and income, and a sharp reduction of real transport costs since the middle of the 20th century. The fall in transport costs stemmed from the technological progress in car manufacturing, the massive investment in road infrastructure, and the persistent underpricing of car use in many countries and urban areas (e.g. absence of road pricing, implicit parking subsidies, low end-prices of motor fuels). Urban sprawl has also been encouraged by a shift of preferences towards living in larger dwellings, situated far from environmentally degraded and often expensive city centres. For this reason, urban sprawl was initially considered to be the natural outcome of a desirable and efficient transformation process, rather than a misallocation of resources. This way, it went on for decades to become, in many parts of the world, the dominant form of urban development, possessing a momentum that is hard to reverse.

A common misperception is that it is not a particular form of urban development that is responsible for various environmental problems emerging in cities, but instead that these problems stem from urbanisation *per se*. This misperception is largely driven by the statistical correlation between city size and indicators of environmental pressures. However, such statistical relationships are often found by models failing to control for differences in urban form across cities or over time, so they should be interpreted with caution. In fact, such models often cannot disentangle the effects of city size from the effects of urban form. Attributing the costs of particular urban forms to urbanisation can be problematic when it comes to decision making, since the net benefits of urbanisation would be underestimated. Urbanisation is inextricably connected with modern economic growth and in order for its benefits to be calculated correctly, the exact urban development pattern, i.e. the distribution of population and structures across urban space, must be known in detail.

1.2. Why is a new perspective on urban sprawl needed?

Urban sprawl is still widely regarded as an elusive concept, even though the term has already been in use for about 80 years (Brueckner, 2000; Nechyba and Walsh, 2004). The phenomenon has been defined in numerous ways, and different disciplines have a different understanding of how sprawl manifests itself. Apart from the frequent confusion between urban sprawl and urbanisation delineated above, a common problem occurring with many definitions of urban sprawl is that the underlying phenomenon is confounded with its causes and consequences. This is problematic as it allows for subjective claims for or against urban sprawl. More importantly, it hinders policy makers from identifying the exact cause of various problems occurring at the city level and the right course of action to tackle them. For example, when car dependency is considered as part of the definition of urban sprawl, the latter will be blamed for the environmental consequences of car dependency. In turn, policy makers may direct efforts only to policies promoting the reduction of car use, while completely neglecting the influence of urban form on car dependency.

The confusion over urban sprawl is not limited to the conceptual level: it is also manifested in the measurement of the phenomenon. Approaches to measure urban sprawl differ in a number of aspects, but two of them are of particular importance: i) whether urban sprawl is considered a uni- or multidimensional phenomenon, and ii) what urban form characteristics are used to describe the phenomenon. The most common unidimensional measure of urban sprawl is the average population density in an urban area. As sprawl is assumed to decrease with average population density, the inverse of it, i.e. land uptake per capita, is often used instead. The problem with unidimensional approaches to measuring urban sprawl is that they are too simplistic to describe such a complex phenomenon. Multidimensional approaches are much better suited to capture its different aspects and manifestations. However, the majority of these approaches fail to include important measures of the distribution of population and urban fabric over space. Therefore, they do not provide a complete description of urban sprawl and are of limited use when it comes to investigating the relationship of the phenomenon with environmental, economic and social outcomes and alerting governments about possible needs for policy action.

The lack of a clear and neutral definition of urban sprawl and the disagreement over its measurement has hampered the identification and analysis of its consequences. Despite urban sprawl being intuitively associated with a number of environmental, economic and social problems, many of these relationships are not adequately substantiated by economic theory or empirical evidence. Empirical analysis of the effects of urban sprawl on the environment is particularly scarce, mainly due to the absence of sufficiently long time series of good indicators of urban sprawl for a large number of cities. The absence of empirical evidence for many of the environmental, economic and social pressures attributed to urban sprawl hinders conducting a proper cost-benefit analysis of the phenomenon and thus identifying whether and when policy intervention is desirable.

Various cities have developed policies to tackle urban sprawl and its potential consequences. However, some of these policies may have important side-effects which are not always considered prior to policy implementation. For example, stringent urban containment policies may cause leapfrog development outside of the regulated area. The latter can severely undermine the effectiveness of these policies in inhibiting urban encroachment on e.g. farmland and forestland and in preventing environmental and economic losses. At the same time, certain land-use policies, such as rigid building height restrictions, may themselves encourage urban sprawl. Once again, the confusion over the definition of urban sprawl and the lack of good indicators to measure it has not allowed a proper evaluation of the effects of different policies on the phenomenon. In any case, it is important that policy makers gain a better understanding of the possible implications of different policy options for urban sprawl, the environment, economic growth and social cohesion.

1.3. How does the new perspective presented in this report help address the policy challenge of urban sprawl?

The new perspective on urban sprawl presented in this report aims to help policy makers:

- Better understand the complex phenomenon of urban sprawl, by defining it in a neutral way without references to its causes or consequences;
- Monitor urban sprawl, by providing a set of indicators that reflect the multidimensional nature of the phenomenon and accounts for the distribution of people and urban fabric over space;
- Make comparisons with development patterns in other cities and over time, by measuring these indicators for more than 1 100 urban areas and in 3 different time points;

- Obtain an objective assessment of the environmental and economic consequences of urban sprawl through an extensive review of existing theoretical and empirical work;
- Develop possible courses of action to address the environmental and economic consequences of urban sprawl by providing a menu of policy options grounded in economic theory and empirical evidence.

The following paragraphs explain in more detail these contributions of the report.

The definition of urban sprawl presented in Section 1.1 reflects its multidimensional nature and is based exclusively on the characteristics of this development pattern. The causes and consequences of urban sprawl do not constitute part of its definition and, thus, potential tautologies that could hamper policy analysis are avoided. Urban sprawl can manifest itself through various distributional patterns of population and urban fabric over space. Understanding this basic feature of the phenomenon can shift policy makers' attention away from average population density and towards other characteristics of urban development that determine its environmental, economic and social effects. In line with this, the report highlights several cases in which a considerable fraction of the urban fabric exhibits very low population density levels, while, at the same time, the average population density of the entire urban area is high.

Indicators of urban sprawl are required to enable monitoring the phenomenon, undertaking comparative analyses with other cities and over time, and evaluating its causes and consequences. As sprawl is a multidimensional phenomenon, different indicators are needed to measure its different dimensions. Such dimensions comprise different aspects of the distribution of population density, the fragmentation of urban fabric, and the distribution of urban population between high and low density areas. In addition to the widely used indicator of average urban population density, six indicators are developed in this report:

- Variation of urban population density: the degree to which population density varies across a city;
- Land-to-density allocation: the share of urban footprint in which population density lies below a predefined threshold;
- Population-to-density allocation: the share of population living in areas where urban population density is below a predefined threshold;
- Polycentricity: the number of high population density peaks in an urban area;
- Fragmentation: the number of urban fabric fragments per km^2 of built-up area; and
- Decentralisation: the percentage of urban population residing outside areas of peak density.

It is important to note that the size of the artificial area *per se* is neither considered a dimension of urban sprawl nor among the determinants of the phenomenon. Therefore, it may well be that cities of larger urban footprint are less sprawled than smaller ones.

Some earlier studies of urban sprawl that acknowledged its multidimensional nature constructed composite indicators to measure it. Such indicators essentially combine different dimensions of a concept in a single measure. Despite their usefulness in measuring the evolution of the phenomenon over time in a certain geographical context, composite indicators have a number of drawbacks. The first disadvantage of composite indicators is that they are much more difficult to interpret than their components. Their second disadvantage is that they are not very informative for policy development and evaluation. The reason for this is that they do not enable pinpointing the exact dimension(s) of urban sprawl that are problematic and need to be targeted by policy action. Furthermore, weighting methods used to construct composite indicators often seem ad-hoc. Discouraged by these drawbacks, this report abstains from constructing a composite indicator of urban sprawl. On the contrary, it relies on the set of indicators mentioned above to provide a comprehensive assessment of different dimensions of urban sprawl and facilitate the identification of problematic development patterns in different urban settings.

The different dimensions of urban sprawl have been quantified for an unprecedented combination of geographical and time coverage. The seven urban sprawl indicators have been computed for more than 1 100 urban areas in 29 OECD countries and for three time points: 1990, 2000 and 2014. The analysis has been enabled by a unique combination of satellite, administrative and other GIS data sources offering a granular level of spatiotemporal information. The calculation of these indicators for such a geographical and time coverage allows monitoring the evolution of urban sprawl in a 25-year period and making comparisons of the phenomenon across cities and countries. It also enables conducting retrospective analyses of the causes and effects of different dimensions of urban sprawl in a cross-country context.

The indicators are used to assess the current state of urban sprawl in the examined cities and countries, as well as the trends of the phenomenon over time. The analysis reveals that there is great diversity in the way that different dimensions of urban sprawl have evolved across OECD cities. A close look at the distributional characteristics of urban population density – referring here only to population density in functional urban areas (the OECD's economic definition of a city) – reveals interesting patterns. In some OECD countries, average urban population density has substantially decreased, driven primarily by rapid suburbanisation. In contrast, a process of densification is observed in the urban areas of other OECD countries, which is, however, far from homogeneous. In some, low-density areas have grown faster than high-density ones, implying that suburbanisation has co-evolved with densification. Focusing on the other dimensions of urban sprawl, cities in most OECD countries have become more fragmented, but also more centralised, i.e. a larger share of their population lives in urban centres (areas of peak density).

The report assesses the drivers and the environmental and economic consequences of urban sprawl drawing upon a voluminous empirical literature, which spans several scientific disciplines, including economics, biology, and environmental and agricultural sciences. Causes and consequences of different dimensions of urban sprawl which are substantiated by empirical evidence are highlighted. However, the report also mentions cases in which a link is likely to exist, despite not being adequately supported by empirical evidence. Furthermore, the review distinguishes the consequences of urban sprawl from those of other forms of urban expansion, such as infill development. Missing this semantic detail may redirect the interest of policy makers from interventions aiming to discontinue problematic development patterns to others aiming to curb urbanisation.

Urban sprawl is caused by various demographic, economic, geographic, social and technological factors. As demand for floor space is very sensitive to income changes, the increase of real incomes in the past decades has significantly contributed to urban sprawl. Demand for floor space particularly increased in suburban areas where land prices were lower than those closer to urban centres. Rising real incomes induced low-density development in suburban areas and fragmentation of the urban fabric. Another important driver of the phenomenon is individual preferences for more space, comfort and privacy, which have also encouraged low-density and fragmented development. Such preferences are not only reflected in residential location choices, but also in transport mode choices: car use is partially driven by similar considerations. Technological progress in car production has further facilitated urban sprawl, as it has allowed covering longer distances more safely, comfortably, reliably and at substantially lower costs. Urban development pressures combined with physical conditions that hamper contiguous development also contribute to fragmentation of urban development.

The factors listed above are important determinants of urban sprawl, but certain policies have also implicitly encouraged the phenomenon. Stringent maximum density (e.g. building height) restrictions have induced low-density urban development. When combined with urban containment policies, they have often also led to leapfrog development in remote areas. The long-lasting underpricing of car use – stemming from a lack of road pricing, low on-street parking prices and in some cases low motor fuel taxes – and massive investments in road infrastructure have also encouraged households to move away from urban centres and their job location and form low-density and fragmented urban structures.

Higher emissions from road transport and loss of open space and environmental amenities in suburban areas are relatively well-established environmental consequences of urban sprawl. Fragmented and low-density development induces car dependency, which in turn translates to higher emissions of greenhouse gases and air pollutants. Furthermore, low density implies higher losses of open space, as more land needs to be developed to house a given population. Urban sprawl has also been claimed to harm biodiversity more than other forms of urban development. However, different dimensions of urban sprawl may have different and, in some cases, opposite effects on biodiversity. Low-density development is generally harmful to biodiversity, as larger urban footprints translate in higher losses of periurban biodiversity. In contrast, higher fragmentation of urban development is harmful to biodiversity only to the extent that it leads to higher fragmentation of natural habitats. This depends on the initial development pattern and on where new development takes place. Urban sprawl has also been suggested to have other consequences for the environment and health, including degraded water quality and higher obesity rates. However, such claims are not equally substantiated by empirical evidence.

The economic and social consequences of urban sprawl include higher costs to provide public services to low-density areas, as well as significant losses of time and productivity due to longer commuting distances. Furthermore, the increased costs of providing public services often cause pressures on local public finance. Among the dimensions of urban sprawl, costs of providing public services are heavily influenced by the share of population residing in low-density areas (e.g. below 3 500 inhabitants per km^2). The higher that share is, the more costly it becomes for governments to provide those services. Commuting distances and infrastructure requirements and maintenance costs also increase with fragmentation, but the impact of low density on the costs and profitability of public investments is generally higher. From a social perspective, low-density development has been associated with social inequality and segregation, as the regulatory mechanisms that are used to maintain it may severely affect housing affordability.

The multiple private benefits of urban sprawl should be weighed against the social (private and external) costs entailed by its consequences. Market forces fail to take these external costs into account and, thus, policy intervention is necessary in many urban settings to address environmental problems and restore economic efficiency. As explained above, the new perspective of sprawl presented in this report provides the necessary tools and information to policy makers to help them evaluate the state of the phenomenon and determine whether policy action needs to be taken. To help policy makers further with developing possible courses of action, the report also provides a menu of policy options that can steer urban development to more sustainable patterns. Beyond this framework, customised and more elaborate solutions can be developed with the use of a case-study approach. Such an approach allows utilising detailed land-use data, elaborate socioeconomic and institutional information, and state-of-the-art modelling techniques, and can provide useful policy insights for a specific urban area. A case-study approach goes beyond the scope of this report, but it could be pursued as a separate stream of future work.

Policy action needs to focus on promoting socially desirable levels of population density and fragmentation through policies that often bear fruit in a relatively longer time horizon. In line with that objective, the report examines a series of relevant policy options: relaxation of stringent maximum density restrictions, adjustment of urban containment policies to deter leapfrog development, reforms of property taxation to encourage infill development and incentives for developers to provide public infrastructure for new constructions.

At the same time, urban policies need to directly address the car dependency caused by sprawl and mitigate its environmental and economic consequences. With regard to this objective, the report discusses a menu of possible policy interventions: the introduction of road pricing mechanisms; the abolishment of minimum parking requirements; the pricing of on-street parking at its marginal social cost; the increase of motor fuel taxes where the latter do not fully account for the external costs of fuel consumption; and the shift of focus from investments in road network expansions to the development of infrastructure for public transport, walking and cycling.

New land-use and transport policies and related reforms will interact with the existing policy framework, so governments should carefully consider the possible outcomes of such interactions before implementing them. The relevant framework contains policies set by national or local authorities that affect urban development despite pursuing other objectives, as well as land-use and transport policies under the jurisdiction of local authorities in neighbouring urban areas that may give rise to policy competition.

1.4. Navigation through the report

In the remainder of this report, the new perspective on urban sprawl is developed in two parts. The first part (Chapters 2 and 3) explains in detail how the definition of urban sprawl provided here differs from earlier definitions of the phenomenon and describes the indicators used to measure it. It also presents a comparative analysis of the current state and trends of urban sprawl across 29 countries and over a period of 40 years. The second part (Chapters 4 and 5) provides a critical assessment of the causes and consequences of the phenomenon and a detailed discussion of their implications for policy-making.

Chapter 2 develops a conceptual framework in which the various characteristics of urban sprawl are systematically categorised. The chapter discusses how the definition of urban sprawl reflects its multidimensional nature and the critical differences of the phenomenon from other urban development patterns. The various ways through which sprawl manifests itself are explained in detail and depicted schematically.

Chapter 3 operationalises the definition of urban sprawl. The sprawl dimensions described in Chapter 2 are represented by indicators which can be computed by widely available granular data on land cover, and enable both an analysis of the current state of the phenomenon and its evolution over time. The chapter elaborates on the methodology employed to compute the indicators and on the global datasets used to that end. The indicators are computed for more than 1 100 cities in 29 OECD countries and for three time points spanning the period from 1990 to 2014. The results of this work are used in a cross-country analysis, in which country rankings are provided for the state and evolution of each sprawl indicator. This analysis provides useful insights into the current state and trends of different dimensions of urban sprawl. The chapter also provides a comprehensive summary of the most interesting findings for each country.

Chapter 4 discusses in detail the causes and consequences of urban sprawl. The analysed drivers of urban sprawl include individual preferences, expectations of property owners, technological progress, physical geography, and certain policy instruments. The chapter also discusses a wide array of impacts ranging from the more well-established consequences, such as car dependency, emissions and inefficient provision of public services, to more disputable propositions, including the impact of sprawl on water quality and biodiversity. It also covers a series of hypotheses that have been formed inconsistently, have been falsified or have received limited empirical support.

Chapter 5 focuses on policies to steer urban development to more sustainable pathways. The chapter discusses in detail concrete policy actions that can help control urban sprawl and mitigate its environmental consequences. It also offers some general directions for addressing concerns over urban sprawl and promoting more sustainable urban development patterns. Finally, it highlights the importance of considering interactions between policy instruments and following an integrated approach to designing and implementing urban policies.

References

Angel, S. et al. (2011), *Making Room for a Planet of Cities*, Policy Focus Report/Code PF027, Lincoln Institute of Land Policy, Cambridge, MA, Available online at: *www.lincolninst.edu/sites/default/files/pubfiles/making-room-for-a-planet-of-cities-full_0.pdf*.

Brueckner, J.K. (2000), "Urban sprawl: Diagnosis and remedies", *International Regional Science Review*, Vol. 23/2, pp. 160-171.

Nechyba, T.J. and R.P. Walsh (2004), "Urban sprawl", *The Journal of Economic Perspectives*, Vol. 18/4, pp. 177-200.

OECD (2016), *Making Cities Work for All: Data and Actions for Inclusive Growth*, OECD Publishing, Paris, *http://dx.doi.org/10.1787/9789264263260-en*.

OECD (2006), *Competitive Cities in the Global Economy*, OECD Publishing, Paris, *http://dx.doi.org/10.1787/9789264027091-en*.

United Nations (2008), *State of the World's Cities 2008/2009: Harmonious Cities*, United Nations Human Settlements Programme, Nairobi, Kenya.

United Nations, Department of Economic and Social Affairs, Population Division (2014), *World Urbanization Prospects: The 2014 Revision, Highlights*, (ST/ESA/SER.A/352), New York, NY, *https://esa.un.org/unpd/wup/Publications/Files/WUP2014-Highlights.pdf*.

PART I

Urban Sprawl – Definition and measurement

Rethinking Urban Sprawl
Moving Towards Sustainable Cities

PART I

Chapter 2

Urban sprawl as a multidimensional phenomenon

This chapter develops a conceptual framework in which the characteristics of urban sprawl are systematically categorised and disentangled from its causes and consequences. Furthermore, it provides a functional definition of urban sprawl that reflects its multidimensional nature and its main differences from other forms of urban development. Using a series of graphical illustrations, the chapter describes various features of urban development that determine urban sprawl: average population density and its variation across urban space; the share of urban footprint and population in areas where population density lies below certain thresholds; fragmentation of urban land; number of peaks of high population density; and the fraction of urban population residing outside these peaks.

2.1. Introduction

This chapter develops a conceptual framework for the phenomenon of urban sprawl, in which its various intrinsic characteristics are isolated from its causes and effects and are disentangled from each other. This effort results in a definition that is based exclusively on different features of a development pattern: urban sprawl manifests itself through various ways population and built environment may be distributed across urban space. This multidimensional definition can help in redirecting part of the policy makers' attention, which in many cases is concentrated on average population density, to other features of the development pattern.

The chapter highlights several cases in which a considerable fraction of the urban fabric may be bound to problematic development patterns, while the average population density of the entire urban area is high. Urban sprawl's potential consequences, such as reduced accessibility, car dependency and environmental degradation, as well as others discussed in Chapter 4, do not constitute part of its definition. Such a value-free definition facilitates policy analysis, as it allows for an objective assessment of the effects of urban sprawl. Importantly, several manifestations of the phenomenon are not necessarily detrimental from an environmental or economic viewpoint. For example, fragmentation of urban fabric and low population density may simply reflect physical limitations, rather than policy constraints affecting urban development. The definition of urban sprawl provided in this chapter is subsequently operationalised in Chapter 3, where the various sprawl dimensions are being measured in more than 1 100 urban areas of 29 OECD countries.

2.2. The multiple dimensions of urban sprawl

Urban sprawl has been defined in various ways in different scientific disciplines: economists, geographers, environmental scientists, urban and transport planners have attached a different meaning to it. For economists, sprawl is the *excessive* spatial growth of cities (Brueckner, 2000). The term excessive refers to the part of the urban growth driven by an increasing land uptake *per capita*, rather than by the increasing population of a city. Therefore, sprawl is a synonym of low population density and an antonym of compactness. The latter is associated with high population density and a small *per capita* uptake of land.

The definition used by economists has been criticised by other disciplines as being too simplistic to describe such a complex phenomenon as sprawl. Geographers and urban planners offer a series of alternative definitions of urban sprawl, whereby it is described as a specific pattern of urban development. In most of the cases, definitions are implicit. In order to extract the sprawl definition implicitly adopted in each study, someone has to examine the measurable attributes used to construct complex sprawl indicators. For instance, Tsai (2005) defines sprawl as a function of the degree to which economic activity is evenly distributed and the extent to which high-density suburbs are clustered in space. Torrens (2008) measures sprawl by combining different metrics that describe the location of artificial areas within a city, the allocation of activity across them and the degree to which these areas are fragmented, decentralised and accessible. Galster et al. (2001) define sprawl as a condition of land use that is represented by low values on one or more of the following urban form metrics: density, continuity, concentration, clustering, centrality, nuclearity, mixed uses, and proximity. Frenkel and Ashkenazi (2008) imply that urban sprawl is indicated, among others, by the degree of irregularity in the shape of artificial areas and the degree to which land use is mixed, including presence of public facilities and institutions.

Many of these approaches to define and measure urban sprawl are problematic for various reasons. The first reason is that the phenomenon of urban sprawl is confused with its own potential causes or consequences. This leads to tautological definitions that attempt to maximise the correlation between the proposed sprawl indicators and a series of other phenomena including reduced accessibility, car dependency and environmental degradation. Following these approaches, sprawl can be any set of characteristics that may be environmentally and economically detrimental in an urban context. Consequently, a city is sprawled because such negative features are present.

Second, many of the proposed metrics of urban form in the literature seem arbitrary. These include, for instance, measures of porosity and peculiarity in the shape of individual fragments of built area. While the latter may be strongly correlated with undesirable phenomena attributed to urban sprawl, there is limited empirical justification that such correlations could represent causal channels in a valid theoretical framework. In some cases, complex sprawl indicators are constructed to encapsulate some of these alleged aspects of sprawl. The outcome has little policy relevance. Even when these indicators are cause- and effect-free, it is hard to interpret them and even harder to determine policy interventions based on them.

This report defines urban sprawl as an *urban development pattern characterised by low population density that can be manifested in multiple ways*. That is, an urban area may be sprawled because the population density is, on average, low. Furthermore, urban areas characterised by high average density can be considered sprawled if density varies widely across their footprint, leaving a substantial portion of urban land exposed to very low density levels. Urban sprawl can also be manifested in development that is discontinuous, strongly scattered and decentralised, where a large number of unconnected fragments are separated by large parts of non-artificial surfaces.

This definition departs from the main viewpoint of the economics discipline on the phenomenon, namely that sprawl is described exclusively by the average population density in an urban area. Following the proposition of other scientific disciplines (see, for example, Ewing and Hamidi, 2014), the definition is modified to account for the entire distribution of population density across an urban area, rather than its average value. Apart from the average population density in a given urban area, sprawl is characterised and measured by: i) the variation of that density across space; ii) the percentage of population living below different population density thresholds; iii) the degree to which population density peaks in one or several locations; iv) the extent to which the density distribution is fragmented; and v) the percentage of population living in artificial areas with relatively high population.

The various dimensions of urban sprawl are summarised in descriptive terms in Table 2.1. In Chapter 3, each of these characteristics is operationalised by one or more sprawl indicators that are computed for more than 1 100 urban areas in 29 OECD countries. To ensure cross-country comparability, the analysis is conducted at the level of the *functional urban area* (FUA), OECD's economic definition of a city. An FUA comprises a set of contiguous local administrative units, which are characterised by relatively high commuting flows between each other (OECD, 2012).

Table 2.1. **Characterisation of urban sprawl**

Dimension	Explanation
Average urban population density	The average number of inhabitants in a square kilometre of land of an urban area.
Population-to-density allocation	The share of population living in areas where population density is below a certain threshold.*
Land-to-density allocation	The share of urban footprint occupying areas where population density lies below a certain threshold.*
Variation of urban population density	The degree to which population density varies across the city.
Fragmentation	The number of fragments of urban fabric per km^2 of built-up area.
Polycentricity	The number of high-density peaks in an urban area.
Decentralisation	The percentage of population residing outside the high-density peaks of an urban area.

* The thresholds used in the corresponding calculations are 1 500, 2 500 and 3 500 inhabitants per km^2 (for details, see Section 3.4).

Figure 2.1. **Geographic distribution of population in two monocentric cities with different total land uptake**

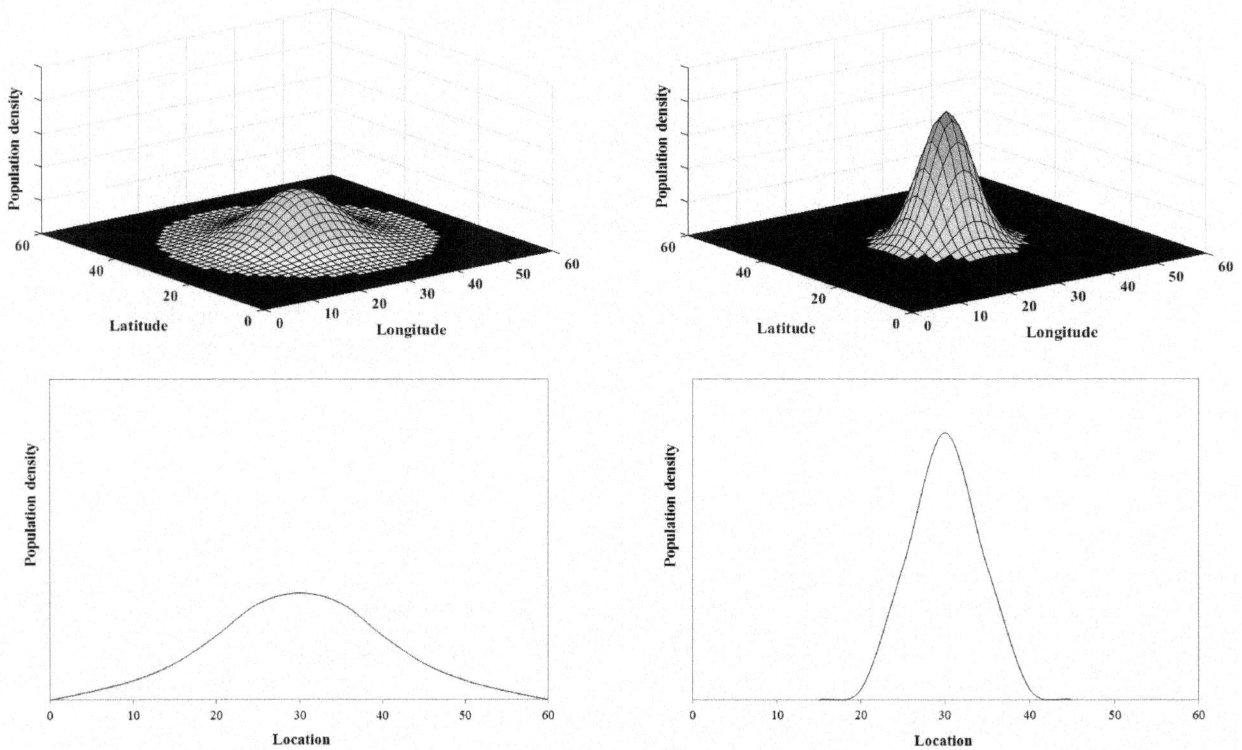

Note: The left panels display a city where built-up area per capita is high (low average population density), whereas the right panels display a city where built-up area per capita is low (high average population density).

The characteristics of urban sprawl considered in this report are illustrated in Figures 2.1-2.7. To simplify discussion and avoid any loss of generality, the footprints of all urban areas are depicted as squares of equal surface that accommodate the same population size. The coloured parts of the footprints (squared pattern) designate artificial areas, i.e. areas covered by buildings, roads and other structures, while the black parts denote undeveloped land within the urban area, where population density is zero by definition. In each figure, the upper panels depict the *geographic distribution of population*.

This function associates every location within an urban area with a local population density. To simplify the exposition, lower panels in each figure provide illustrative, two-dimensional examples of the population density.[1]

Figure 2.1 depicts two urban areas of equal population that differ fundamentally with respect to their total artificial footprint. As a result, the *per capita* land uptake and its inverse, average population density, i.e. the average number of people per square kilometre, differ widely between the two cases. The left panels of the figure display an urban area that is sprawled as average population density is low. In this case, low average density results from the expansion of the urban fabric into periurban areas.

In contrast to Figure 2.1, Figure 2.2 depicts two cities of equal population and urban footprint. That is, the average population density is identical in the two cases. However, population density displays a larger *variation* across urban space in the latter case (right panels), with a substantial part of the urban footprint being characterised by either very high or very low population density.

Figure 2.2. **Geographic distribution of population in two monocentric cities with identical population and land uptake**

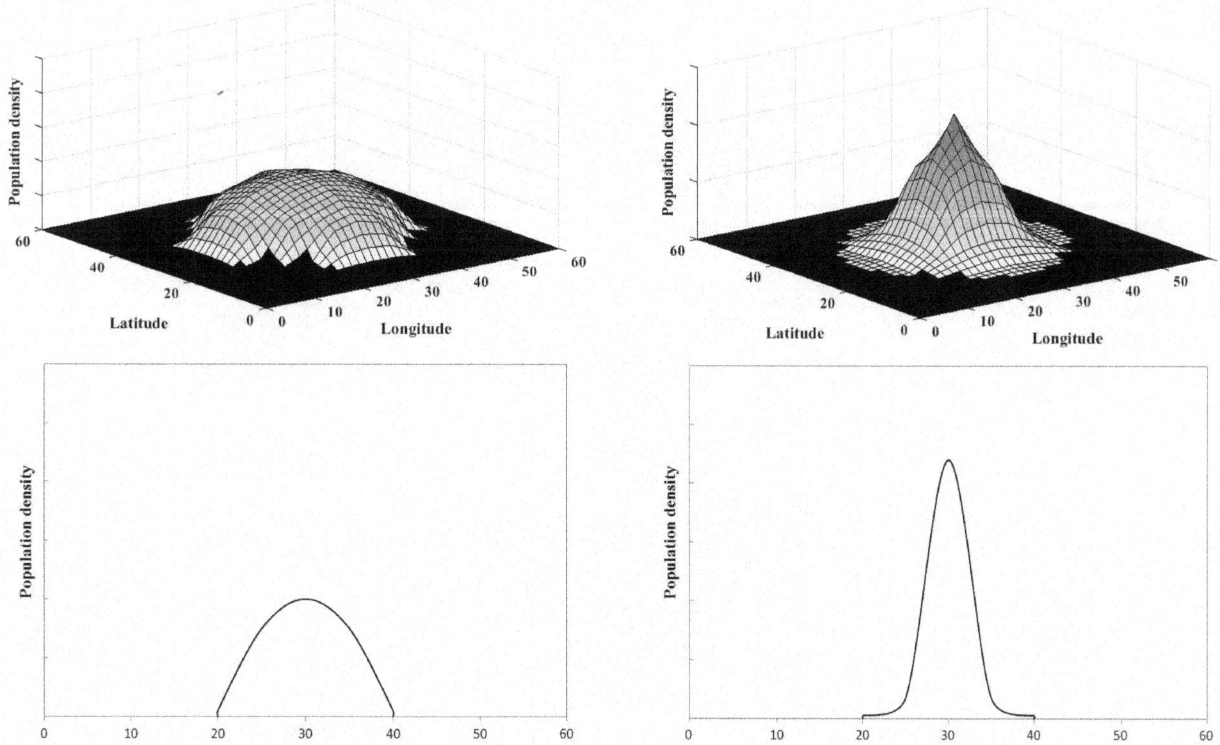

The implications of density variation across urban space are further examined in Figure 2.3 and Figure 2.4. In both figures, the upper panels illustrate the distribution of population density over space in two hypothetical cities with the same land uptake and population. Figure 2.3 illustrates the derivation of a *land allocation function* from the geographic distribution of population. The land allocation function associates any level of population density in an urban area with the percentage of artificial surface where population density lies beyond that level. For example, approximately 80% of the urban area depicted in the right panels of Figure 2.3 hosts residential densities below d_4 (lower right panel). In the upper right panel, this percentage corresponds to the ratio of the length of the long-dashed arrows (i.e. the sum of intervals *ae* and *e'a'*, which represent urban land hosting density below d_4) to the length of the solid arrow (i.e. interval *aa'*, which represents the total populated area). Similarly, more than 60% of the same urban area hosts density levels below d_2. This corresponds to the ratio of the length of the short-dashed arrows (i.e. the sum of intervals *ad* and *d'a'*) to the length of the solid arrow (i.e. interval *aa'*) in the upper right panel.

Figure 2.3. **Derivation of the land-allocation function from the geographic distribution of population in two cities with identical land uptake and population**

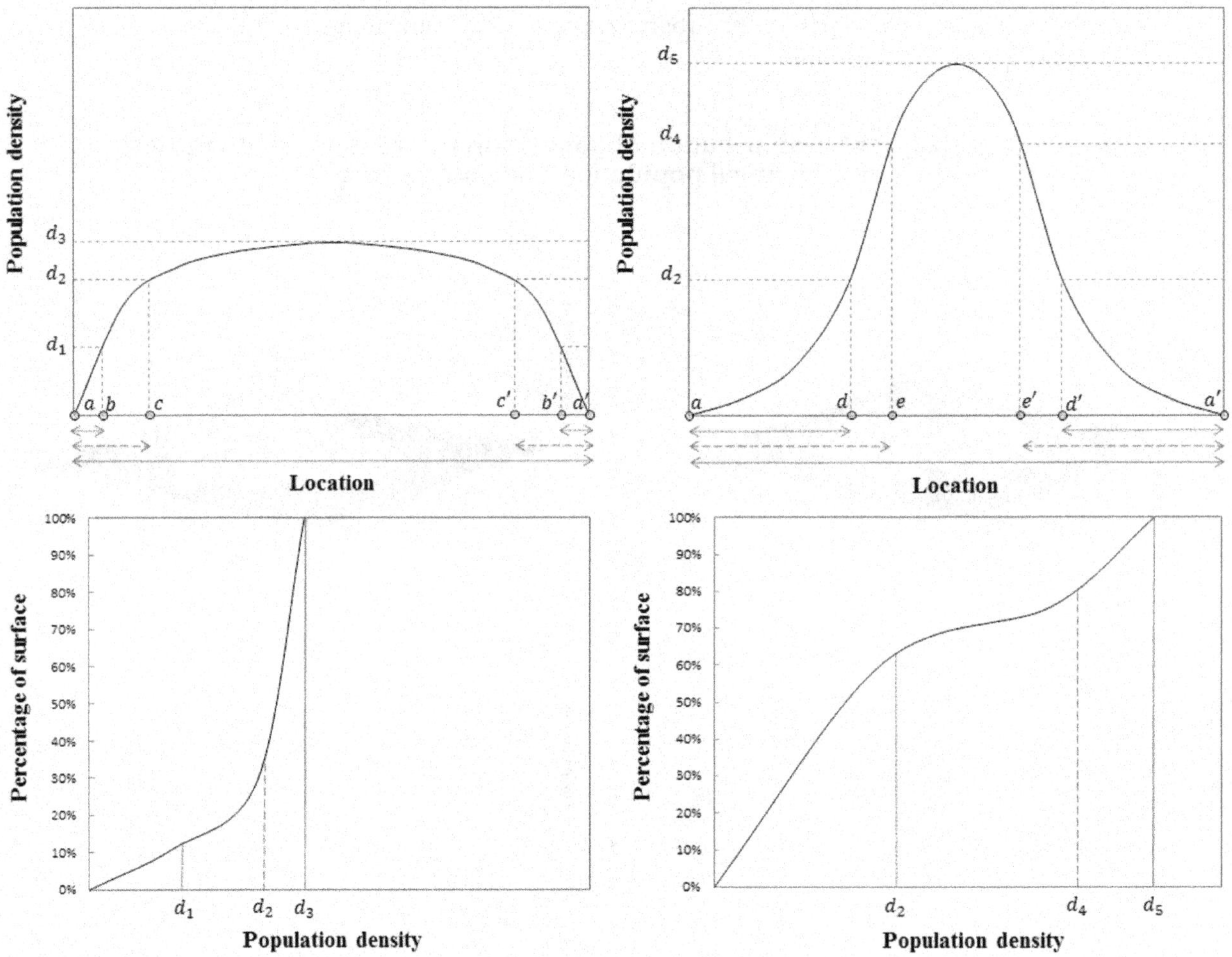

The land allocation function encapsulates important information about the internal structure of cities and the social cost of providing local public goods, such as roads, and services, such as public transport and water supply. In the city depicted in the right panels of Figure 2.3, a substantially larger share of surfaces are exposed to low population density than in the city depicted in the left panels.[2] Hence, public goods and services subject to economies of density, as those mentioned above, may be significantly more expensive to provide in the city of the right panels.

The derivation of a *population allocation function* from the geographic distribution of population is illustrated in Figure 2.4 (lower panels). That function indicates the percentage of population residing in all locations of the city where density lies below a certain number. For example, roughly 60% of the urban area depicted in the right panels of Figure 2.4 hosts residential densities below d_4 (lower right panel). In the upper right panel, this percentage corresponds to the ratio of the population residing in areas of density below d_4 (i.e. the sum of the light and dark grey shaded areas) to the total population of the city (i.e. the total area below the density curve). Similarly, less than 30% of the population resides in areas where density is lower than d_2, which is the portion of the total area under the density curve shaded in dark grey.

While the land-allocation function and population allocation function are strongly correlated, the information they provide is complementary. For example, while both cities displayed in the illustration host roughly 30% percent of their population in areas of density below d_2 (lower panels of Figure 2.4), the percentage of urban land occupied by these areas differs by approximately thirty percentage points (35% versus 65%), as suggested by the lower panels of Figure 2.3.

Figure 2.4. **Derivation of the population-allocation function from the geographic distribution of population in two cities with identical land uptake and total population**

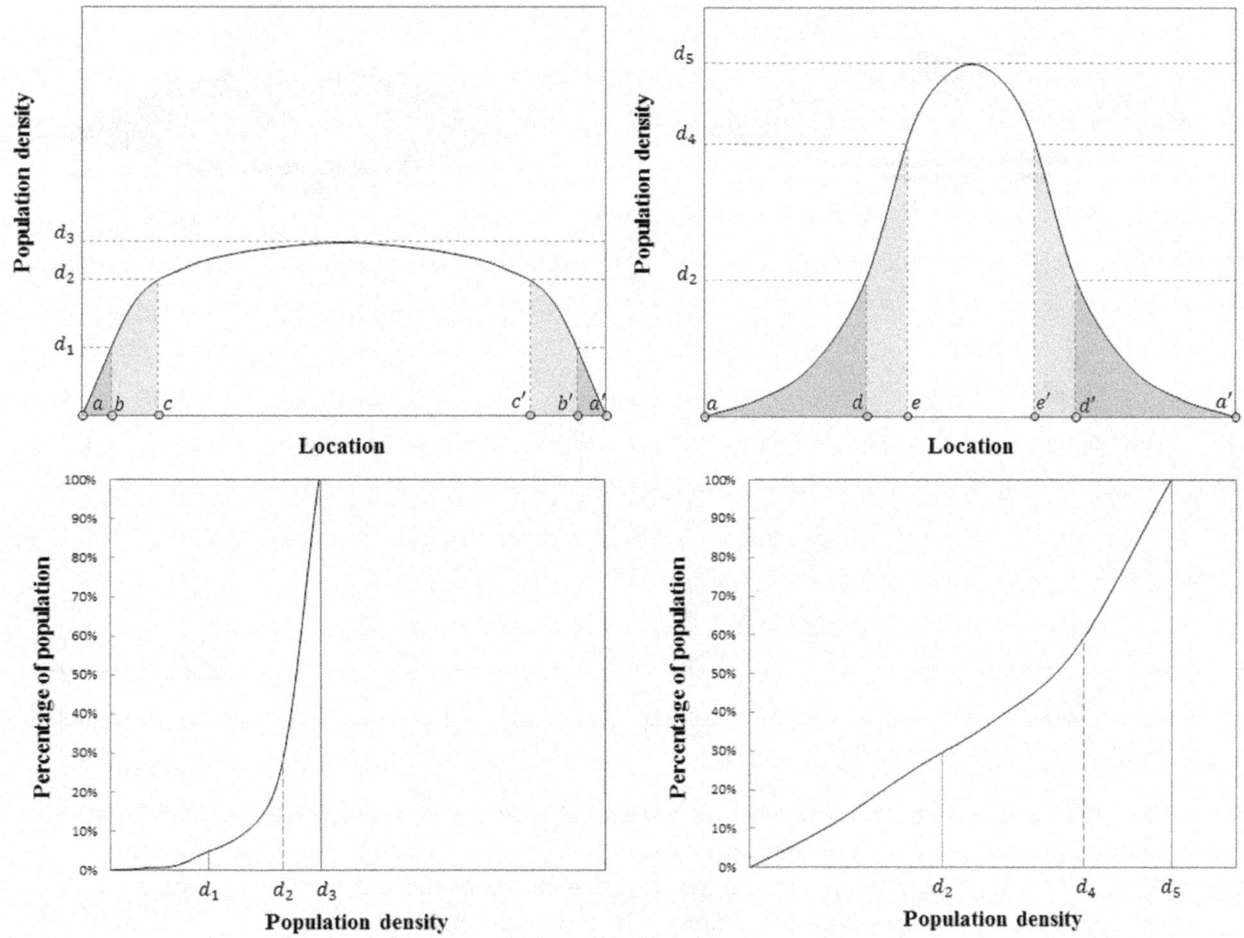

By taking into account the entire distribution of population density, it becomes clear that urban sprawl can occur even in cities of high average population density. As illustrated in Figure 2.3 and Figure 2.4, urban areas of identical footprint and average population density may be characterised by completely different internal structures. That aspect has either been neglected by a large number of earlier studies on urban sprawl, or its importance has not been articulated in a clear way. The implications of residential density variation are clarified further in Chapter 4, where the impacts of urban sprawl are discussed in detail.

The difference between monocentric and polycentric urban settings is depicted in Figure 2.5. In a polycentric setting, residential density peaks at multiple locations that lie at considerable distance from each other. Polycentric settings are likely to require a larger urban footprint to accommodate a given population, even though this will not necessarily be the case in all types of urban structure. The environmental implications of adjusting residential density in monocentric and polycentric urban areas are discussed in Chapter 4.

Figure 2.5. **Polycentric versus monocentric cities of identical population**

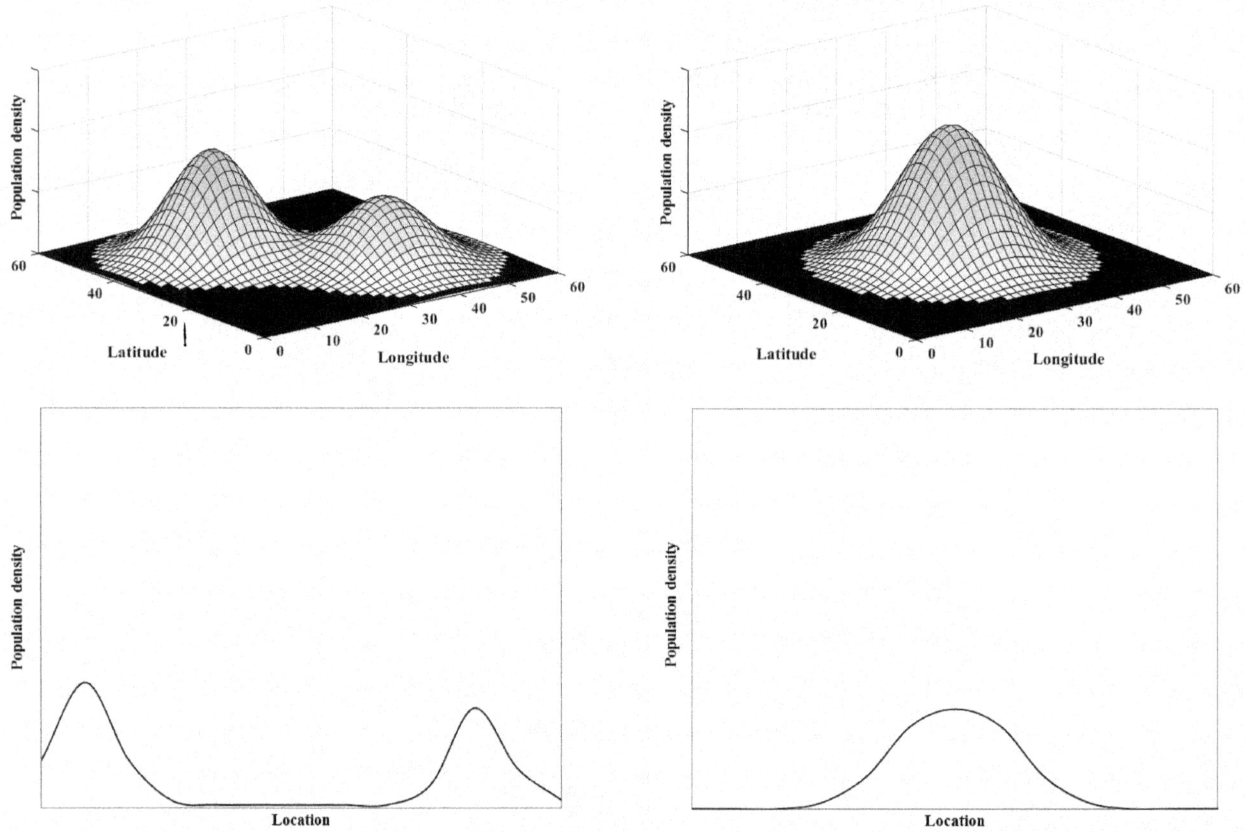

Note: Left panels display a bicentric city, i.e. a city with a pair of peaks in population density. Right panels display a monocentric city, i.e. a city with a single peak in population density.

The concept of fragmentation is illustrated in Figure 2.6. A fragmented urban fabric is not contiguous. Instead, it is split into a set of *patches* that are scattered across the urban area. While fragmentation is used to describe the extent of discontinuity in a city's built environment, it contains no information on how population is distributed on the various patches of urban fabric.

Figure 2.6. **Urban areas of low and high fragmentation**

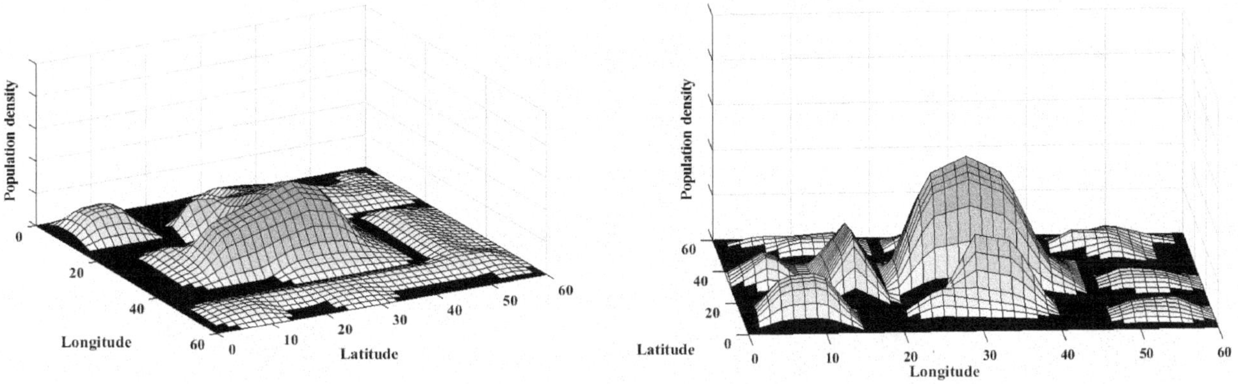

Note: Left panel displays a city with relatively low fragmentation, while right panel displays a city with relatively high fragmentation.

Decentralisation reveals how unequally population is distributed between areas of peak density and the rest of the urban area. The concept is graphically shown in Figure 2.7.

Figure 2.7. **Centralised and decentralised urban areas**

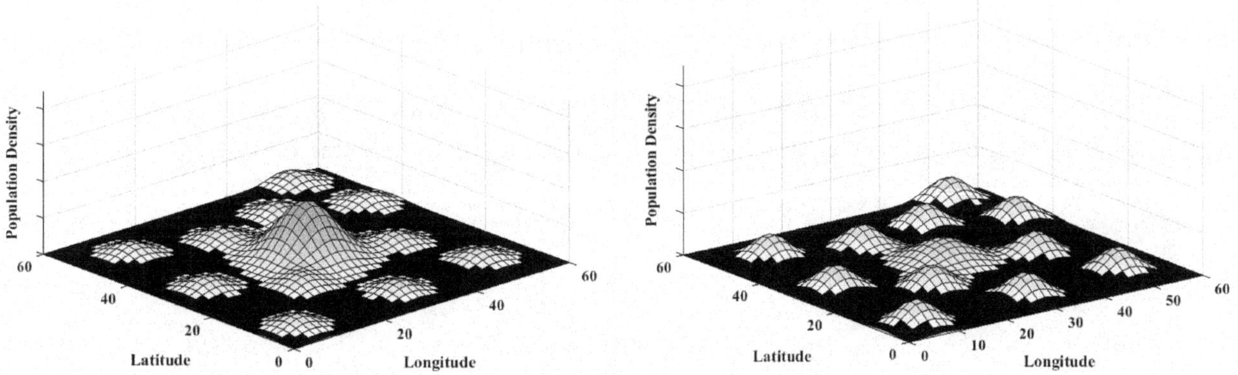

Note: Left panel displays a centralised city, while right panel displays a decentralised one.

2.3. Summary

This chapter provided a new definition of urban sprawl that is based entirely on the intrinsic characteristics of an urban development pattern, rather than on its causes or effects. Sprawl is defined through several features characterising the distribution of population and built surfaces across an urban area. Therefore, the definition allows different manifestations of the phenomenon beyond low average population density: high variation of population density across space; a high share of urban footprint and population occupied by areas in which population density lies below certain thresholds; fragmentation of the urban fabric; a large number of high-density peaks within a city; and a low fraction of urban population residing in them. Some of these sprawl dimensions, which are further operationalised and measured in Chapter 3, are not always detrimental from an environmental or economic viewpoint. Chapter 4 provides an extensive literature review that attempts, whenever possible, to map the causes and effects of urban sprawl to the different sprawl dimensions presented in this chapter.

Notes

1. Each density peak in the lower panels is represented by a single location in the horizontal axis, e.g. x^*, and the density in a certain location, e.g. x_A, can be considered as an approximation of the average population density in any location at distance $|x^* - x_A|$ from the density peak. For example, the density in location $x_L = 20$ can be considered as the average population density in locations whose longitude is smaller than 30 and whose distance from the density peak point $x^* = (30,30)$ is equal to 10 kilometres. Similarly, the density in location $x_R = 40$ can be considered as the average population density in locations whose longitude is bigger than 30 and whose distance from the density peak point $x^* = (30,30)$ is 10 kilometres.
2. For example, for density level d_2 the difference is large: roughly 35% for the city in the left versus more than 60% for the city in the right.

References

Brueckner, J.K. (2000), "Urban sprawl: Diagnosis and remedies", *International Regional Science Review*, Vol. 23/2, pp. 160-171.

Ewing, R. and S. Hamidi (2014), *Measuring Sprawl 2014*, Report prepared for *Smart Growth America*, available online at: *www.smartgrowthamerica.org/app/legacy/documents/measuring-sprawl-2014.pdf.*

Frenkel, A. and M. Ashkenazi (2008), "Measuring urban sprawl: How can we deal with it?", *Environment and Planning B: Planning and Design*, Vol. 35/1, pp. 56-79.

Galster, G. et al. (2001), "Wrestling sprawl to the ground: Defining and measuring an elusive concept", *Housing Policy Debate*, Vol. 12/4, pp. 681-718.

OECD (2012), *Redefining "Urban": A New Way to Measure Metropolitan Areas*, OECD Publishing, Paris, *http://dx.doi.org/10.1787/9789264174108-en.*

Torrens, P. (2008), "A toolkit for measuring sprawl", *Applied Spatial Analysis and Policy*, Vol. 1/1, pp. 5-36.

Tsai,Y. (2005), "Quantifying urban form: Compactness versus sprawl". *Urban Studies*, Vol. 42/1, pp. 141-161.

PART I

Chapter 3

Sprawl in OECD urban areas

This chapter operationalises the conceptual definition of urban sprawl offered in Chapter 2 and provides a cross-city and cross-country analysis of the phenomenon. The different dimensions of sprawl are represented by indicators that are computed using three data sources: two high-resolution global datasets on land cover and population, and the geographic delimitation of functional urban areas. The indicators are computed for 1 156 urban areas in 29 OECD countries. They are then used in cross-city and cross-country comparisons, as well as in a country-level analysis of urban sprawl. The findings show that many cities and countries have been sprawling since 1990, even though this process is manifested in heterogeneous ways. Among the dimensions of urban sprawl, fragmentation of urban land, variation of urban population density and the share of urban land allocated to very low density levels have grown in most countries since 1990. At the same time, urban areas in some countries, including Austria, Canada, Slovenia and the United States, rank high in multiple dimensions of sprawl, while cities in other countries, such as Czech Republic, Denmark, France, Hungary, Poland and Slovak Republic have been sprawling along most of the considered dimensions since 1990.

3.1. Introduction

Urban sprawl is a concept that can be operationalised and measured exclusively within city limits; therefore, well-defined delimitations of urban areas are a prerequisite for the effective study of the phenomenon. This chapter provides an inter-temporal, cross-country analysis of sprawl in OECD urban areas. The analysis is based on the measurement of urban sprawl that has been conceptualised in Chapter 2. That is, each indicator proposed in this chapter corresponds to an urban sprawl dimension discussed in that chapter. In contrast to several complex sprawl indicators analysed in earlier studies, the metrics[1] proposed here can be more directly related to the effects of certain policies, such as the ones discussed in Chapter 4. The urban form indicators are measured for 1 156 urban areas in 29 OECD countries. Data from three different sources are combined to compute them: i) a unique dataset that identifies built-up areas globally with a resolution of 38 m × 38 m at three different time points (1990, 2000 and 2014); ii) a dataset on global population density with a 250 m × 250 m resolution observed for the same time points; and iii) a geospatial dataset designating the borders of OECD urban areas.

The outline of the chapter is as follows. Section 3.2 provides a systematic review and classification of metrics used to operationalise the multiple and diverse definitions of urban sprawl in the literature. Section 3.3 describes the three main data sources used in the current study, where special attention is paid to the dataset on geographic delimitation of urban areas. Section 3.4 briefly describes the urban sprawl indicators used in the study, and visualises and discusses the most important findings from a cross-country analysis of these indicators. Section 3.5 presents some results of the country-level analysis, which is further elaborated in Appendix 3.B. Section 3.6 concludes.

3.2. Background literature

Urban sprawl has been analysed by various disciplines such as landscape ecology, transport planning, geography and urban economics, each with their own point of view on the concept (Arribas-Bel, Nijkamp and Scholten, 2011). There is no consensus on the definition of sprawl and the way to quantify it. However, it is widely accepted that urban sprawl is a multidimensional concept whose definition on the basis of average population density or occupied urban footprint may be too simplistic. As highlighted in Chapter 2, the distribution of population may vary widely across urban areas with identical average population density, even if the areas occupy the same footprint. Therefore, the entire distribution of population across space is central in comparing urban areas. Compact development around major public transport nodes can provide an average density that is equally low to that of a suburban zone where development is scattered. However, the environmental, economic and energy profiles of the two suburban areas may be diametrically opposed. Therefore, several dimensions are required to describe urban sprawl in a meaningful way (see e.g. Galster et al., 2001; Su and DeSalvo, 2008; Torrens and Alberti, 2000).

Another issue is whether the measurement of sprawl through the rate of change of certain stock variables, such as various density indicators proposed in the literature, is sufficient for policy analysis. Some studies have used approaches paying attention only to the rate at which urban areas and populations are growing and completely neglecting the current state of these areas. Then, cities are sprawling if the growth rate of urban built-up area is bigger than the growth rate of population.

Measures of urban morphology

The most widely used measures of urban morphology are urban land cover, fragmentation and centrality.

Urban land cover

Urban land cover can be measured in two ways: i) as the total amount of urban built-up area (Angel et al., 2011; Jaeger and Schwick, 2014; Oueslati, Alvanides and Garrod, 2015), or ii) as the ratio of the size of the built-up areas to the total area of the reporting unit (Angel et al., 2011; EEA, 2016). Built-up areas comprise buildings and other man-made constructions. Most land cover datasets do not distinguish between urban and non-urban built-up areas. Therefore, a method should be applied to distinguish urban built-up areas from villages, towns and remote developments.

Fragmentation

Fragmentation measures quantify the degree of discontinuity or scattering of the urban development (Frenkel and Ashkenazi, 2008). In its most simple form, fragmentation is measured as the ratio of the number of urban patches to total artificial area (Irwin and Bockstael, 2007; Oueslati, Alvanides and Garrod, 2015) or to population (Arribas-Bel, Nijkamp and Scholten, 2011) in a city. Other measures include the mean patch size (Frenkel and Ashkenazi, 2008; Irwin and Bockstael, 2007; Solon, 2009) and the degree of openness, measured by the amount of undeveloped land surrounding the area around an average grid-cell classified as built-up land (Angel et al., 2011; Burchfield et al., 2006; Frenkel and Ashkenazi, 2008; Siedentop and Fina, 2010). Another group of indicators measures exclusively the speed at which fragmentation of urban areas occurs over time (Angel et al., 2011, Bockstael, 2007).

Centrality

Centrality indicators measure the degree to which urban fragments agglomerate close to urban cores, i.e. contiguous areas of considerable population density that occupy substantial footprints. Huang, Lu and Sellers (2007) measure centrality as the average distance of different patches to the largest patch of the urban area, which is considered to be the central business district (CBD). As this index is sensitive to the overall size of the urban area, distances are corrected for that. The drawback of this indicator is that it is based on the monocentric city model and is, therefore, less suitable for cities with more than one centre.

Measures of internal composition

Indicators of internal composition explain the distribution of population, buildings and jobs across patches of urban fabric. These indicators can be categorised into measures of density, distribution, centralisation, polycentricity and land-use mix.

Residential and job density

Density indicators are the most widely used type of urban form metrics. Density is defined as the number of inhabitants (population density), residences (residential density) or jobs (employment density) per square kilometre of land. Areas with more inhabitants, residences or jobs per km^2 are considered to be more intensively used and thus less sprawled (EEA, 2016). It is important to distinguish between *gross density*, which is calculated in terms of the number of people, residences, or jobs per km^2 of *total urban area* that includes non-artificial surfaces,[2] and *net density*, which denotes the number of people, residences, or jobs per km^2 *of artificial area*. The larger the fraction of the total urban area occupied by non-artificial surfaces, the larger the deviation of net density from its gross counterpart.

Distribution of density

Average density alone provides no information on how activity is distributed within an urban area. Measures of the spatial distribution of population density can provide more information on how density varies across urban space. Such measures reveal the degree to which population is equally distributed across the built-up parts of an urban area or concentrated in a relatively small fraction of them. Various indices, such as the Gini coefficient, Theil's index, Delta index and entropy measures have been used in earlier studies for this purpose (Galster et al., 2001; Gordon, Richardson and Wong, 1986; Small and Song, 1994; Tsai, 2005; Veneri 2017). Several measures of spatial autocorrelation can be used to detect the degree to which urban parts of similar density are clustered together or dispersed widely across urban areas (Arribas-Bel and Schmidt, 2013; Torrens, 2008; Tsai, 2005; Zhao, 2011).

Centralisation

Centralisation measures are similar to the centrality indicator discussed before, with the difference that they are weighted by the population or employment in each unit of land (Galster et al., 2001, Veneri 2017). They can be considered more meaningful metrics than centrality, as they indicate e.g. how far the average person lives from the centre, instead of only taking into account the location of the urban patches.

Polycentricity

Polycentricity (also defined as *nuclearity*) measures assess the presence of multiple urban centres. Urban centres are "places with a high concentration of population and economic activities that functionally organise their surrounding territory" (Brezzi and Veneri, 2015). The quantification of polycentricity starts with the identification of the centres. Urban centres can be detected by examining local peaks of population or employment density (Amindarbari and Sevtsuk, 2012; Galster et al., 2001; Veneri 2017). Several metrics result from the identification of such peaks, such as the share of the population that lives in centres, the fraction of urban surface occupied by them, their relative size, and the distance between them. It is important to note that polycentricity measures are conceptually different from dispersion ones. Dispersion measures express the global clustering of people and jobs in a city whereas polycentricity measures how those high-density clusters are organised in centres (Arribas-Bel, Nijkamp and Scholten, 2011).

Land-use mix

Mixed land use indicators measure the balance between different types of land use, such as residential and business. The index of dissimilarity (Arribas-Bel and Schmidt, 2013), the exposure index (Galster et al., 2001) and entropy measures (Cervero, 1989; Frank and Pivo, 1995; Zhao, 2011) are somewhat similar indicators used to describe the degree to which different land-use categories are distributed in a homogenously and non-mixed way.

3.3. Data

This report makes use of three distinct datasets to compute the various urban form metrics proposed in Section 3.4. These data include the spatial delimitation of urban areas across OECD countries, as well as development intensity and population density across space at three time points (1990, 2000 and 2014).

Identifying urban areas

Each *Functional Urban Area* (FUA) comprises a set of contiguous local administrative units. In Europe, these administrative units correspond to municipalities.[3] In the rest of the OECD countries, the local units composing FUAs are the smallest administrative areas for which national commuting data are available. Despite being constructed on the basis of administrative boundaries, functional urban areas are defined on the basis of commuting flows. Therefore, they are of economic significance, as they represent highly self-contained labour markets. The set of administrative units out of which an FUA is constructed is identified in a series of different steps, which are explained below. The reader is referred to OECD (2012) for more details.

The first step involves an examination of population raster maps[4] to detect areas (cells) in which population density is high enough for them to be considered as urban.[5] The population density threshold for cells to be considered as urban is set at 1 500 inhabitants per km^2 in Europe, Japan, Korea and Mexico and at 1 000 people per km^2 in the US and Canada, where several metropolitan areas develop in a less compact manner (OECD, 2012). Contiguous population raster cells with a density over the aforementioned thresholds form clusters. Any such *high-density cluster* is considered further when its total population, i.e. the sum of inhabitants across its contiguous grid cells, exceeds a certain threshold. This threshold is set to 50 000 people in Europe, Canada and the US and to 100 000 people in Japan, Korea and Mexico (OECD, 2012). The final part of the first step involves the construction of *municipal urban cores*. Any municipality whose population resides by at least by 50% in a high-density cluster qualifies as part of an urban core, i.e. it is a core municipality. Any pair of adjacent core municipalities belongs to the same urban core. Thus, urban cores comprise one or more municipalities. Figure 3.1 illustrates the process of construction of urban cores out of population grid and municipal delimitation data.

The next step involves deciding which of the urban cores identified in the previous step are going to be considered part of the same functional urban area. Any pair of urban cores (A,B) with considerable cross-commuting flows, i.e. with over 15% of the population of urban core A commuting to urban core B and/or *vice versa*, are automatically considered to be part of the same FUA. This procedure is illustrated in Figure 3.2. The criteria used to assign cores to functional urban areas allow the latter to represent polycentric metropolitan areas containing a central city with a large population nucleus and a set of smaller sub-centres integrated with the nucleus. The final step in the construction of functional urban areas is the identification of *hinterland municipalities*. These are municipalities outside the urban core, i.e. municipalities with less than 50% (even 0%) of their population residing in a high-density population cluster, which however display significant commuting flows to the urban core of the FUA they are assigned to.

Figure 3.1. **Obtaining municipal urban cores from municipal delimitations and population density data**

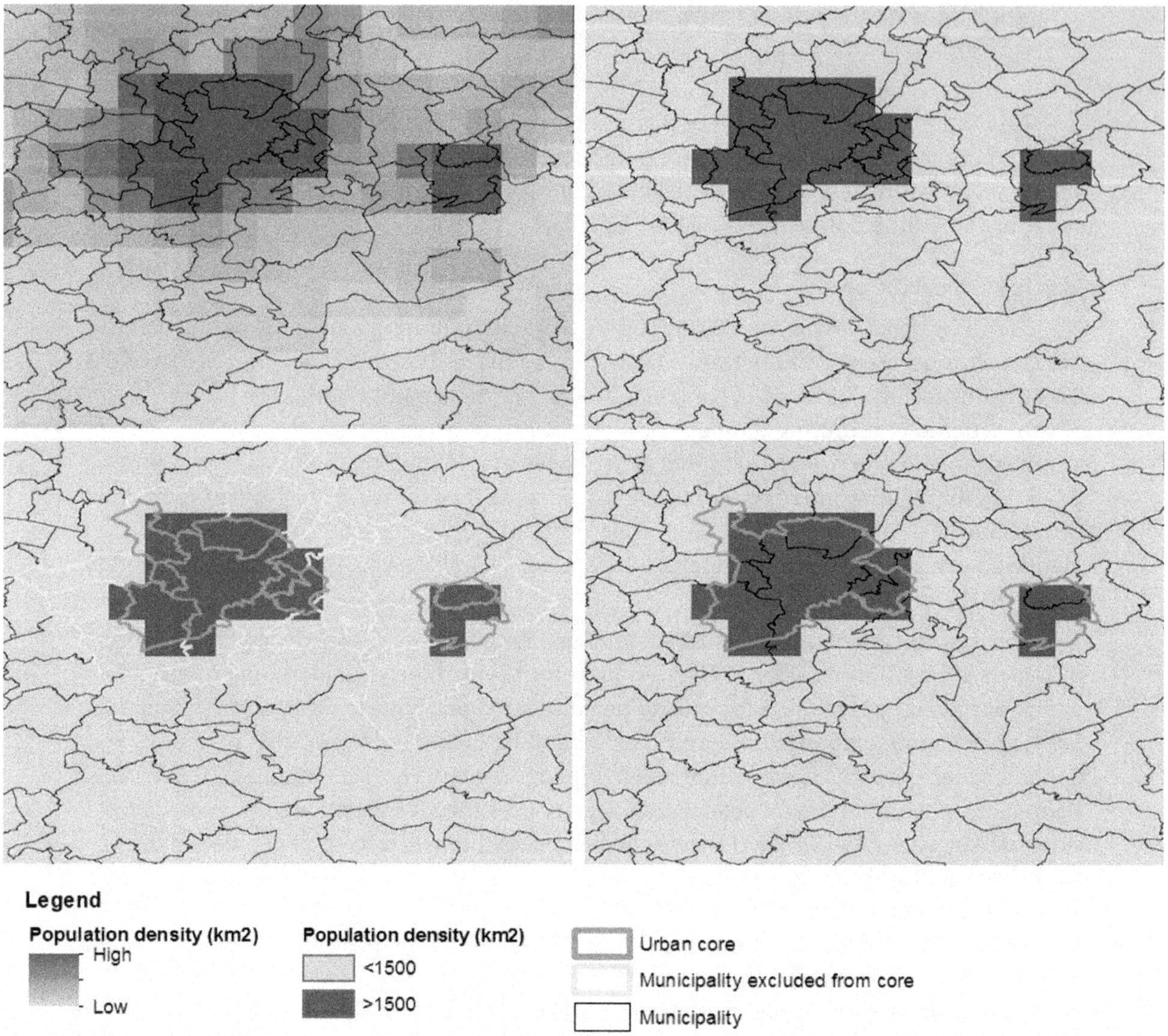

Notes: Upper left panel: population raster cells of 62 500 m^2 (250 m × 250 m) superimposed on a layer representing municipalities. Upper right panel: the two high density clusters derived from the population raster using the threshold of 1 500 inhabitants per km^2 are superimposed on the layer of municipalities. Lower left panel: municipalities with at least 50% of their inhabitants residing in one of the two high density clusters are highlighted with red limits. Municipalities with some, but less than 50% of their inhabitants residing inside high density clusters are highlighted with yellow limits. Implicit assumption: uniform distribution of population within municipalities. None of the inhabitants in non-highlighted municipalities resides in high-density clusters. Lower right panel: The two high density clusters yield two urban municipal cores, highlighted in red.

Furthermore, two urban cores, for instance B and C in Figure 3.3, may belong to the same FUA even if cross-commuting between them is low. In that case, there is at least a third urban core (i.e. core A in Figure 3.3), such that the cross-commuting condition is satisfied both for pair (A,C) and for pair (A,B). Figure 3.3 juxtaposes the latter case (left panel) against the case in which the labour force of one of the cores, i.e. core C, is mostly self-contained (right panel).

Figure 3.2. **Obtaining functional urban areas from municipal urban cores**

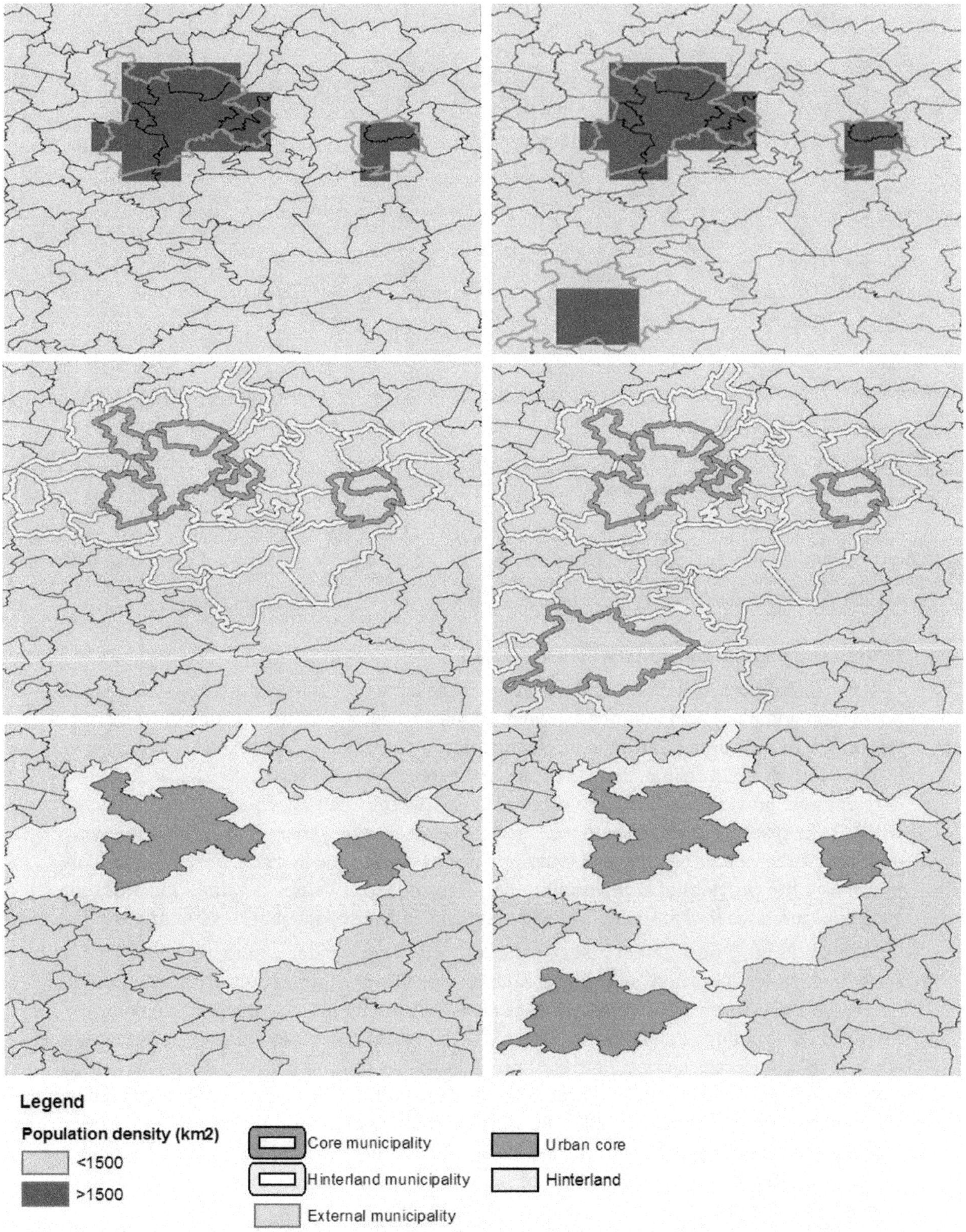

Notes: Upper panels: municipal urban cores superimposed on the high density clusters they are derived from. Middle panels: urban core municipalities (highlighted in dark red borders) and hinterland municipalities (highlighted in light yellow borders). Lower panels: functional urban areas derived after considering the commuting flows between urban cores and from hinterland to urban cores.

Figure 3.3. **The decisive role of cross commuting flows in delimiting functional urban areas**

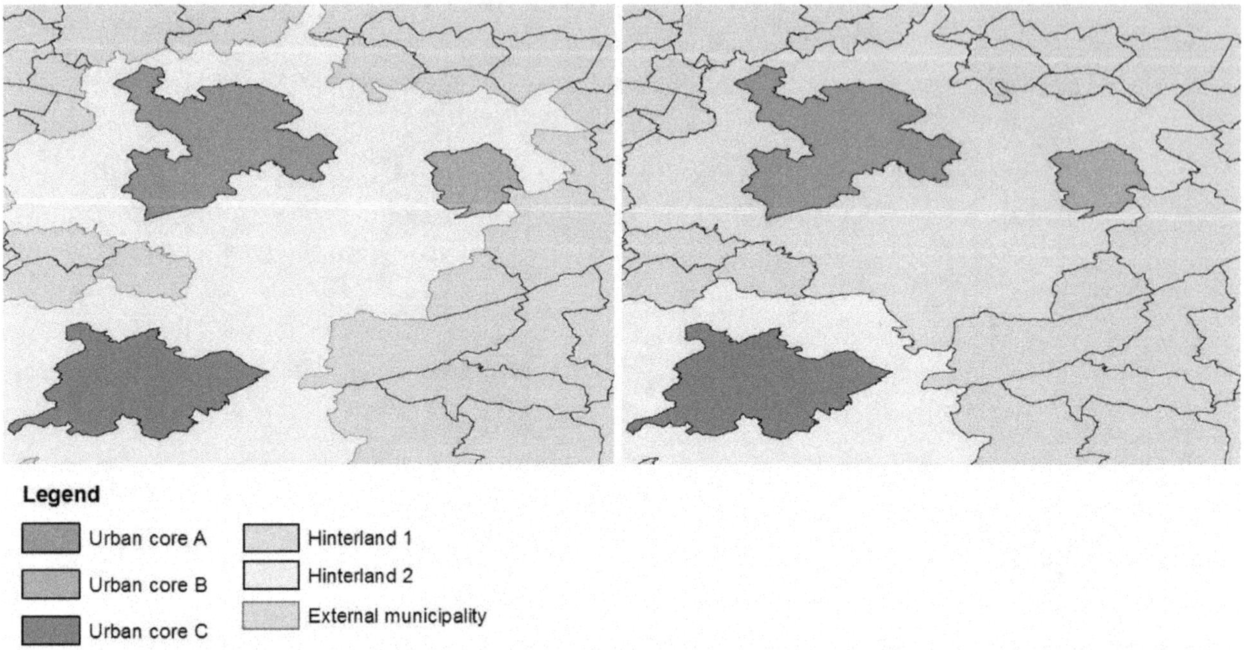

Notes: Left panel: three municipal urban cores grouped into a single functional urban area, assuming that more than 15% of residents in cores B and C commute to core A. Right panel: the same municipal urban cores grouped in two functional urban areas, assuming that: i) less than 15% of core C inhabitants commute to core A and *vice versa*, ii) less than 15% of core C inhabitants commute to core B and *vice versa* and iii) at least 15% of population in core A commutes to B and/or *vice versa*.

Estimating population density across space

The Global Human Settlement (GHS) built-up area dataset (Pesaresi et al., 2015) and the GHS population grid (European Commission, Joint Research Centre (JRC) and Columbia University, Center for International Earth Science Information Network – CIESIN, 2015)[6] are used in conjunction with FUA delimitations to compute the indicators proposed in Section 3.4. The two GHS datasets provide worldwide coverage of development intensity and population density with a high spatiotemporal resolution. The worldwide coverage ensures that the underlying data used to compute the proposed indicators are homogeneous in terms of resolution. This minimises the problem of comparability between indicator values obtained for different geographic units, as they are computed with data of identical spatiotemporal resolution.

The GHS built-up area data (Pesaresi et al., 2015) are provided in raster cells of high resolution (38m × 38m) derived from satellite images.[7] The building intensity at each cell is expressed as the fraction of the cell's surface area, i.e. 1 444 m^2 (0.00144 km^2), occupied by the footprints of buildings, related structures and civil works. This fraction ranges from zero, when a cell's surface is estimated to contain no buildings or other structures, to one, which is the case when that surface is estimated to be fully built up. This exercise is illustrated in Figure 3.4. Settlement data display the highest temporal resolution among land-cover datasets available at global scale. The recording of settlement intensity at three time points (1990, 2000, 2014) facilitates the analysis of land-cover changes and the identification of time trends in development intensity.

The GHS population grid dataset (European Commission, Joint Research Centre (JRC) and Columbia University, Center for International Earth Science Information Network – CIESIN, 2015) provides worldwide population density maps. Population data are provided in grid

Figure 3.4. **From satellite images to land cover and settlement data**

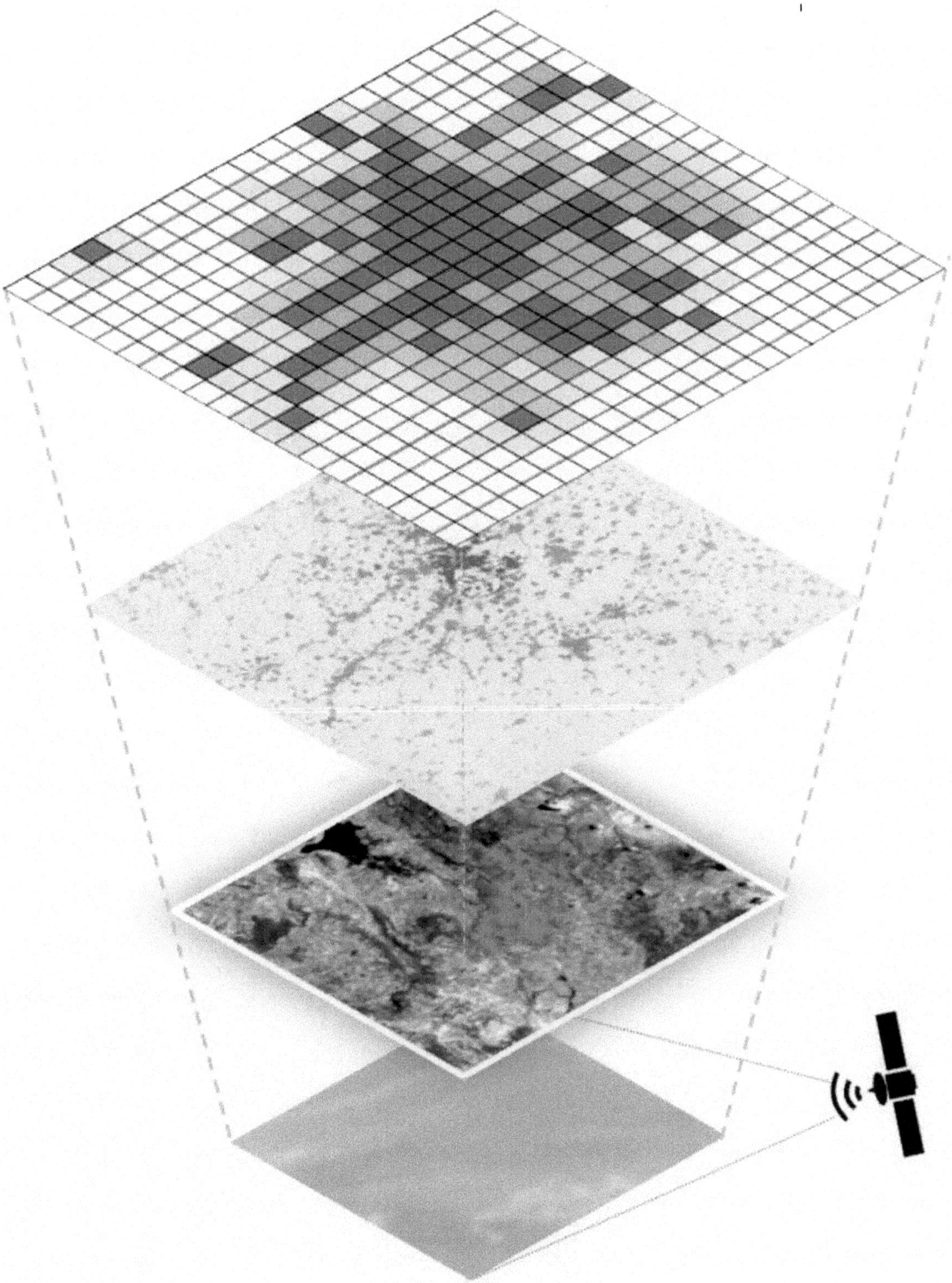

Notes: Bottom panel: Earth surface. 2nd panel: Earth observation satellites provide images of earth's surface in the form of raster files. 3rd panel: Extraction of built-up areas, i.e. surface areas covered by buildings and other structures. Top panel: Built-up area raster, expressing the fraction of built-up area in the total size of a grid cell.
Source: Own illustration, based on the presentation of the procedure provided in the GHS website: *http://ghslsys.jrc.ec.europa.eu/data.php#GHSLBasics*. Satellite photo credit: MaxxL/Wikimedia Commons/CC BY-SA 3.0.

Figure 3.5. **Constructing a population raster out of a built-up area raster and census population data**

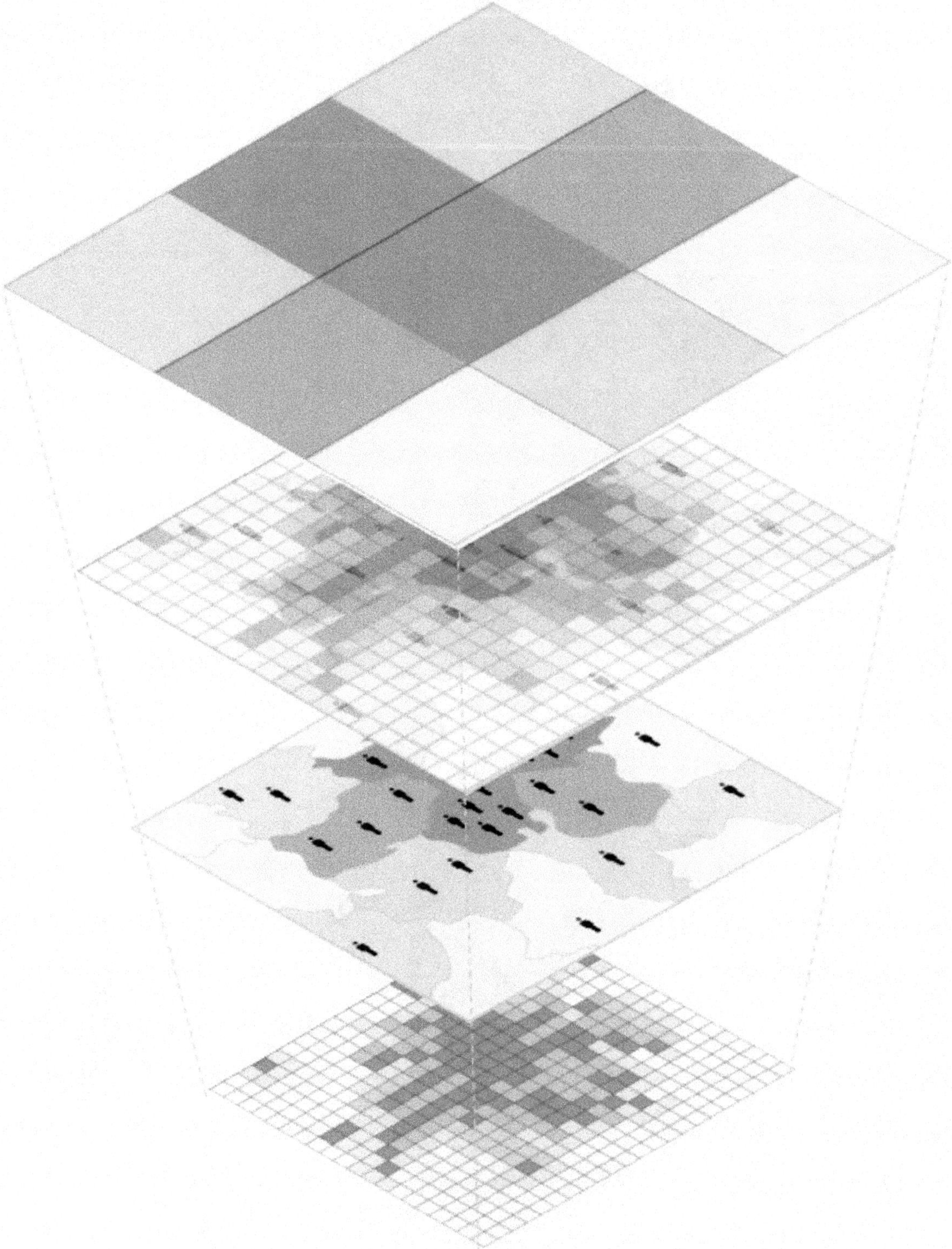

Notes: Bottom panel: Built-up area raster (see also Figure 3.4). 2nd panel: Census data. 3rd panel: Combining census data on population (e.g. at the census tract level) with the built-up area raster. Top panel: Population raster, expressing the number of inhabitants per grid cell.
Source: Own illustration, based on the presentation of the procedure provided in the GHS website: *http://ghslsys.jrc.ec.europa.eu/data.php#GHSLBasics*.

cells of 250 m × 250 m, with the estimated number of inhabitants within each cell surface of 62 500 m^2 (0.0625 km^2) being reported for 1990, 2000 and 2015. The reported estimates are derived by combining the population figures recorded for administrative areas or census tracts with the high-resolution settlement data derived from satellite images for the same time period. In this context, population estimates for 2015 are combined with built-up area data for 2014. The procedure followed to combine the two datasets is shown in Figure 3.5. A larger development intensity in the underlying settlement grid cells and a larger number of inhabitants in the underlying administrative units imply a larger number of inhabitants allocated to a 250 m × 250 m cell.[8]

Estimating the spatial distribution of population and built-up land within urban areas

For the computation of the urban sprawl indicators introduced in Section 3.4, the Global Human Settlement datasets are delimited by each of the FUA boundaries. This procedure is illustrated in Figure 3.6.

Figure 3.6. **Raster cells of built areas and population density of a given functional urban area**

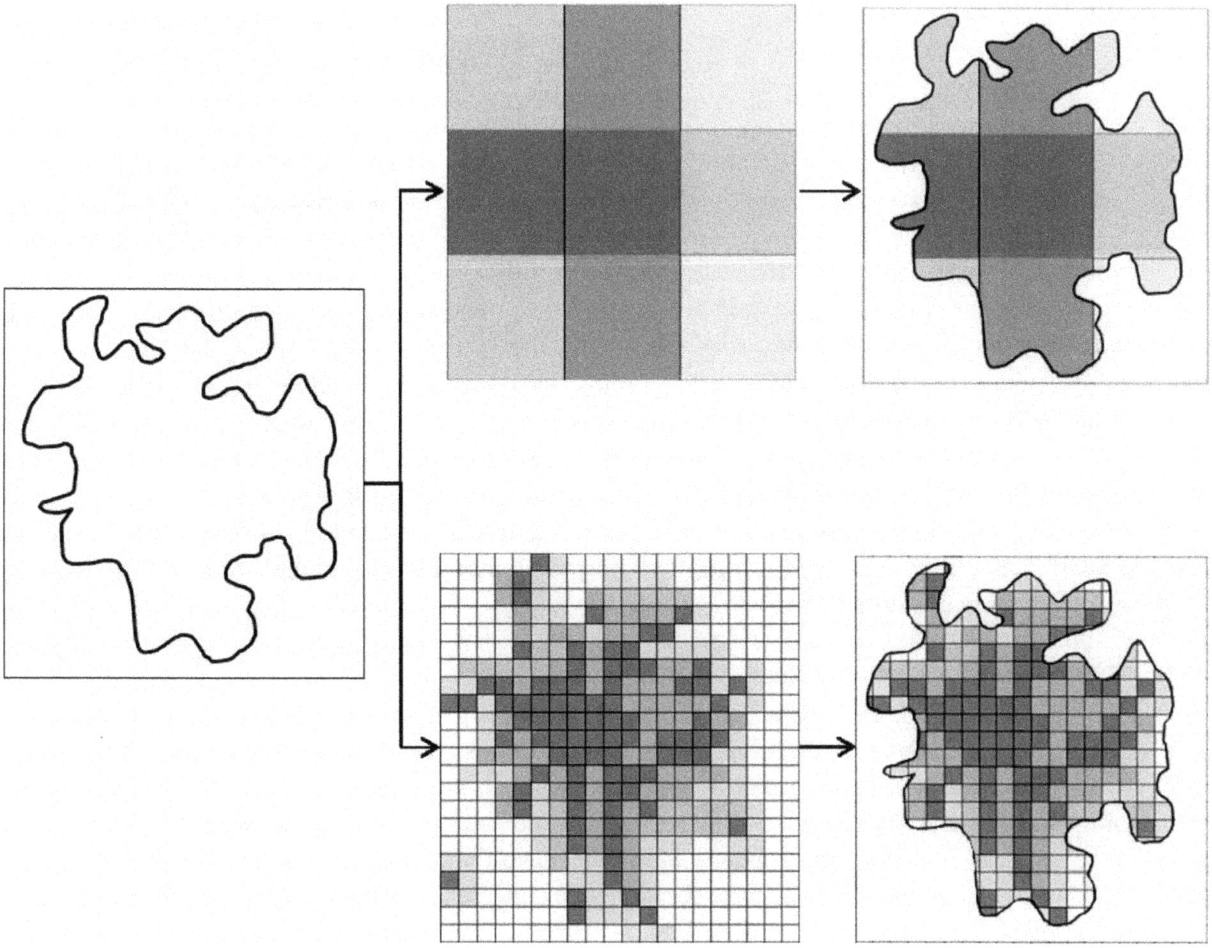

Notes: Left panel: delimitation of a functional urban area (FUA). Upper middle panel: selected cells from population raster map. Lower middle panel: selected cells from a built-up area raster map. Upper right panel: selection of population cells that make up the FUA. Lower right panel: selection of built-up raster cells that make up the FUA.

3.4. Cross-country analyses of urban sprawl indicators

The indicators of urban sprawl used in this study are matched to the urban sprawl dimensions presented in Chapter 2 in Table 3.1. These indicators are selected on the basis of a number of criteria. First, they should enable an analysis of sprawl at certain points in time and facilitate the examination of its changes over time. Second, the different dimensions of sprawl should be conceptually distinct from each other. Third, they should allow for polycentric urban structures, because there is a considerable number of FUAs with more than one centre. The mathematical formulas used for the calculation of each indicator at the FUA level, as well as those used for aggregating the city-level indicators to the country level, are presented in Appendix 3.A.

Table 3.1. **Indicators of urban sprawl**

Dimension	Indicator
Average urban population density	Arithmetic mean of the number of inhabitants per km^2 of populated urban space.
Population-to-density allocation	Percentage of population living in areas with a density below a certain threshold.*
Land-to-density allocation	Percentage of urban footprint occupying areas of density below a certain threshold.*
Variation of urban population density (dispersion)	Coefficient of variation (relative standard deviation) of urban population density.
Fragmentation	Number of urban fabric fragments per km^2 of built-up area.
Polycentricity	Number of urban centres, i.e. population-density peaks, in an urban area.
Decentralisation	Share of urban population residing outside of the urban centres of an FUA.

* The thresholds used in the corresponding calculations are 1 500, 2 500 and 3 500 inhabitants per km^2.

This section provides static and intertemporal cross-country comparisons based on these indicators. Static comparisons are performed using *average* values *at the country level* for the year 2014, which is referred to as the *current situation*. In addition, the provided cross-country comparisons report the FUAs in which indicators obtain their minimum and maximum values in each country. This facilitates a visual inspection of the range of values taken by different indicators across the FUAs of a country.

On the other hand, intertemporal comparisons are entirely based on the evolution of indicator values at the country level, which are obtained for 29 countries (all OECD member countries, except for Estonia, Iceland, Israel, Latvia, New Zealand and Turkey) in three time points: 1990, 2000 and 2014.[9] Countries are ranked according to the total change occurred between 1990 and 2014. The changes that took place in the periods 1990-2000 and 2000-14 are displayed together with the corresponding total changes. All changes are computed and reported in absolute terms.

Average urban population density

The average population density of an urban area is the average number of inhabitants per km^2 of populated urban space. This is the ratio of the urban area's total population to the total inhabited surface within that urban area. The indicator is computed at the urban area level using Equation (1) in Appendix 3.A. The value of the indicator at the country level is computed using Equation (2) of the appendix and is equivalent to the average population density that would be observed had all FUAs of the country been concatenated in a single urban area.

Current situation

Statistics of the average population density of urban areas for the 29 OECD countries included in the study are provided in Figure 3.7. Countries are ranked from highest to lowest mean of average population density levels in 2014. The figure also displays the minimum and

Figure 3.7. **Average population density in urban areas of 29 OECD countries, 2014**

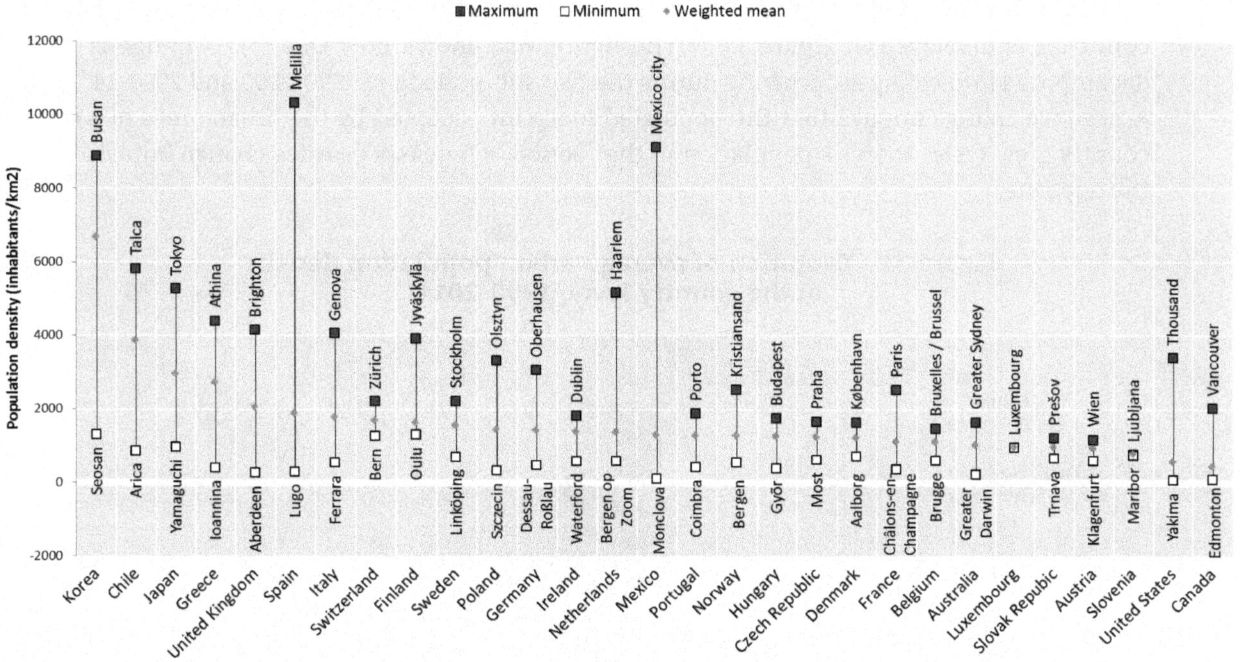

Notes: Red diamond-shaped points indicate average urban population densities at the country level. Minimum and maximum values of the indicator at the city level are indicated with white and blue squares respectively.

Source: Own calculations, based on GHS built-area data (Pesaresi et al., 2015), GHS population data (European Commission, Joint Research Centre (JRC) and Columbia University, Center for International Earth Science Information Network – CIESIN, 2015) and FUA delimitations (OECD, 2012).

maximum values of average population density at the FUA level and the names of the corresponding urban areas.

As revealed by the ranking of countries, urban areas of Canada and the United States are, on average, the least dense. However, urban areas of both countries are heterogeneous and display average densities that lie in a wide range. Specific functional urban areas, such as New York and Vancouver, have an average population density that exceeds the average density observed in most European cities. For example, Vancouver is much denser than Copenhagen or Prague, despite urban areas of Denmark and Czech Republic being on average much denser than those of Canada. On the other hand, the least dense FUAs in these countries display densities that fall below the threshold of 150 people per km^2, which is the threshold used to define rural areas (OECD, 2011). To ensure that country mean densities are not affected by outlier values, North American functional urban areas with a density below 80 inhabitants per km^2 were excluded from the study.[10]

The average population density of urban areas obtains values between 1 000 and 2 000 people per km^2 for the majority of countries. However, within-country variation is remarkably high, primarily across urban areas of Mexico and Spain, and secondarily of Korea, The Netherlands and Chile. Greece and the United Kingdom are the only European countries where density of urban areas exceeds the threshold of 2 000 people per km^2. The figure also reveals that urban areas in Korea and Japan are, on average, some of the densest worldwide. However, both countries contain diverse urban areas with local averages that vary widely, peaking in the cities of Busan and Tokyo respectively. Chile is the second densest country among the ones analysed here, with the majority of its urban areas being very dense.

Trends 1990-2014

The evolution of average urban population density between 1990 and 2014 in the 29 OECD countries is displayed in Figure 3.8.[11] The figure also shows how this total change is decomposed into changes occurring during the two sub-periods of 1990-2000 and 2000-14. A negative change implies that the populated footprint occupied by the urban areas of a country grew faster than its population in that period, whereas a positive change implies the opposite.

Figure 3.8. **Evolution of average urban population density at the country level, 1990-2014**

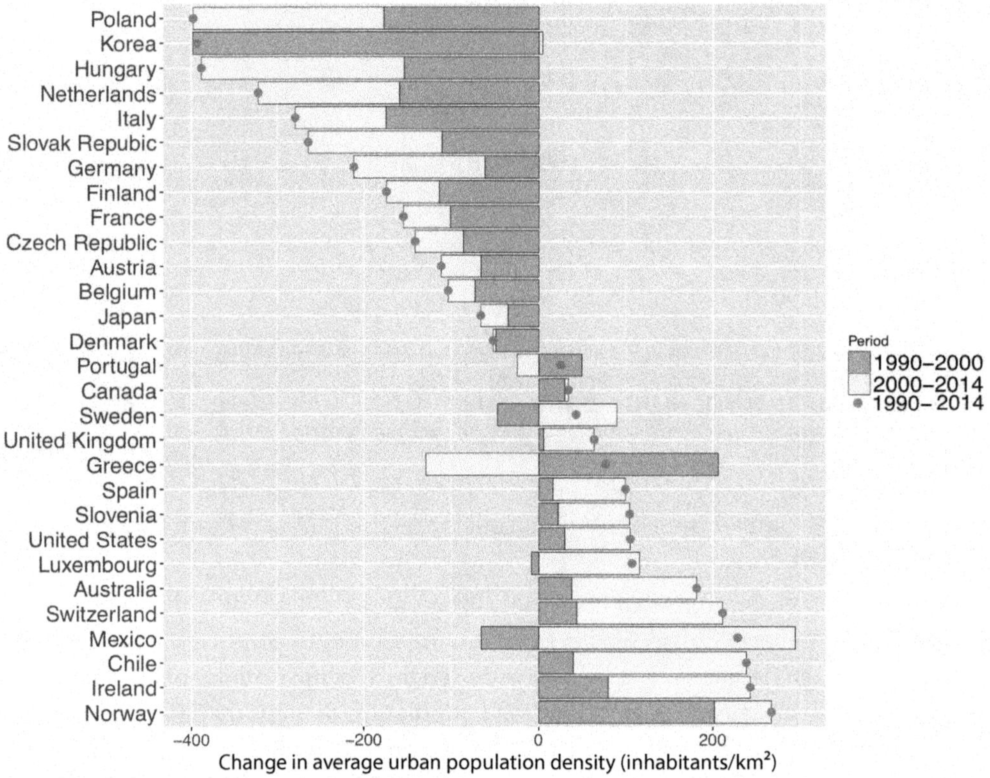

Notes: Red dots represent the total change in average urban population density in the period 1990-2014. The bars decompose the total change into changes occurring during the periods 1990-2000 (darker blue) and 2000-14 (lighter blue).

Source: Own calculations, based on GHS built-area data (Pesaresi et al., 2015), GHS population data (European Commission, Joint Research Centre (JRC) and Columbia University, Center for International Earth Science Information Network – CIESIN, 2015) and FUA delimitations (OECD, 2012).

Since 1990, average urban population density has increased in 15 countries and has declined in 14. Despite density having increased in most of the countries, reductions of urban population density are, on average, much larger than relevant increases. This is mainly due to important reductions of population density in several countries, such as Korea and Italy, during the period 1990-2000. The most important reductions of average urban population density are observed in Poland, Korea, Hungary and the Netherlands. In Korea, the large decline of population density in the period 1990-2000 was followed by a minor increase in density in the period 2000-14. On the other hand, in Germany and the Slovak Republic, a relatively large share of the density decline has occurred after 2000.

The largest increases of average urban population density since 1990 have occurred in Norway, Ireland, Chile and Mexico. These increases have mainly occurred after 2000 (except for Norway), with Mexico showing the greatest increase in absolute terms among the examined countries in the period 2000-14. Average urban population density has increased in all three countries with the lowest density in 2014: Slovenia, United States and Canada. In Greece and Portugal, densification of the period 1990-2000 was slightly reversed in the period 2000-14, when urban population density declined in both countries.

Population-to-density allocation

The allocation of population to areas of relatively low density is captured by the share of population living in areas where density is below a certain threshold. Three thresholds are considered in this report: 1 500, 2 500 and 3 500 inhabitants per km^2. The lower threshold of 1 500 people per km^2 matches the threshold value used by the OECD (2012) to identify areas which can be considered as urban. Under the conditions presented in Section 3.3 such areas make up the urban cores, the fundamental building block of a functional urban area. The higher threshold of 3 500 people per km^2 is based on the study by Newman and Kenworthy (2006). Using data from 58 higher-income cities, that study suggests the existence of a critical urban density threshold, placed at approximately 3 500 inhabitants (or workers) per km^2, above which car dependency is significantly reduced. Finally, the middle threshold of 2 500 people per km^2 is a natural intermediate step between the other two values. It should also be mentioned that areas with population density up to 150 inhabitants per km^2 are not considered in the calculation of the indicator, as this is the threshold below which areas are considered as rural (OECD, 2011).

At the city level, the share of population living in areas of the FUA where density lies below one of the three aforementioned thresholds is computed using Equation (3) in Appendix 3.A. At the country level, the indicator reflects the share of urban population residing in areas of all FUAs of the country where density is below the selected threshold. This indicator is calculated using Equation (4) in Appendix 3.A. In the cross-country analysis of the indicator that follows, the selected threshold is the lowest of the ones presented above, i.e. 1 500 inhabitants per km^2.

Current situation

The statistics associated with the share of population residing in areas where density is between 150 and 1 500 people per km^2 are provided in Figure 3.9. The 29 countries considered in the report are ranked, from highest to lowest, with respect to the share of their urban population that was residing in such areas in 2014. The figure also displays the minimum and maximum values obtained by the indicator at the FUA level, as well as the names of the corresponding urban areas.

The resulting ranking of countries differs substantially from the cross-country ranking of average population density provided in Figure 3.7. First, the countries with the lowest urban population density are not found at the top of the ranking. For instance, less than 15% of the urban population of Canada resides in areas of very low population density, a value that lies far below the maximum recorded in Luxemburg (30.5%). Second, countries with moderate levels of average population density can be found at the lower end of the ranking. For instance, only a very small portion of Mexico's urban population resides in locations where density lies between 150 and 1 500 inhabitants per km^2. Korea, Chile,

Figure 3.9. **Percentage of urban population living in areas with a density of 150-1 500 people per km² in 29 OECD countries, 2014**

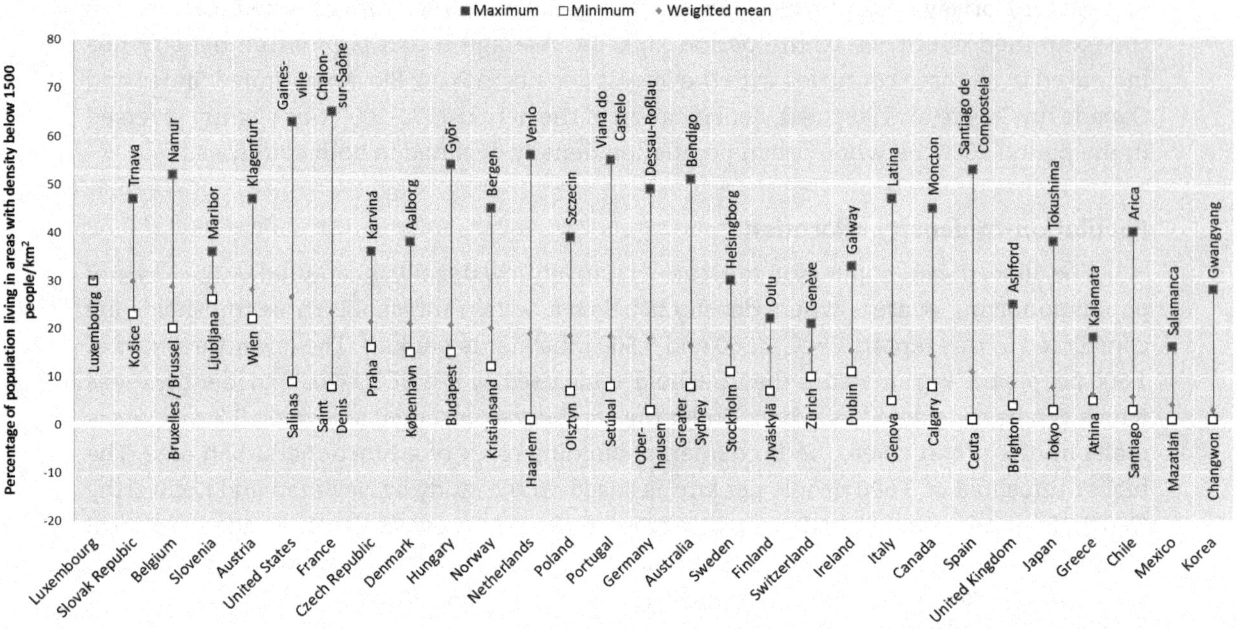

Notes: Red diamond-shaped points indicate the average share of population residing in areas with density of 150-1 500 inhabitants/km² at the country level. Minimum and maximum values of the indicator at the city level are indicated with white and blue squares respectively.
Source: Own calculations, based on GHS built-area data (Pesaresi et al., 2015), GHS population data (European Commission, Joint Research Centre (JRC) and Columbia University, Center for International Earth Science Information Network – CIESIN, 2015) and FUA delimitations (OECD, 2012).

Greece and Japan score similarly in both indicators in 2014: their urban areas are dense and only a very low share of their population resides in those parts of their FUAs where density is very low.

Trends 1990-2014

The intertemporal changes in the percentage of population residing in areas of very low population density (150-1 500 inhabitants per km²) for the 29 OECD countries considered in the analysis are displayed in Figure 3.10. The total change between 1990 and 2014, which is denoted by dots, is also decomposed into changes occurring during the two sub-periods: 1990-2000 and 2000-14.

Overall, the share of population living in areas of very low density has increased in about half of the countries. The largest increase of the indicator is observed in Slovak Republic (about 6 percentage points), followed by the Netherlands, Hungary and Poland. On the other hand, the largest decline of the share of population living in areas of very low density since 1990 occurred in the urban areas of Australia (about 12 percentage points), Luxembourg, Canada and the United States. In all countries mentioned above, a major part of the observed changes has occurred in more recent years, i.e. during the period 2000-14.

The increases of the indicator displayed in Figure 3.10 may be driven by different forces. First, the indicator may have increased because some low-density areas (150-1 500 inhabitants/km²) have densified without their density exceeding the threshold of 1 500 inhabitants per km². Another reason for the observed increases may be that new areas that were previously

Figure 3.10. **Evolution of country-specific percentages of urban population living in areas of density 150-1 500 people/km², 1990-2014**

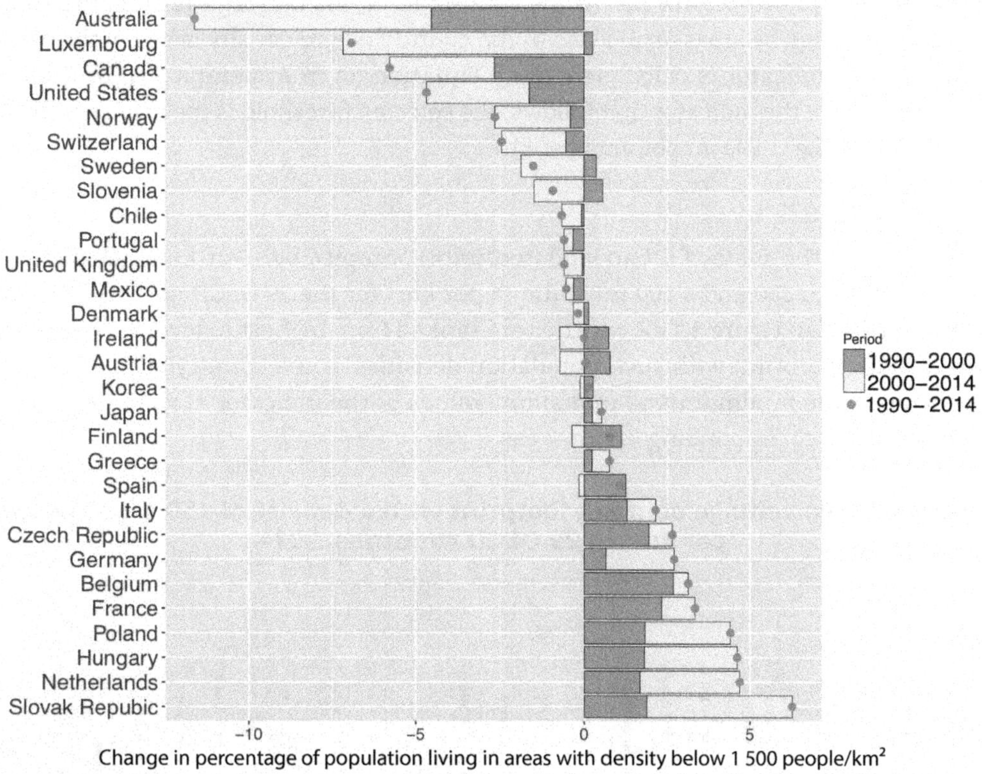

Notes: Red dots represent the total change in the share of population residing in areas with density of 150-1 500 inhabitants/km² in the period 1990-2014. The bars decompose the total change into changes occurring during the periods 1990-2000 (darker blue) and 2000-14 (lighter blue).

Source: Own calculations, based on GHS built-area data (Pesaresi et al., 2015), GHS population data (European Commission, Joint Research Centre (JRC) and Columbia University, Center for International Earth Science Information Network – CIESIN, 2015) and FUA delimitations (OECD, 2012).

undeveloped are converted to low-density locations or that density decreases in areas where it has previously been slightly above 1 500 inhabitants per km². To identify whether the evolution of the indicator is driven by the latter type of change, the values of the population-to-density allocation indicator should be examined in conjunction with the corresponding values of the land-to-density allocation indicator, which is provided in Figures 3.11 and 3.12 below.

Another important insight provided by Figure 3.10 is that in a few European countries, such as Greece and Spain, both average urban population density and the percentage of population residing in areas with population density of 150-1 500 inhabitants per km² have increased. This finding indicates that in some of the urban areas of these countries densification has been accompanied by suburbanisation. This phenomenon is examined in more detail separately for each country in the sheets available in Appendix 3.B.

Land-to-density allocation

The allocation of urban land to areas of relatively low density is captured by the share of urban land occupied by areas where density lies below a certain threshold. As with the population-to-density allocation, the thresholds considered are 1 500, 2 500 and 3 500 inhabitants per km² (for the rationale behind selecting these thresholds, see the relevant discussion in the presentation of the population-to-density allocation). At the city level, the share of land occupied by areas where density lies below a threshold value is computed using Equation (5) in Appendix 3.A. At the country level, the indicator reflects the share of urban land occupied by areas of all FUAs of the country where density is below the selected threshold. This indicator is calculated using Equation (6) in Appendix 3.A. In the cross-country analysis of the indicator that follows, the selected threshold is the lowest of the ones presented above, i.e. 1 500 inhabitants per km^2.

Current situation

Statistics of the share of urban land (footprint) occupied by areas in which population density is between 150 and 1 500 inhabitants per km^2 for the 29 OECD countries analysed here are provided in Figure 3.11. Countries are ranked from highest to lowest average share of urban land (footprint) with such population densities at the country level in 2014. The figure displays the minimum and maximum values of the indicator at the FUA level, and the names of the corresponding urban areas.

Figure 3.11. **Percentage of urban footprint with a density of 150-1 500 people per km^2 in 29 OECD countries, 2014**

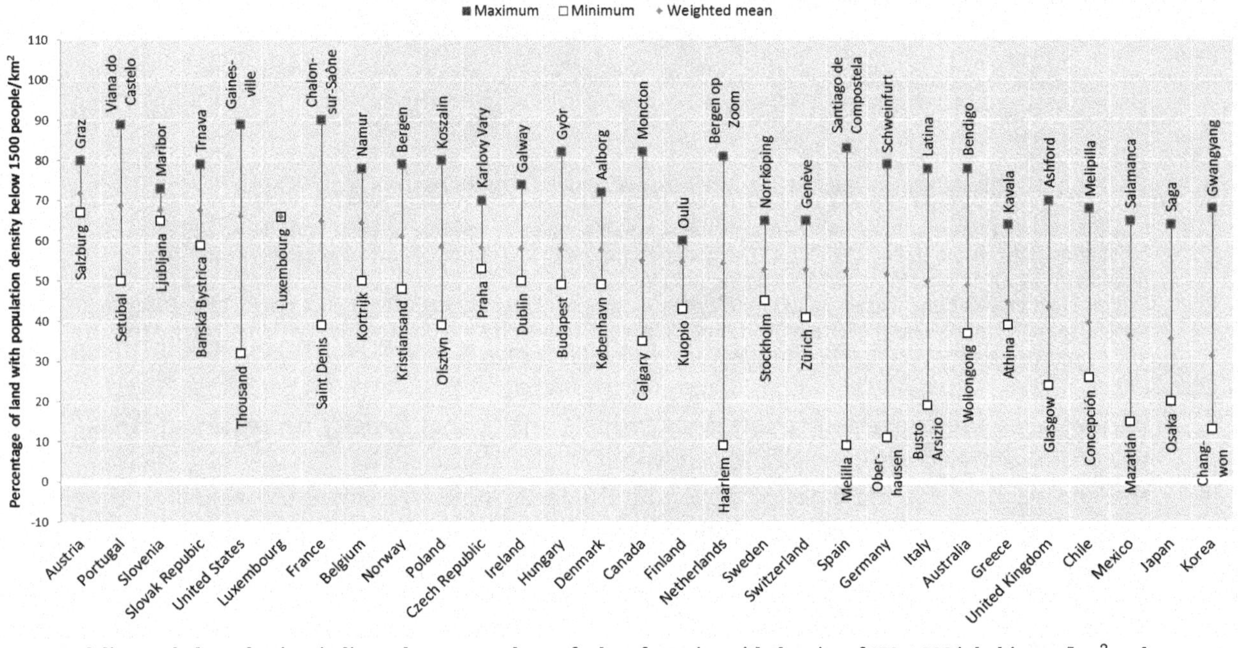

Notes: Red diamond-shaped points indicate the average share of urban footprint with density of 150-1 500 inhabitants/km^2 at the country level. Minimum and maximum values of the indicator at the city level are indicated with white and blue squares respectively.
Source: Own calculations, based on GHS built-area data (Pesaresi et al., 2015), GHS population data (European Commission, Joint Research Centre (JRC) and Columbia University, Center for International Earth Science Information Network – CIESIN, 2015) and FUA delimitations (OECD, 2012).

In many respects, the ranking resembles that of the share of population residing in areas of very low density, displayed in Figure 3.9, with the same set of six countries found in the lower end of the two rankings (even though in a different order). That is, functional urban areas in Korea, Japan, Mexico, Chile, United Kingdom and Greece contain the smallest percentages of land exposed to very low density levels, all below 45%. On the other hand, the national average values in Belgium, France, Luxembourg, United States, Slovak Republic, Slovenia and Austria all lie above 64%.

The share of urban footprint occupied by areas where population density is very low is strongly correlated with the share of population residing in areas of such density levels, but the two indicators provide complementary information.[12] This is highlighted in the case of Portugal, where the share of population residing in areas of very low density is modest, i.e. about 18%, but the share of urban footprint occupied by areas of very low density obtains the second largest value recorded in the national ranking, i.e. about 69%. Such a large divergence can mainly be attributed to a considerably lower population density in areas with less than 1 500 inhabitants per km^2 than the one in areas where density exceeds that threshold. In case of such large differences between the two indicators, population density is likely to display a large variation across the urban surfaces of a country. The analysis of the next indicator (variation of population density) supports this hypothesis.

Trends 1990-2014

The intertemporal changes in the share of urban footprint hosting areas of population density below 1 500 inhabitants per km^2 for the 29 OECD countries are presented in Figure 3.12. The total change between 1990 and 2014, which is denoted by the red dots, is also decomposed into changes occurring during the two sub-periods: 1990-2000 and 2000-14.

Figure 3.12. **Evolution of country-specific percentages of urban footprint with density of 150-1 500 people/km², 1990-2014**

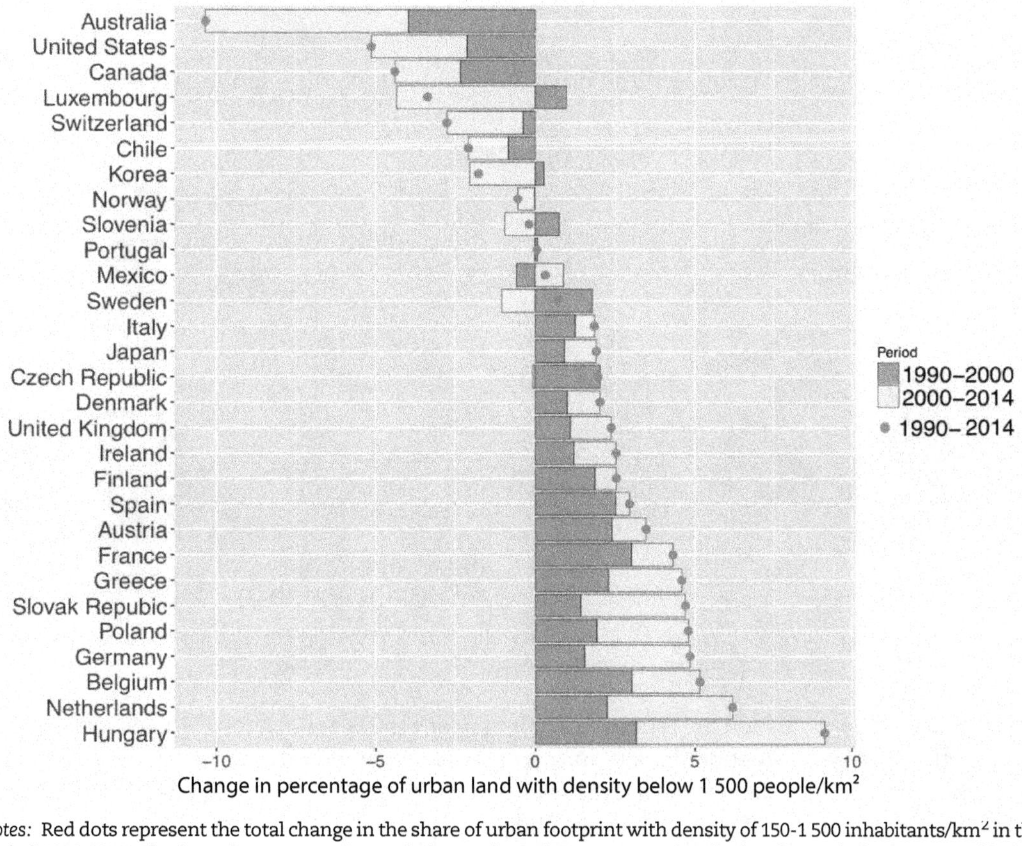

Notes: Red dots represent the total change in the share of urban footprint with density of 150-1 500 inhabitants/km² in the period 1990-2014. The bars decompose the total change into changes occurring during the periods 1990-2000 (darker blue) and 2000-14 (lighter blue).

Source: Own calculations, based on GHS built-area data (Pesaresi et al., 2015), GHS population data (European Commission, Joint Research Centre (JRC) and Columbia University, Center for International Earth Science Information Network – CIESIN, 2015) and FUA delimitations (OECD, 2012).

In the majority of countries, the share of urban footprint in very low density areas increased since 1990, with the largest growth recorded in Hungary (9 percentage points), the Netherlands, Belgium, Germany and Poland. On the other hand, the largest reductions are recorded in Australia (10 percentage points), the United States and Canada. To a large extent, these changes reflect the evolution of the share of population residing in areas of very low density in the aforementioned countries, shown in Figure 3.10.[13]

In some countries, especially in Europe (Greece, Ireland, Spain, Sweden and the United Kingdom), both average urban population density and the percentage of urban footprint occupied by areas of very low density (150-1 500 inhabitants per km^2) have increased. This reflects that in some of the urban areas of these countries densification has co-evolved with suburbanisation. However, this trend is also observed in cities of other countries. Box 3.1 displays the case of Santiago, the capital of Chile, whose functional urban area experienced both a growth in average population density and an increase in the share of urban land allocated to very low density levels (150-1 500 inhabitants per km^2) between 1990 and 2014.

Box 3.1. **Densification and suburbanisation in Santiago, Chile (1990-2014)**

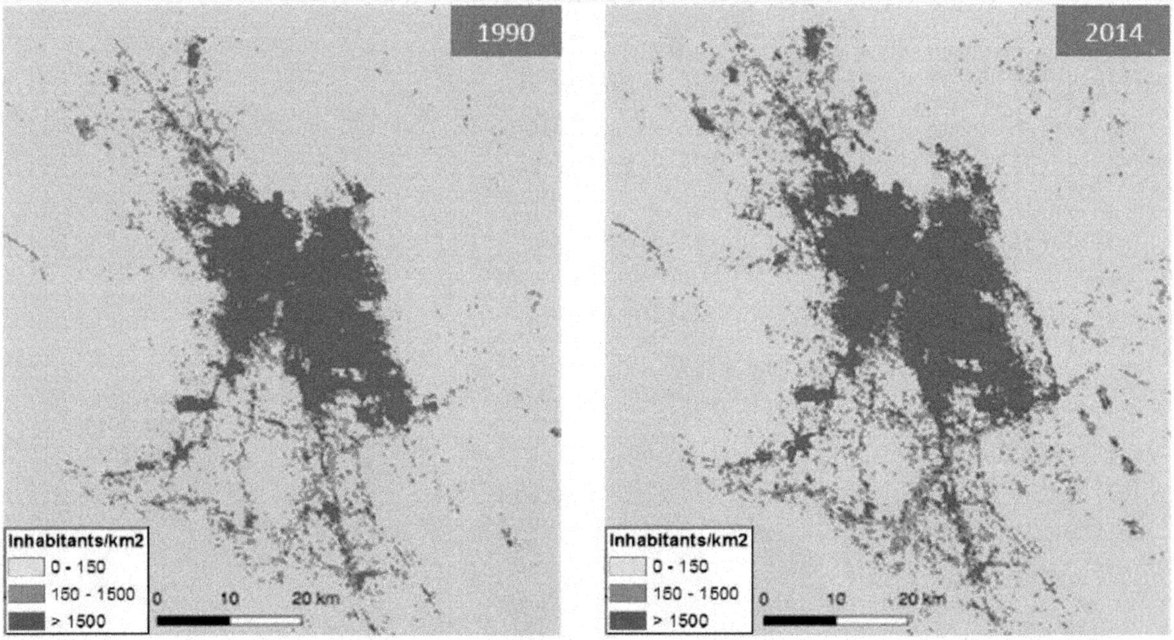

Notes: Left panel: Distribution of population density across three intervals (< 150, 150-1 500, and > 1 500 inhabitants per km^2) in Santiago in 1990. Right panel: Distribution of population density across the same intervals in 2014.

The coevolution of densification and suburbanisation over time is reflected well in the case of Santiago. Back in 1990, the average population density in the parts of the functional urban area hosting more than 150 inhabitants per km^2 (the coloured parts in the figure on the left) was approximately 5 606 inhabitants per km^2. In the same year, roughly 29% of that surface was hosting densities below 1 500 inhabitants per km^2. That area is represented by the red pixels of the figure.

The urban area of Santiago expanded significantly in the period from 1990 to 2014, as indicated by the difference in the number of coloured surfaces between the two panels. While average density in the areas

Box 3.1. Densification and suburbanisation in Santiago, Chile (1990-2014) *(cont.)*

represented by these coloured surfaces increased by 2.2% between 1990 and 2014, the composition of developed land changed in favour of low-density areas. By 2014, the share of developed land hosting density levels below 1 500 inhabitants per km^2 (red pixels) had increased by 3.3%, while the share of population residing in areas of such density had increased by 4.2%. This is depicted in the growth of red pixels, which is faster than the growth of blue pixels in the examined period.

Source: Own elaboration, based on GHS built-area data (Pesaresi et al., 2015), GHS population data (European Commission, Joint Research Centre (JRC) and Columbia University, Center for International Earth Science Information Network - CIESIN, 2015) and FUA delimitations (OECD, 2012).

Variation of urban population density

Population density often varies substantially among different areas of a city. The indicator used to measure the level of variation of urban population density is the coefficient of variation (also known as relative standard deviation). At the city level, the indicator is equal to the ratio of the standard deviation of population density in an FUA over the mean of population density in that FUA. The mathematical formula used to compute the coefficient of variation at the city level is presented in Equation (8) of Appendix 3.A. At the country level, the indicator shows the ratio of the standard deviation of population densities at all locations in the FUAs of a country from the national mean of urban population density over that mean. The indicator at the country level is calculated using Equation (10) of Appendix 3.A.

Current situation

The statistics associated with the variation of urban population density for the 29 OECD countries are provided in Figure 3.13. Countries are ranked from highest to lowest coefficient of variation of urban population density at the country level in 2014. The figure also displays the minimum and maximum values of the coefficient of variation at the FUA level and the names of the corresponding urban areas.

Urban areas of Canada, Mexico and the United States are characterised, on average, by the largest coefficient of variation among the examined OECD countries. However, urban areas of these countries are heterogeneous, thus the coefficient values at the FUA level range widely across cities. On the other hand, the lowest variation of urban population density is observed in The Netherlands, Germany and Japan.

The relationship between the mean and the coefficient of variation of urban population density at the country level is not particularly strong. Indeed, cities in countries including Chile, Finland, Italy, Japan and Switzerland are dense and have a relatively low coefficient of variation of density, and urban areas in Canada, France and the United States are rather sparsely populated and have a high coefficient of variation of density. However, countries may be placed closer to the lower end in the coefficient of variation ranking while their average urban population density is also relatively low. For instance, Luxembourg and the urban areas of Czech Republic have relatively low population density but are, on average, also among the ones with the lowest coefficient of variation across OECD countries. On the other hand, the coefficient of variation is relatively high in Korea, Greece and Spain, despite these countries ranking high in terms of average urban population density.

Figure 3.13. **Coefficient of variation of population density across OECD urban areas and countries, 2014**

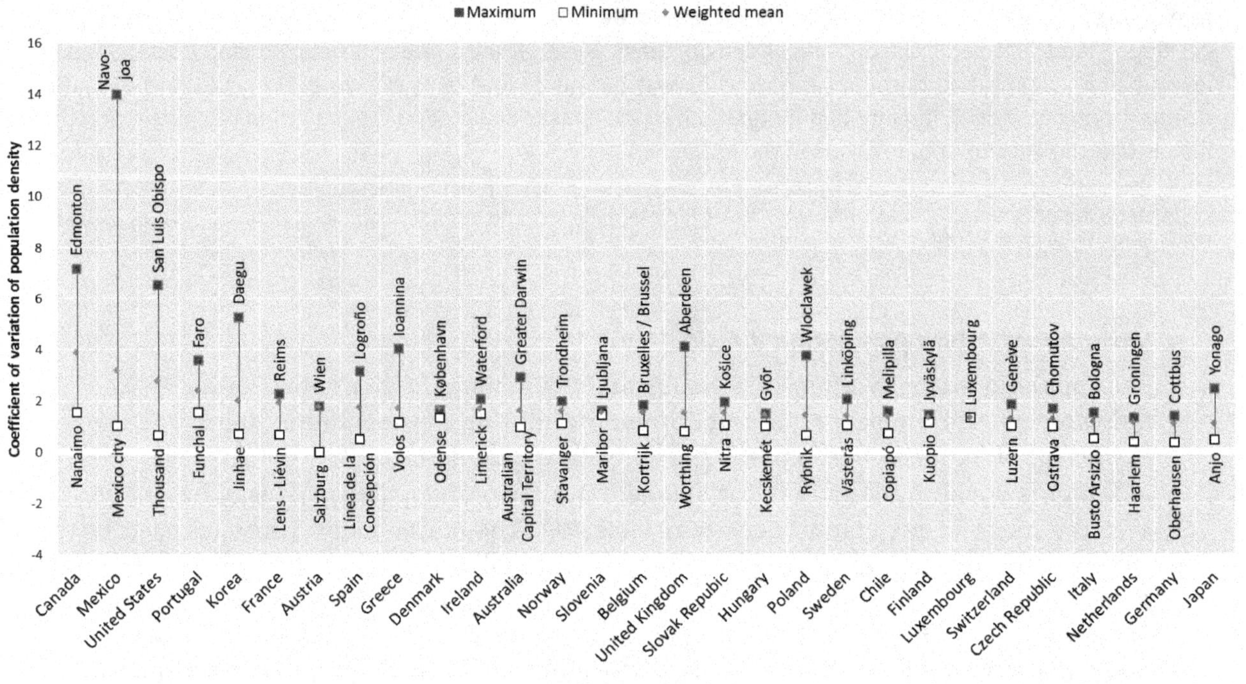

Notes: Red diamond-shaped points indicate the average coefficient of variation of urban population density at the country level. Minimum and maximum values of the indicator at the city level are indicated with white and blue squares respectively.

Source: Own calculations, based on GHS built-area data (Pesaresi et al., 2015), GHS population data (European Commission, Joint Research Centre (JRC) and Columbia University, Center for International Earth Science Information Network – CIESIN, 2015) and FUA delimitations (OECD, 2012).

Trends 1990-2014

The intertemporal changes of the coefficient of variation of urban population density for the 29 studies included in the analysis are shown in Figure 3.14. The total change between 1990 and 2014, which is denoted by the red dots, is also decomposed into changes occurring during the two sub-periods: 1990-2000 and 2000-14, denoted by bars of different colours.

The variation of urban population density has increased over time in most of the countries included in the analysis. In absolute terms, increases in the coefficient of variation since 1990 have been particularly high in Denmark, Hungary, Belgium, while the largest increase since 2000 is observed in Korea. On the contrary, variation of urban population density has declined sharply in Mexico, especially since 2000. The United States, Chile and Ireland have also seen large reductions in the variation of urban population density in the period 1990-2014.

Fragmentation

The fragmentation index measures the number of urban fabric fragments per km^2 of built-up area. At the city level, the indicator is computed using Equation (11) of Appendix 3.A. At the country level, the fragmentation index is obtained by dividing the total number of fragments identified in all functional urban areas of the country by the total amount of artificial land in the same areas. The formula used to compute the indicator at the country level is provided in Equation (12) of the same appendix.

Figure 3.14. **Evolution of the coefficient of variation of urban population density, 1990-2014**

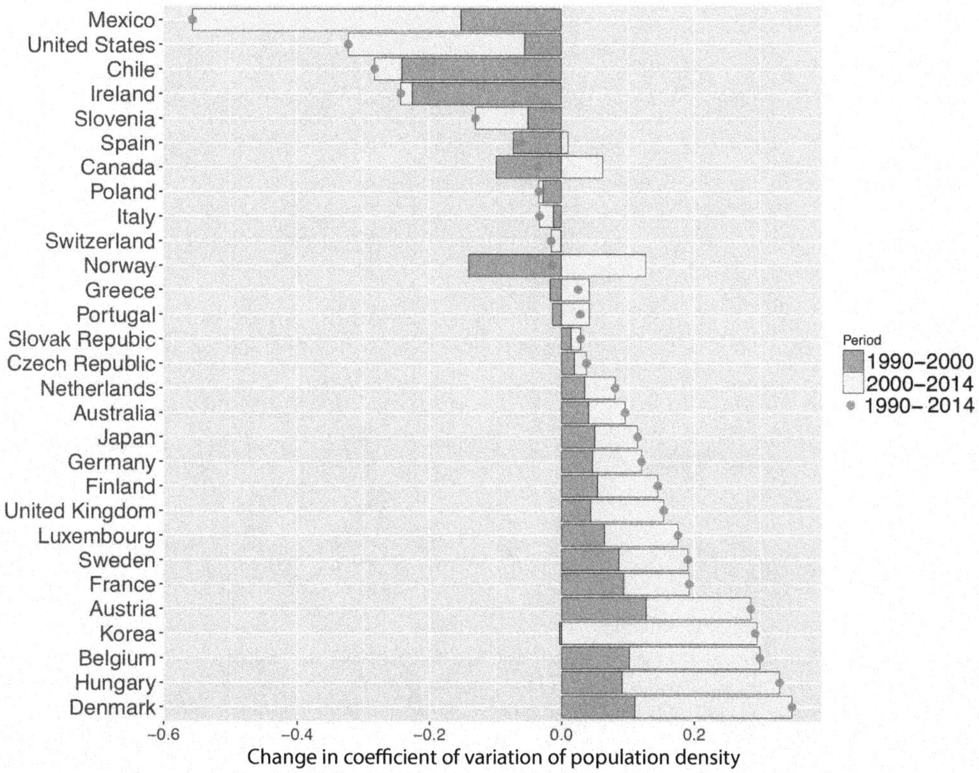

Notes: Red dots represent the total change in the coefficient of variation of urban population density at the country level in the period 1990-2014. The bars decompose the total change into changes occurring during the time periods 1990-2000 (darker blue) and 2000-14 (lighter blue).
Source: Own calculations, based on GHS built-area data (Pesaresi et al., 2015), GHS population data (European Commission, Joint Research Centre (JRC) and Columbia University, Center for International Earth Science Information Network – CIESIN, 2015) and FUA delimitations (OECD, 2012).

Current situation

Statistics of the fragmentation of urban fabric for the 29 OECD countries analysed here are provided in Figure 3.15. Countries are ranked from highest to lowest average fragmentation of urban fabric in 2014. The figure also displays the minimum and maximum values of fragmentation at the FUA level and the names of the corresponding urban areas.

In 2014, fragmentation at the country level ranged from 4.91 fragments per km^2 of artificial area in Japan to around 15.21 in Slovenia. Fragmentation is relatively high in the urban areas of Chile, Austria and Finland and relatively low in the urban areas of the United Kingdom, Germany and the Netherlands. The within-country variation of the indicators, i.e. the variation of fragmentation among cities of the same country, is very high. That is, in many cases the value of the fragmentation index at the country level lies far below the values recorded in multiple FUAs of a given country. On the other hand, large metropolitan areas usually exhibit rather low levels of fragmentation, as the fragmentation index in these areas is often found to lie below the corresponding index at the country level.

The relationship between fragmentation of urban fabric and urban population density does not turn out to be particularly strong at the country level. On the one hand, urban

Figure 3.15. **Number of urban fabric fragments per km² across OECD countries, 2014**

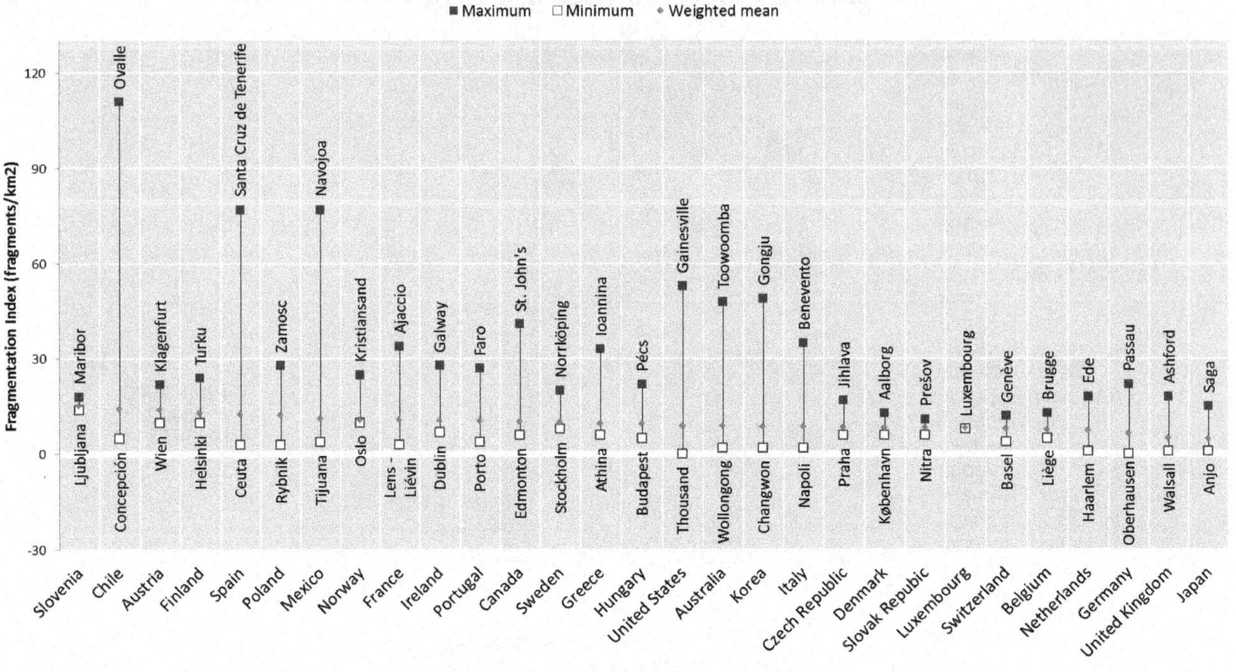

Notes: Red diamond-shaped points indicate average fragmentation of urban fabric at the country level. Minimum and maximum values of the indicator at the city level are indicated with white and blue squares respectively.

Source: Own calculations, based on GHS built-area data (Pesaresi et al., 2015) and FUA delimitations (OECD, 2012).

areas in countries including Japan, the United Kingdom and Switzerland are both dense and not very fragmented, and areas in Austria and Slovenia are both fragmented and sparsely populated. On the other hand, cities in Belgium, Luxembourg and Slovak Republic display relatively low population density, but also quite low fragmentation. Other examples are Chile and Spain, where urban fabric is rather fragmented, despite these countries ranking high in terms of average urban population density.

Trends 1990-2014

The evolution of fragmentation of urban fabric over time for the 29 countries considered in the analysis is provided in Figure 3.16. The total change in the average number of fragments per km² of artificial area between 1990 and 2014, which is denoted by the red dots, is also decomposed into changes occurring during the two sub-periods: 1990-2000 and 2000-14, denoted by bars of different colours.

Fragmentation has increased in 18 of the 29 countries included in the analysis since 1990. The largest increases are recorded in Hungary (more than two fragments per km²), Austria, the United Kingdom and Slovak Republic, while increases of more than one fragment per km² have been recorded in Denmark and Sweden. Fragmentation has also increased significantly in Chile and Belgium from 2000 onwards. By contrast, the largest decreases in fragmentation since 1990 are observed in Portugal (about 1.7 fragments per km²), Korea, Norway and Spain (all by more than one fragment per km²). The largest decline of fragmentation in the period 2000-14 has been recorded in Norway, the Netherlands and Finland.

Figure 3.16. **Evolution of fragmentation in OECD countries, 1990-2014**

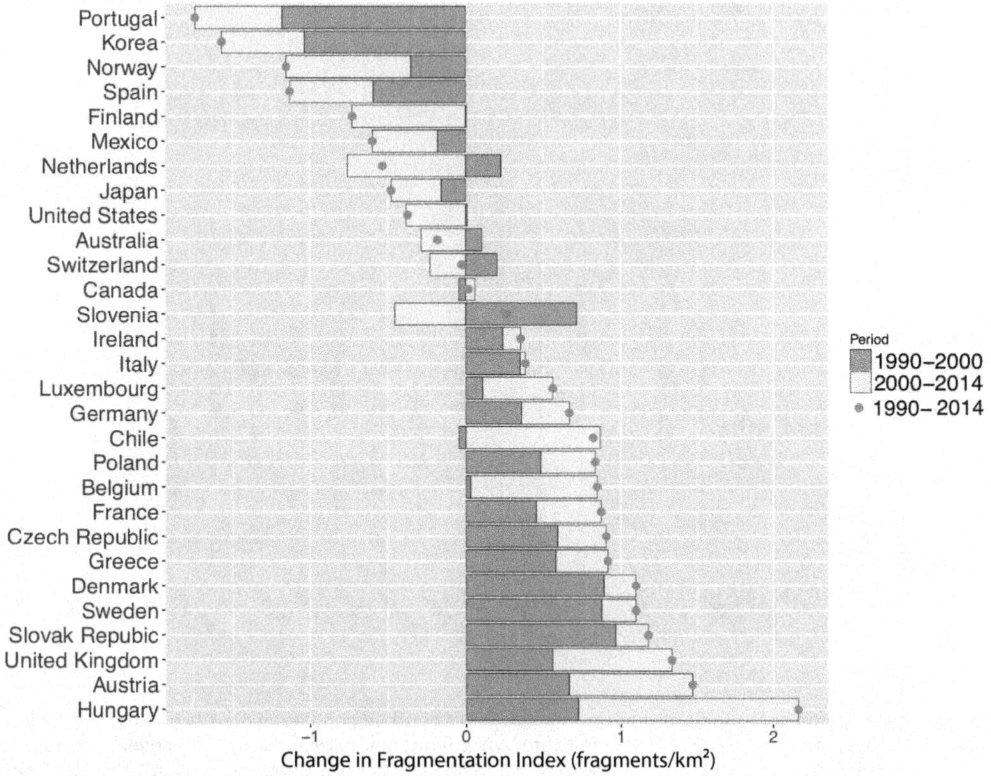

Notes: Red dots represent the total change in fragmentation of urban fabric at the country level in the period 1990-2014. The bars decompose the total change into changes occurring during the time periods 1990-2000 (darker blue) and 2000-14 (lighter blue).

Source: Own calculations, based on GHS built-area data (Pesaresi et al., 2015) and FUA delimitations (OECD, 2012).

Polycentricity

The polycentricity indicator is defined as the number of urban centres, i.e. the number of population-density peaks in an urban area. The approach followed to identify these centres is explained in detail in Appendix 3.A. At the country level, the polycentricity index is computed by dividing the total number of high-density peaks identified in the FUAs of a country by the total number of FUAs in that country.

Current situation

The statistics of polycentricity for the 29 OECD countries considered in the report are provided in Figure 3.17. Countries are ranked, from highest to lowest, according to the average number of centres identified in their FUAs in 2014. The figure also displays the minimum and maximum values of fragmentation at the FUA level and the names of the urban areas attaining the maximum values.

Urban areas with multiple density peaks are identified in every country, apart from Greece, where all FUAs were found to be monocentric. Both FUAs of Slovenia have two density peaks (centres) and the only FUA in Luxembourg has four. The range in the rest of the countries varies between one and a maximum which is often observed in the country's largest urban area (e.g. Brussels in Belgium, Toronto in Canada, Copenhagen in Denmark, Helsinki in Finland, Dublin in Ireland, Amsterdam in the Netherlands, Oslo in Norway, Warsaw in Poland and London in the United Kingdom, Washington in the United States) or

Figure 3.17. **Number of high-density peaks in the urban areas of OECD countries, 2014**

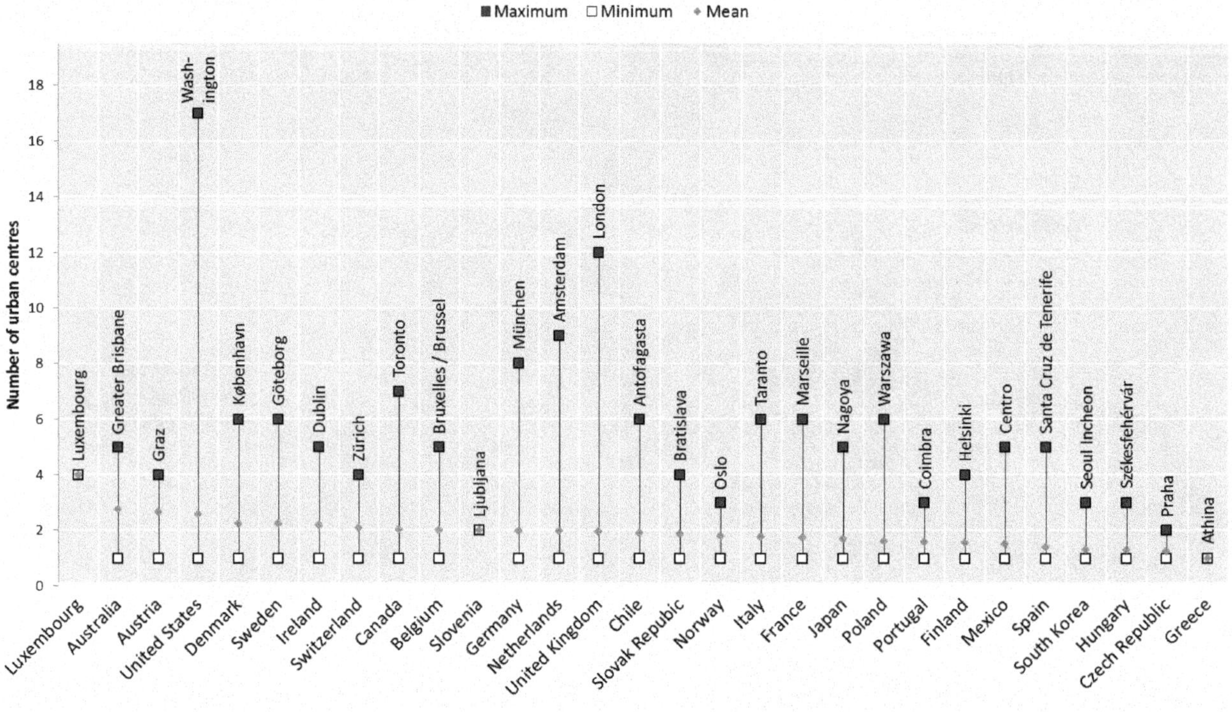

Notes: Red diamond-shaped points indicate the average number of peaks of urban population density at the country level. Minimum and maximum values of the indicator at the city level are indicated with white and blue squares respectively. A minimum value of one implies that at least one urban area in the country has been found to be monocentric. Cities corresponding to minimum values are not reported since in most countries the minimum value of one applies to multiple cities. All urban areas in Slovenia are found to have two centres. All urban areas in Greece are found to be monocentric. Country averages are not weighted, i.e. dots represent the expected number of centres in a randomly selected urban area of a country.

Source: Own calculations, based on GHS built-area data (Pesaresi et al., 2015), GHS population data (European Commission, Joint Research Centre (JRC) and Columbia University, Center for International Earth Science Information Network – CIESIN, 2015) and FUA delimitations (OECD, 2012).

in one of the biggest FUAs (Greater Brisbane in Australia, Graz in Austria, Marseille in France, Munich in Germany, Gothenburg in Sweden). The highest average numbers of urban centres after Luxembourg are observed in Australia, Austria and the United States, whereas the lowest ones after Greece are recorded in Czech Republic, Hungary and Korea.

Trends 1990-2014

Intertemporal changes in the average number of peak-density points in the FUAs of OECD countries are presented in Figure 3.18. The total change of the indicator between 1990 and 2014, which is denoted by the red dots, is also decomposed into changes occurring during the two sub-periods: 1990-2000 and 2000-14, denoted by bars of different colours.

The number of urban centres (urban peak-density points) has increased in the majority of countries since 1990. Some of the largest increases in this number are observed in Ireland, Denmark, Slovak Republic and Chile. In these countries, population density has adjusted in a way that new urban centres have emerged within existing urban areas. Since 2000, the greatest increases have been recorded in Denmark, the Slovak Republic and Slovenia, where a new urban centre has emerged in every second urban area of the country. However, it is important to note that the magnitude of the changes observed in Slovenia and Luxembourg, where the indicator declined by one urban centre since 2000, could be partially attributed to the fact that the two countries contain only one and two FUAs

Figure 3.18. **Evolution of polycentricity in OECD countries, 1990-2014**

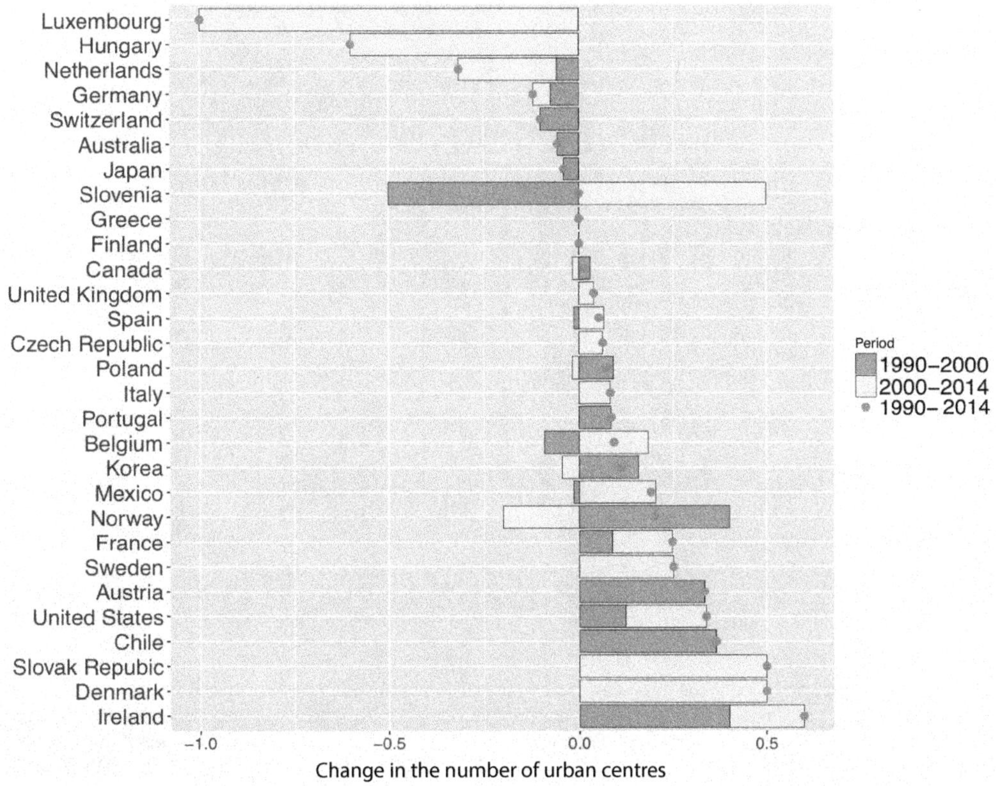

Notes: Red dots represent the total change in the polycentricity index at the country level in the period 1990-2014. The bars decompose the total change into changes occurring during the time periods 1990-2000 (darker blue) and 2000-14 (lighter blue).

Source: Own calculations, based on GHS built-area data (Pesaresi et al., 2015), GHS population data (European Commission, Joint Research Centre (JRC) and Columbia University, Center for International Earth Science Information Network – CIESIN, 2015) and FUA delimitations (OECD, 2012).

respectively. Following Luxembourg, the largest decreases of polycentricity have occurred in Hungary, the Netherlands and Germany.

Decentralisation

The decentralisation index shows the share of urban population residing outside of the urban centres of a FUA. The approach followed to identify urban centres in each FUA is described in detail in Appendix 3.A. The mathematical formula used to compute decentralisation at the city level is provided in Equation (15) of the appendix. At the country level, the indicator reflects the share of urban population residing outside of all urban centres of the FUAs of a country. This share is computed using Equation (16) in Appendix 3.A.

Current situation

The statistics associated with decentralisation, i.e. the share of urban population residing outside FUA centres, for the 29 OECD countries considered in the analysis are provided in Figure 3.19. Countries are ranked according to the values of the decentralisation index recorded for 2014, from highest to lowest. The figure also displays the minimum and maximum values of the decentralisation indicator at the FUA level, as well as the names of the corresponding urban areas.[14]

Figure 3.19. **Share of urban population residing outside urban centres in OECD countries, 2014**

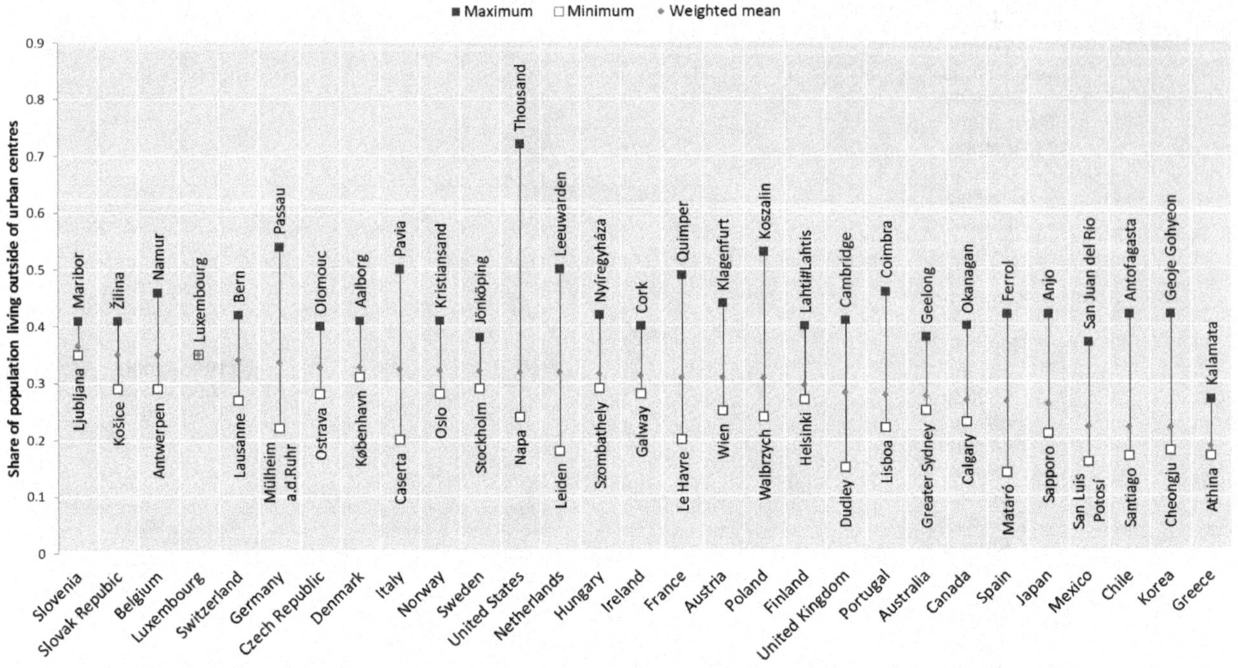

Notes: Red diamond-shaped points indicate the average fraction of urban population residing outside FUA centres at the country level. Minimum and maximum values of the indicator at the city level are indicated with white and blue squares respectively.

Source: Own calculations, based on GHS built-area data (Pesaresi et al., 2015), GHS population data (European Commission, Joint Research Centre (JRC) and Columbia University, Center for International Earth Science Information Network – CIESIN, 2015) and FUA delimitations (OECD, 2012).

Average decentralisation in urban areas varies substantially across OECD countries, with values ranging from 19% in Greece to 37% in Slovenia. Following Slovenia, decentralisation is highest in the Slovak Republic, Belgium, and Luxembourg, where the percentage of population living outside FUA centres is 35% or higher. The average share of urban population residing outside FUA centres in the 29 countries considered in the analysis is about 30%. Greece, Korea, Chile and Mexico are the only countries in which that percentage lies below 25%.

Trends 1990-2014

Intertemporal changes in the average fraction of population residing outside urban centres, but still within FUA boundaries of OECD countries, are presented in Figure 3.20. The total change of the decentralisation indicator between 1990 and 2014, which is denoted by the red dots, is also decomposed into changes occurring during the two sub-periods: 1990-2000 and 2000-14, denoted by bars of different colours.

In contrast to most other indicators of urban sprawl developed in this study, decentralisation has declined in the majority of countries since 1990. It has only grown in 10 countries, with the largest increases observed in Czech Republic (about 4 percentage points increase), Slovak Republic, Ireland and Korea.[15] In the rest of the countries where decentralisation increased, its growth was lower than 2 percentage points. On the other hand, the strongest centralisation forces in the period 1990-2014 are observed in Canada (about 4 percentage points decline), Finland, Hungary and Australia. It is also noteworthy that the separate changes that took place during the two sub-periods (1990-2000 and 2000-14) point to the same direction (positive or negative) for all countries analysed here except for Chile, Slovenia and Spain.

Figure 3.20. **Evolution of decentralisation in OECD countries, 1990-2014**

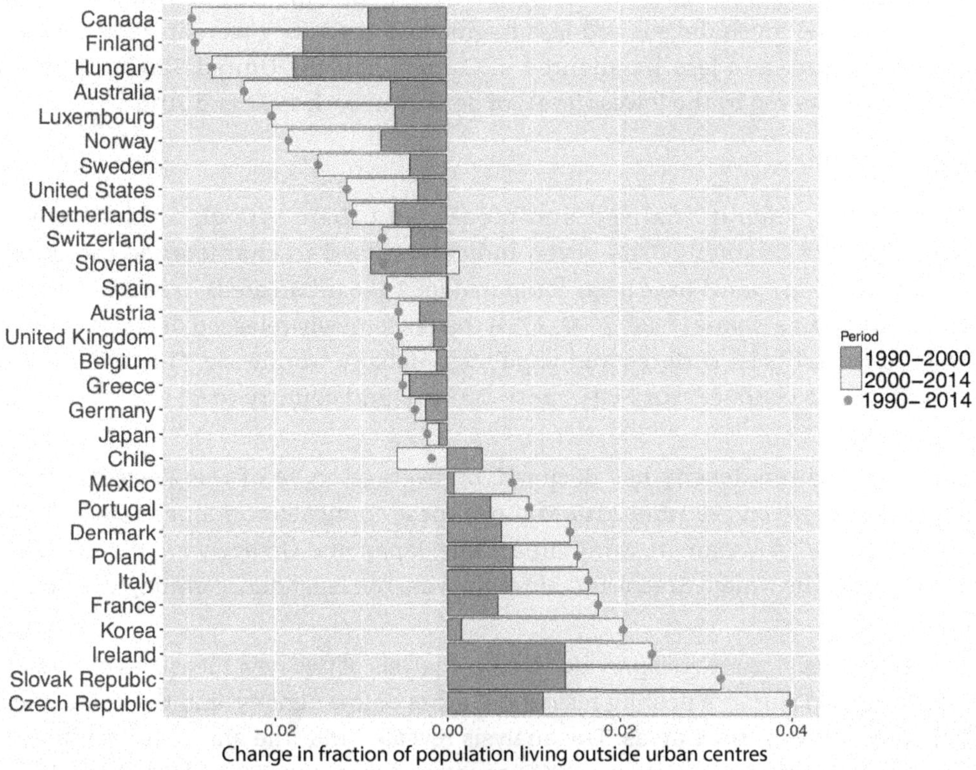

Notes: Red dots represent the total change in the decentralisation index at the country level in the period 1990-2014. The bars decompose the total change into changes occurring during the time periods 1990-2000 (darker blue) and 2000-14 (lighter blue).

Source: Own calculations, based on GHS built-area data (Pesaresi et al., 2015), GHS population data (European Commission, Joint Research Centre (JRC) and Columbia University, Center for International Earth Science Information Network – CIESIN, 2015) and FUA delimitations (OECD, 2012).

3.5. Country-level analysis

This section presents the main findings from the analysis of the current state of urban sprawl and its evolution over time for each country separately. A detailed presentation of that analysis is provided in the country sheets of Appendix 3.B, which contain one-page summaries of the state and evolution of urban sprawl for each of the 29 countries analysed here.

The country-level analysis reveals that urban areas in some countries in Central Europe and North America, such as Austria and Slovenia, and Canada and the United States, are among the most sprawled ones. This is manifested in their high rank in most dimensions of urban sprawl. Cities in Canada and the United States are on average more sparsely populated than cities in these European countries, and urban population density varies much more within them.

Another small group of countries score low in most dimensions of urban sprawl. Greece, Japan, Korea and the United Kingdom are at the bottom of the ranking of multiple indicators of sprawl. Chile, Mexico and Spain also seem to perform well in multiple dimensions of sprawl, but their urban areas are still relatively fragmented.

Focusing on the evolution of urban areas over time, cities in Denmark, France, and several Central European countries, such as Czech Republic, Hungary, Poland and

Slovak Republic have sprawled along most of the dimensions examined since 1990. On the other hand, urban sprawl has declined in Australia, Spain and Switzerland, where urban areas have become much denser and less fragmented than they were in 1990. Cities have also become denser and less fragmented in Canada and the United States, which were characterised, however, by the lowest levels of density in both 1990 and 2014.

3.6. Summary

This chapter operationalised and measured urban sprawl, as the latter was conceptualised in Chapter 2. The seven indicators used to characterise the different dimensions of urban sprawl have been computed for 1 156 urban areas in 29 OECD countries and for different time points (1990, 2000, 2014) thanks to newly released datasets that follow the evolution of artificial surfaces and population density worldwide. The indicators have then been used to conduct cross-city, cross-country and country-level analyses of urban sprawl.

Urban population density has declined, on average, in 14 of the 29 OECD countries examined here between 1990 and 2014. Some of these countries contained relatively dense areas in 1990. In 2014, urban areas in Korea, Chile, Japan and Greece were the densest and those of Canada, the United States and Slovenia were the least dense among the examined OECD countries.

Interesting insights are also provided by the analysis of two new measures of sprawl: the share of developed surfaces hosting residential areas of low density, and the share of urban population residing in those areas. The analysis revealed that the sharp decline in average population density observed in many OECD countries between 1990 and 2014 was driven by rapid suburbanisation. This is indicated by a substantial increase of the share of urban developed surfaces hosting residential areas of very low density, i.e. 150-1 500 inhabitants per km^2, observed in that period. However, in some countries (Greece, Ireland, Spain, Sweden and the United Kingdom) both average urban population density and the percentage of urban footprint occupied by areas of very low density (150-1 500 inhabitants per km^2) have increased. This shows that in some of the urban areas of these countries densification coincided with the above suburbanisation process, either because initial urban population density was, on average, very low or because population in already dense parts of urban space increased even further.

At the same time, the relationship between urban population density and fragmentation is not particularly strong at the country level. For example, fragmentation of urban areas in Chile and Spain is relatively high, whereas cities in these countries are among the densest of those analysed. Decentralisation is highest in urban areas of Slovenia, Slovak Republic, Belgium, and Luxembourg, where the percentage of population living outside the urban core exceeds 35%. Greece, Korea, Chile and Mexico are the only countries where that percentage lies below 25%.

Some countries, including Austria and Slovenia rank relatively high in most dimensions of urban sprawl. Other countries, such as Canada and the United States, are very sparsely populated, but score lower in indicators of fragmentation and decentralisation. Looking at the evolution of cities since 1990, urban areas in Czech Republic, Denmark, France, Hungary, Poland and Slovak Republic have been sprawling along most of the considered sprawl dimensions.

Notes

1. The terms "indicator" and "metric" are used interchangeably throughout this chapter.
2. Non-artificial surfaces inside urban areas may include, among others, agricultural areas, forests, grasslands and water bodies.
3. In the terminology used by Eurostat, this translates into Local Administrative Units (LAU) level 2, formerly known as NUTS level 5. An exception is Portugal, for which commuting data are available at the LAU-1 level.
4. A raster map is organizes geographic information using a grid consisting of equally sized cells.
5. The population grid data used in the identification of urban cores have been derived from population census data at the municipality level using downscaling techniques. Such techniques provide an allocation of the municipal populations, which are usually available through census data, to higher resolution grid cells using land cover and land-use data, coupled with interpolation techniques. The latter techniques are used to distribute population in a high-resolution manner. The former are used to ensure that the spatial distribution will accord to the observed land-cover and land-use patterns. Thus, population will be allocated only to artificial and not to, for example, agricultural or forest areas. In the case of Europe, the population grid was derived by the Joint Research Centre (JRC) at 1 km^2 resolution combining census data at the LAU-2 level with CORINE land cover and other data sources for land use. For all non-European countries, harmonised gridded population data from the Landscan project are used.
6. For more information, see *http://ghsl.jrc.ec.europa.eu/index.php*.
7. The intermediate steps of orthorectification, georeferencing, spectral calibration and radiometric corrections that are followed between the receipt of satellite images and the production of settlement data are out of the scope of this discussion.
8. It should be noted that the employed datasets for human settlements can neither distinguish between different types of land use (i.e. residential, commercial, industrial etc.), nor account for vertical intensity of development, i.e. building height. Therefore, the derived grid population data will overestimate population in cells where floor space is predominantly industrial or commercial. Population density may be overestimated in areas where structural density (i.e. the floor-to-area ratio) is low and underestimated where it is high. Despite the above imperfections, the allocation of population within the grid cells of an administrative area is a valid approximation at the aggregate level.
9. Functional urban area boundaries have not yet been specified for Iceland, Israel, Latvia, New Zealand and Turkey, and, thus, indicator values could not be computed for these countries. Global Human Settlement data at the functional urban area level for Estonia were not considered reliable enough, and the country was not included in the analysis to avoid misleading conclusions.
10. The 80 inhabitants/km^2 lower bound filters out FUAs that emerged from the presence of a high density cluster whose surface is very small compared to the total surface of the administrative units that overlap with it. This can typically occur when the high density clusters (i.e. contiguous areas of population density above 1 000 inhabitants/km^2 that host more than 50 000 people) of a functional urban area are hosted in a very small fraction of the overlapping administrative units and a substantial portion of the latter is occupied by inhabited rural areas of very low density. Furthermore, the application of the lower bound filters out areas that may not fulfil the criteria used to characterise an area as urban in time points 1990 and 2000, i.e. prior to the collection of census data on population and commuting flows used to identify the functional urban areas.
11. Urban population density refers here only to population density in functional urban areas (FUAs): small cities not forming part of a functional urban area are not considered in the analysis.
12. The correlation between the two allocation indicators is about 0.92.
13. The changes in the two allocation indicators are highly correlated.
14. It should be noted that the decentralisation indicator is not strongly correlated with the polycentricity indicator, as the correlation between the two indicators is around 0.14. Cities with multiple high-density peaks may be characterised by high decentralisation if these peaks occupy relatively small surfaces of the urban footprint.
15. The change reported here is the absolute value of the change of a variable expressed in percentage terms. This change should not be confused with the percentage change in the variable of interest.

References

Amindarbari, A. and A. Sevtsuk (2012), "Measuring growth and change in metropolitan form", *Sciences*, Vol. 104/17, pp. 7301-7306.

Angel, S. et al. (2011), *Making Room for a Planet of Cities*, Policy Focus Report/Code PF027, Lincoln Institute of Land Policy, Cambridge, MA, Available online at: *www.lincolninst.edu/sites/default/files/pubfiles/making-room-for-a-planet-of-cities-full_0.pdf*.

Arribas-Bel, D., P. Nijkamp and H. Scholten (2011), "Multidimensional urban sprawl in Europe: A self-organizing map approach", *Computers, Environment and Urban Systems*, Vol. 35/4, pp. 263-275.

Arribas-Bel, D. and C.R. Schmidt (2013) "Self-organizing maps and the US urban spatial structure", *Environment and Planning B: Planning and Design*, Vol. 40/2, pp. 362-371.

Brezzi, M. and P. Veneri (2015), "Assessing polycentric urban systems in the OECD: Country, regional and metropolitan perspectives", *European Planning Studies*, Vol. 23/6, pp. 1128-1145.

Burchfield, M. et al. (2006), "Causes of sprawl: A portrait from space", *The Quarterly Journal of Economics*, Vol. 121/2, pp. 587-633.

Cervero, R. (1989), *America's Suburban Centers: The Land Use-Transportation Link*, Unwin Hyman, Boston, MA.

EEA (2016), *Urban sprawl in Europe – joint EEA-FOEN report*, EEA Report No. 11/2016, Publications Office of the European Union, Luxembourg.

European Commission, Joint Research Centre (JRC) and Columbia University, Center for International Earth Science Information Network – CIESIN (2015), "GHS population grid, derived from GPW4, multitemporal (1975, 1990, 2000, 2015)" (database), European Commission, Joint Research Centre (JRC), *http://data.europa.eu/89h/jrc-ghsl-ghs_pop_gpw4_globe_r2015a*.

Frank, L.D. and G. Pivo (1995), "Impacts of mixed use and density on utilization of three modes of travel: Single occupant vehicle, transit, and walking", *Transportation Research Record*, Vol. 1466, pp. 44-52.

Frenkel, A. and M. Ashkenazi (2008), "Measuring urban sprawl: How can we deal with it?", *Environment and Planning B: Planning and Design*, Vol. 35/1, pp. 56-79.

Galster, G. et al. (2001), "Wrestling sprawl to the ground: Defining and measuring an elusive concept", *Housing Policy Debate*, Vol. 12/4, pp. 681-718.

Gordon, P., H.W. Richardson and H.L. Wong (1986), "The distribution of population and employment in a polycentric city: The case of Los Angeles" *Environment and Planning A: Economy and Space*. Vol. 18/2, pp. 161-173.

Huang, J., X.X. Lu and J.M. Sellers (2007), "A global comparative analysis of urban form: Applying spatial metrics and remote sensing", *Landscape and Urban Planning*, Vol. 82/4, pp. 184-197.

Irwin, E.G. and N.E. Bockstael (2007), "The evolution of urban sprawl: Evidence of spatial heterogeneity and increasing land fragmentation", *PNAS*, Vol. 104/52, pp. 20672-20677.

Jaeger, J.A.G. and C. Schwick (2014), "Improving the measurement of urban sprawl: Weighted Urban Proliferation (WUP) and its application to Switzerland", *Ecological Indicators*, Vol. 38, pp. 294-308.

Newman, P. and J. Kenworthy (2006), "Urban design to reduce automobile dependence", *Opolis*, Vol. 2/1, pp. 35-52.

OECD (2012), *Redefining "Urban": A New Way to Measure Metropolitan Areas*, OECD Publishing, Paris, *http://dx.doi.org/10.1787/9789264174108-en*.

OECD (2011), "Distribution of population and regional typology", in *OECD Regions at a Glance 2011*, OECD Publishing, Paris, *http://dx.doi.org/10.1787/reg_glance-2011-7-en*.

Oueslati, W., S. Alvanides and G. Garrod (2015), "Determinants of urban sprawl in European cities", *Urban Studies*, Vol. 52/9, pp. 1594-1614.

Pesaresi, M. et al. (2015), "GHS built-up grid, derived from Landsat, multitemporal (1975, 1990, 2000, 2014)" (database), European Commission, Joint Research Centre (JRC), *http://data.europa.eu/89h/jrc-ghsl-ghs_built_ldsmt_globe_r2015b*.

Siedentop, S. and S. Fina (2010), "Monitoring urban sprawl in Germany: Towards a GIS-based measurement and assessment approach", *Journal of Land Use Science*, Vol. 5/2, pp. 73-104.

Small, K.A. and S. Song (1994), "Population and employment densities: Structure and change", *Journal of Urban Economics*, Vol. 36/3, pp. 292-313.

Solon, J. (2009), "Landscape and Urban Planning Spatial context of urbanization: Landscape pattern and changes between 1950 and 1990 in the Warsaw metropolitan area, Poland", *Landscape and Urban Planning*, Vol. 93/3, pp. 250-261.

Su, Q. and J.S. DeSalvo (2008), "The effect of transportation subsidies on urban sprawl", *Journal of Regional Science*, Vol. 48/3, pp. 567-594.

Torrens, P. (2008), "A toolkit for measuring sprawl", *Applied Spatial Analysis and Policy*, Vol. 1/1, pp. 5-36.

Torrens, P.M. and M. Alberti (2000), "Measuring sprawl", *Centre for Advanced Spatial Analysis Working Paper Series*, No. 27, University College London, London.

Tsai, Y. (2005), "Quantifying urban form: Compactness versus sprawl". *Urban Studies*, Vol. 42/1, pp. 141-161.

Veneri, P. (2017), "Urban spatial structure in OECD cities: Is urban population decentralising or clustering?", *Papers in Regional Science*, *http://dx.doi.org/10.1111/pirs.12300*.

Zhao, P. (2011), "Managing urban growth in a transforming China: Evidence from Beijing", *Land Use Policy*, Vol. 28/1, pp. 96-109.

APPENDIX 3.A

Mathematical exposition of urban sprawl indicators

This appendix presents the mathematical formulas used for the computation of the indicators outlined in Section 3.3: average population density, population-to-density and land-to-density allocation, variation of population density, fragmentation, polycentricity and decentralisation.

Average urban population density

The *average population density* of an urban area is the average number of inhabitants per km^2 of populated urban space. This is the ratio of the urban area's total population to the total inhabited surface within that urban area. Equation (1) presents the formula used for the calculation of average population density:

$$PD_{ic} = P_{ic} / L_{Pic} = \underbrace{\left(\sum_y I_{ic}(y) \cdot P_y\right)}_{\text{inhabitants in FUA } i \text{ of country } c} \Bigg/ \underbrace{\left(s_P \cdot \underbrace{\sum_y I_{ic}(y)}_{N_{Pic}}\right)}_{\text{total populated area in FUA } i \text{ of country } c}, \quad (1)$$

where P_{ic} denotes the total population of FUA i in country c and L_{Pic} is the total populated area in the FUA. The binary variable I_{ic} (y) equals one if the population raster cell y belongs to that FUA (zero otherwise), P_y is the population of that cell, and s_P is the surface occupied by each cell in the population raster, i.e. 0.0625 km^2 (250 m × 250 m).

To compute the total population of the urban area, P_{ic}, GIS software iterates across all cells in the population raster, counting the population of all cells belonging to the FUA and disregarding the population of those outside it. This iteration can be visualised in the left panel of Figure 3.A.1, in which the white parts represent non-populated areas within the FUA and coloured cells represent surfaces with various levels of population density. To compute the total populated area within the FUA, L_{Pic}, GIS software iterates across all cells in the population raster, counting the number of population cells lying within the boundaries of that urban area. In the left panel of Figure 3.A.1, this is simply the number of coloured cells, denoted by N_{Pic}. Multiplying that number with s_P yields the total populated area in FUA i of country c.

The average population density *in a country* is given by:

$$PD_c = P_c / L_{Pc} = \underbrace{\left(\sum_y I_c(y) \cdot P_y\right)}_{\text{inhabitants in all FUAs of country } c} \Bigg/ \underbrace{\left(s_P \cdot \underbrace{\sum_y I_c(y)}_{N_{Pc}}\right)}_{\text{total populated area in FUAs of country } c}, \quad (2)$$

where P_c denotes the total urban population of country c; L_{Pc} is the total populated area in all FUAs of the country; I_c (y) equals one if the population raster cell y belongs in *any* functional urban area of the country (zero otherwise).

The mathematical formula in Equation (2) is the expected population density in a randomly selected urban location of a given country. That is equivalent to the average population density that would be observed had all FUAs of country c been concatenated in a single urban area.

Figure 3.A.1. **Population and land cover raster cells**

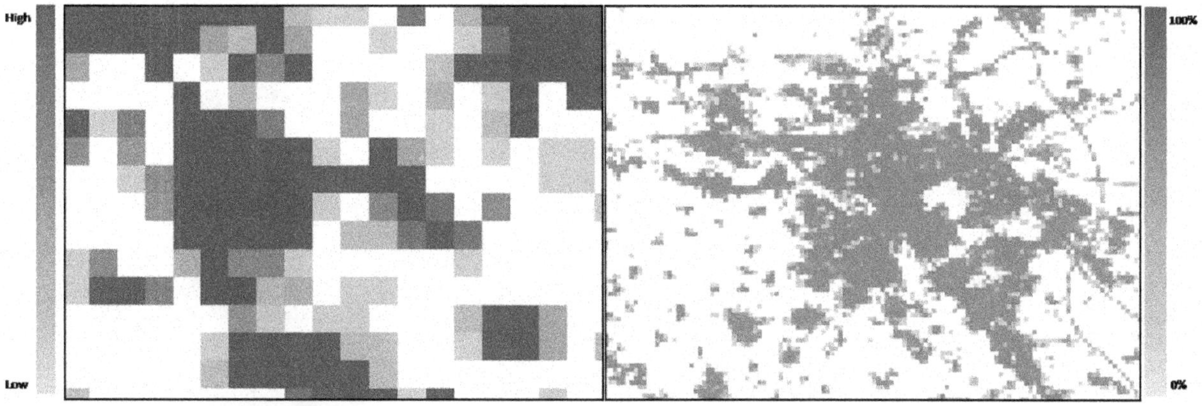

Notes: Left panel: population raster cells of 62 500 m^2 (= 250 m × 250 m). Right panel: land cover raster cells of surface ≈ 0.00146 km^2 (≈ 38.2185 m × 38.2185 m) with gradient representing the percentage of that surface covered by buildings.

Population-to-density and land-to-density allocation

A set of indicators based on population density thresholds that do not vary across FUAs can further facilitate the diagnosis of sprawl. The two indicators developed here are the share of population living in areas where density is below a certain threshold and the share of urban footprint in which density is below that threshold. Areas with population density of 150 inhabitants per km^2 are not considered in the calculation of the two indicators, as this is the threshold below which areas are considered as rural (OECD, 2011). Three thresholds are considered in this report: 1 500, 2 500 and 3 500 inhabitants per km^2 (for the rationale behind selecting these thresholds, see the relevant discussion in Section 3.4). The environmental and socioeconomic importance of the indicators in Equations (3) and (5) is further investigated in Chapter 4. An illustration of the two indicators at the three values of ξ for an FUA with two centres is provided in Figure 3.A.2.

The percentage of population residing in locations where density is lower than a threshold ξ in FUA i of country c is:

$$T_{ic\xi} = \underbrace{\left(\sum_y I_{ic}(y) \cdot I\left(\frac{P_y}{s_P} < \xi\right) \cdot P_y\right)}_{\text{total population in areas of FUA } i \text{ of country } c \text{ where density is below } \xi} \Bigg/ \underbrace{\left(\sum_y I_{ic}(y) \cdot P_y\right)}_{\text{total population of FUA } i \text{ in country } c}, \quad (3)$$

where the indicator $I\left(\frac{P_y}{s_P} < \xi\right)$ equals one if the population density within cell y, i.e. (P_y/s_P) falls short of threshold density ξ and zero otherwise. The corresponding indicator at the country level is:

Figure 3.A.2. **Share of population and urban surface below different density thresholds**

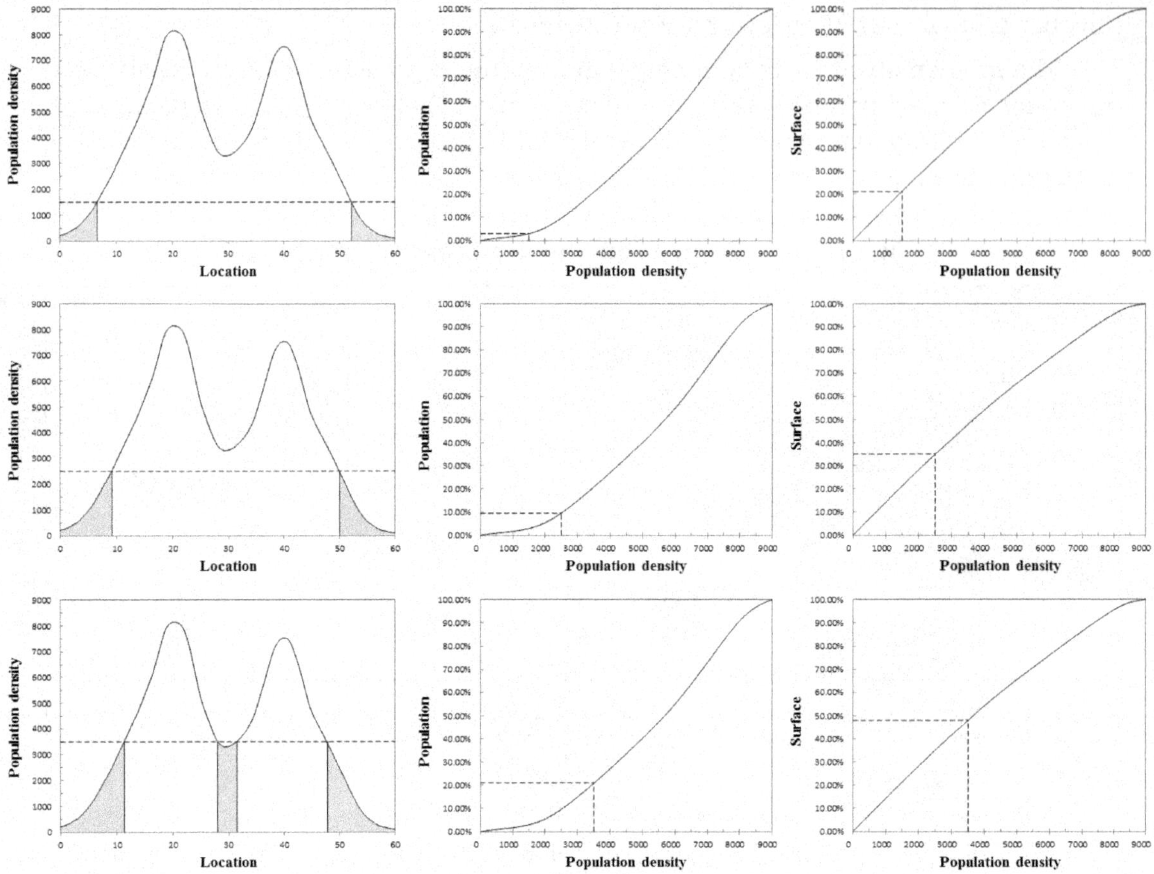

Notes: Left panels: shaded areas represent the mass of population residing in areas with density below threshold levels (horizontal dashed lines). Middle panels: percentage of population living in areas with density below three different thresholds. Right panels: surface of the functional urban area with population density below three different thresholds. Thresholds (inhabitants per km^2): 1 500 (top panels), 2 500 (middle panels), 3 500 (bottom panels).

$$T_{c\xi} = \underbrace{\left(\sum_y I_c(y) \cdot I\left(\frac{P_y}{S_P} < \xi\right) \cdot P_y\right)}_{\substack{\text{total urban population in country c} \\ \text{located in areas where density is below } \xi}} \Bigg/ \underbrace{\left(\sum_y I_c(y) \cdot P_y\right)}_{\substack{\text{total urban population} \\ \text{of country c}}} . \qquad (4)$$

Similarly, the fraction of land with levels of population density below threshold ξ in FUA i of country c is:

$$L_{ic\xi} = \underbrace{\left(S_P \cdot \sum_y I_{ic}(y) \cdot I\left(\frac{P_y}{S_P} < \xi\right)\right)}_{\substack{\text{total populated surface with density} \\ \text{below } \xi \text{ in FUA i of country c}}} \Bigg/ \underbrace{\left(S_P \cdot \sum_y I_{ic}(y)\right)}_{\substack{\text{total populated surface} \\ \text{in FUA i of country c}}} . \qquad (5)$$

The corresponding indicator at the country level is:

$$L_{c\xi} = \underbrace{\left(S_P \cdot \sum_y I_c(y) \cdot I\left(\frac{P_y}{S_P} < \xi\right)\right)}_{\substack{\text{total populated surface with density} \\ \text{below } \xi \text{ in FUAs of country c}}} \Bigg/ \underbrace{\left(S_P \cdot \sum_y I_c(y)\right)}_{\substack{\text{total populated surface} \\ \text{in FUAs of country c}}} . \qquad (6)$$

Variation of urban population density

Population density may vary substantially within a city. A measure of the variation of population density is its standard deviation. The standard deviation of population density in FUA i of country c is defined in Equation (7):

$$SD_{ic} = \sqrt{\frac{1}{N_{Pic}} \cdot \left(\sum_{y} I_{ic}(y) \cdot \left(\frac{P_y}{s_P} - PD_{ic} \right)^2 \right)}, \tag{7}$$

where (P_y/s_P) is the population density (number of inhabitants per km^2) of population cell y, PD_{ic} is the average population density of the urban area and N_{Pic} is the number of population cells that lie within the boundaries of FUA i.[1]

The formula in Equation (7) is used to measure the degree to which population density varies within an FUA. As explained in Chapter 2, this measure is used to detect urban areas which may display a large variation in density, while their overall density (PD_{ic}) is relatively high. An alternative, unit-free measure of density variation is the relative standard deviation of urban population density (also known as coefficient of variation), defined as:

$$CV_{ic} = SD_{ic} / PD_{ic}. \tag{8}$$

The standard deviation of urban population density in a country is given by:

$$SD_{c} = \sqrt{\frac{1}{N_{Pc}} \cdot \left(\sum_{y} I_{c}(y) \cdot \left(\frac{P_y}{s_P} - PD_{c} \right)^2 \right)}, \tag{9}$$

where N_{Pc} is the number of population cells that lie within the boundaries of all FUAs in country c. The rest of the terms are defined earlier in the text. The mathematical formula in Equation (9) is the standard deviation of population densities observed at all locations in the FUAs of a country from the national mean, PD_c. The coefficient of variation at the country level is:

$$CV_{c} = SD_{c} / PD_{c}. \tag{10}$$

Fragmentation

The *fragmentation index* (FI) measures the number of urban fabric fragments per km^2 of built-up area. The mathematical formulation of the indicator is presented in Equation (11):

$$FI_{ic} = F_{ic} / L_{Aic} = F_{ic} \Big/ \underbrace{\left(s_B \cdot \sum_{x} I_{ic}(x) \cdot I(\varphi_{Bx} > \bar{\varphi}) \right)}_{\text{total artificial land in FUA i}}, \tag{11}$$

where F_{ic} is the number of urban fabric fragments in FUA i of country c; $I_{ic}(x)$ equals one if the land-cover raster cell x belongs to that FUA and zero otherwise; φ_{Bx} denotes the fraction of surface in cell x that is covered by buildings or other structures; $I(\varphi_{Bx} > \bar{\varphi})$ equals one if φ_{Bx} exceeds a threshold value $\bar{\varphi}$ and zero otherwise; and s_B is the surface occupied by each cell in the land cover raster, which is approximately equal to 0.00146 km^2 ($\approx$ 38.2185 m $\times$ 38.2185 m). The variable L_{Aic} is the total surface occupied by urban fabric fragments in the FUA.[2]

To calculate L_{Aic}, GIS software iterates across all cells in the land cover raster, focusing on those that fall within the boundaries of the FUA of interest. The algorithm then checks whether cell x belongs to a fragment, i.e. whether the fraction of its footprint occupied by artificial areas is at least $\bar{\varphi}$. In this report, the threshold value $\bar{\varphi}$ was set to 0.5. This means that the indicator $I(\varphi_{Bx} > \bar{\varphi})$ is given the value one whenever 50% or more of the surface of cell x is artificial, and the value of zero otherwise. The sum in the denominator of Equation (11) is the number of land-cover cells that belong to urban fragments in urban area i. In the right panel of Figure 3.A.3, this is the number of coloured cells that results from applying the $I(\varphi_{Bx} > 0.5)$ filter to drop all cells that lie within the FUA but are not sufficiently covered by buildings or other structures. Multiplying that number with s_B yields the total artificial area within the FUA. This is the amount of land occupied by the coloured cells in the right panel of Figure 3.A.3. Constructing distinct fragments in order to obtain the numerator of Equation (11) out of the artificial land cells requires the use of specific algorithms.[3]

Figure 3.A.3. **Obtaining the total artificial area and fragments from land cover data**

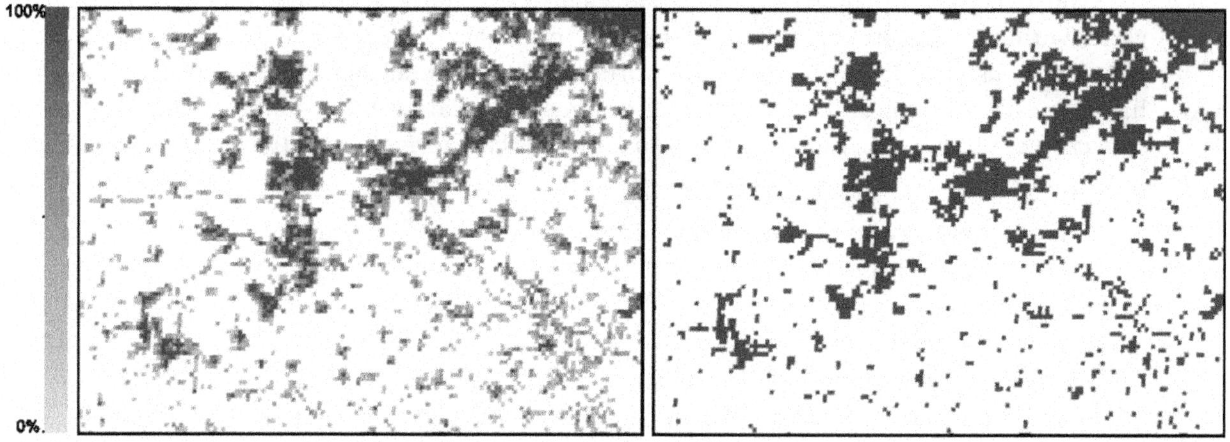

Notes: Left panel: land cover map of building coverage values (φ_{Bx}). Right panel: artificial area map with red colour representing cells where building coverage exceeds 50%.

At the country level, the fragmentation index is obtained by dividing the total number of fragments identified in all functional urban areas of country c by the total amount of artificial land in the same areas. The mathematical formulation for fragmentation at the country level is:

$$FI_c = \underbrace{\left(\sum_i I_{ic} \cdot F_{ic}\right)}_{\substack{\text{total number of} \\ \text{fragments in all FUAs} \\ \text{of country } c}} \Bigg/ \underbrace{\left(s_B \cdot \sum_x I_c(x) \cdot I(\varphi_{Bx} > \bar{\varphi})\right)}_{\substack{\text{total artificial land in all FUAs} \\ \text{of country } c}}, \qquad (12)$$

where I_c (x) equals one if the land cover raster cell x belongs to *any* functional urban area of country c and zero otherwise, and I_{ic} equals one if FUA i belongs to country c and zero otherwise. The mathematical formula in Equation (12) is the expected number of urban fabric fragments per km^2 in a randomly selected urban location of a country. That is equivalent to the average fragmentation observed had all FUAs of country c been concatenated in a single urban area.

Polycentricity

Population density may peak at several locations within an FUA. In this report, urban centres are defined as areas bigger than 5 km^2 where population density is substantially higher than the one observed in their surroundings. The process of extracting urban centres from their surroundings is now described in detail.

First, a moving-average filter is used to smooth the density of each cell y in the population raster. The filtered density is:

Figure 3.A.4. **Obtaining the 3-km moving average filtered density from population density**

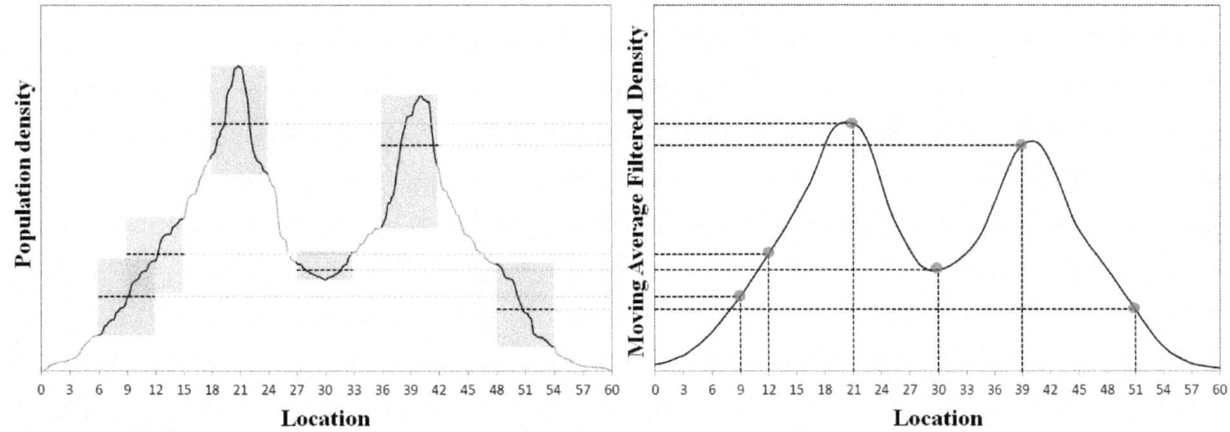

Notes: The figure illustrates the process of obtaining moving average filtered densities at six different locations (9, 12, 21, 30, 39 and 51). Left panel: The width of the highlighted rectangular areas represents the bandwidth at which the moving average filter applies, i.e. 3 km towards each direction. The height of the highlighted areas represents the range of population density values within the smoothing area. The dashed lines represent the moving average population density obtained within the three kilometer bandwidth. Right panel: the values obtained from the smoothing process.

$$M_y = \underbrace{\left(\sum_{y'} I(y,y',d)\cdot P_{y'}\right)}_{\text{population in and around cell c}} \Big/ \underbrace{\left(s_P \cdot \sum_{y'} I(y,y',d)\right)}_{\text{surface in and around cell c}}, \qquad (13)$$

where $I\ (y,\ y',\ d)$ equals one if cells y and y′ fall within the same FUA and the distance between their centres is smaller than d, and zero otherwise.[4] In this study, d is set at 3 km. Figure 3.A.4 provides a detailed illustration of the extraction of moving average filtered densities from the observed population densities.

The filtering process facilitates substantially the extraction of urban centres by smoothing out extremely high or low population density values. Such values may be the result of measurement errors, spatially refined regulatory mechanisms or other idiosyncratic characteristics that vary widely across very small areas. Figure 3.A.5 displays the moving average filtered densities (middle panels) for cities with low (left panels) and high (right panels) local variation of density. In both cases, the proposed filter is shown to be effective in deriving a city-wide picture of population allocation that is free of local specificities.

All cells with filtered population density below a threshold (ϑ) are considered as rural and are therefore removed. Following OECD (2011), the threshold is set to 150 inhabitants per km^2. This population density threshold is represented by the horizontal line in the middle panels of Figure 3.A.3. The outcome of removing rural areas is the smoothed population density displayed by the curves in the lower panels of Figure 3.A.5. The average smoothed density, S_i, is then represented by the horizontal line in those panels. Mathematically, this can be represented by the following fraction:

$$S_i = \underbrace{\left(\sum_{y} I_{ic}(y)\cdot I\left(M_y > \vartheta\right)\cdot M_y\right)}_{\text{sum of filtered population density exceeding }\vartheta} \Big/ \underbrace{\left(\sum_{y} I_{ic}(y)\cdot I\left(M_y > \vartheta\right)\right)}_{\text{sum of cells in which filtered population exceeds }\vartheta}, \qquad (14)$$

where M_y is the filtered population density, and $I\left(M_y > \vartheta\right)$ equals one if the filtered population density exceeds threshold ϑ and zero otherwise.

The set of cells in which filtered population exceeds the average smoothed density given by Equation (14) compose patches similar to those constructed out of land cover cells

Figure 3.A.5. **Obtaining the number of centres (peak-density points) from population density data**

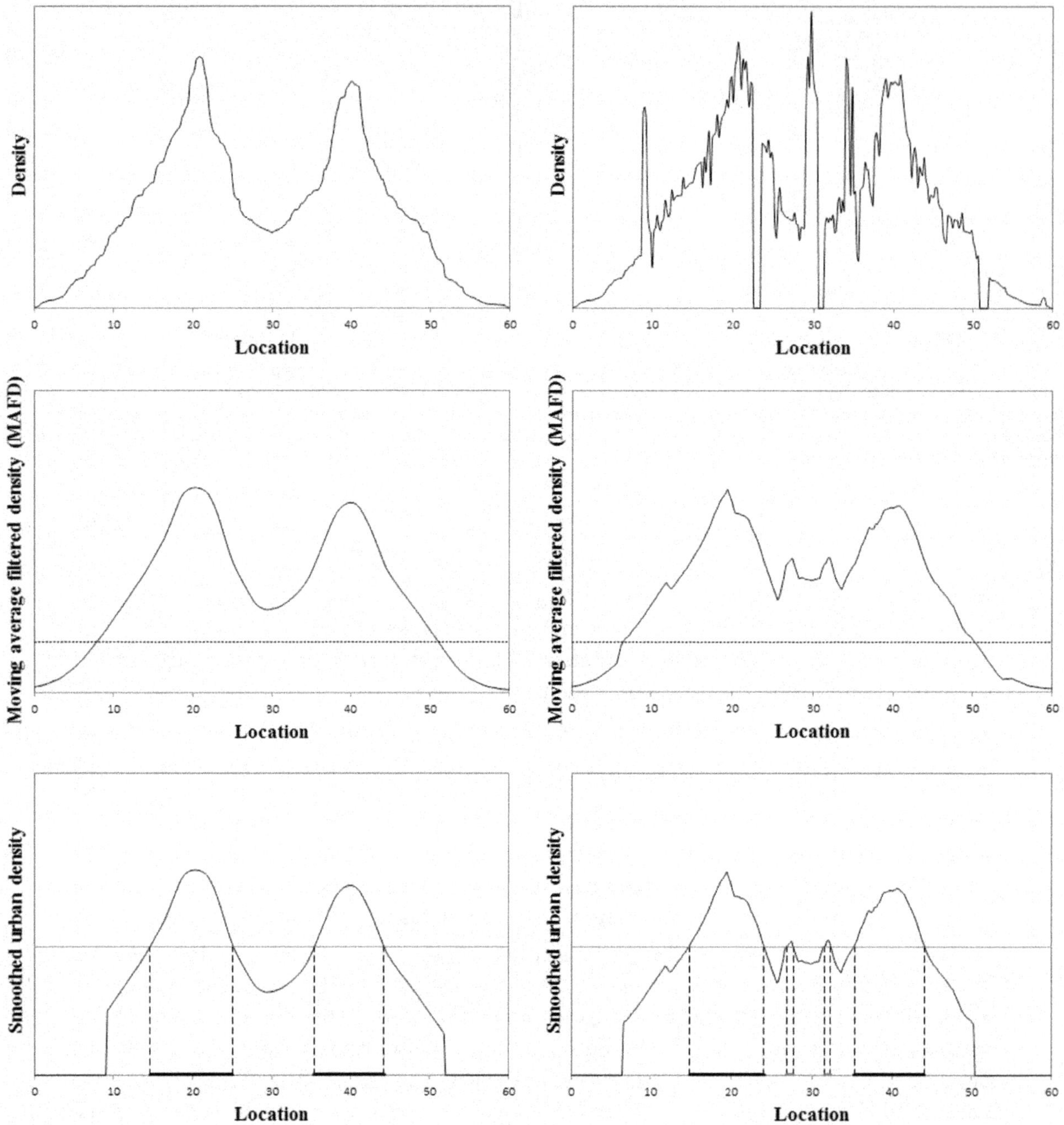

Notes: Upper panels: population density across urban space. Middle panels: smoothed population density derived after applying a moving average filter. Lower panels: identification of urban centres. Left panels: a city with lower variation of local density. Right panels: a city with larger variation of population density.

for built areas (see Figure 3.A.3). Any patch of population cells with total surface over 5 km^2 is considered to be an *urban centre*. In the two dimensional illustration of Figure 3.A.5, both cities turn out to have two urban centres. The city displayed on the left yields two patches of high population density, whose footprints are projected on the horizontal axis. Since both footprints occupy a considerable amount of surface, both patches qualify to be considered as urban centres. The city displayed at the right yields four candidate urban centres; however, only two of them occupy enough space (over 5 km^2) to be considered as urban centres.

The average number of urban centres in an OECD country is given by the ratio of the total number of centres identified in all functional urban areas of the country divided by the number of these urban areas. This is equivalent to the total number of urban centres expected in a randomly selected urban area of the country.

Decentralisation

Decentralisation shows the share of urban population residing outside of the urban centres of an FUA. The formula used to compute decentralisation for FUA i in country c is the one presented in Equation (15):

$$D_{ic} = 1 - \left(\underbrace{\sum_k \left(\sum_y I(y, k_{ic}) \cdot M_y \right)}_{\text{total population in urban centres of FUA i}} \Bigg/ \underbrace{\left(\sum_y I_{ic}(y) \cdot M_y \right)}_{\text{FUA filtered population}} \right), \tag{15}$$

where the indicator $I\ (y,\ k_{ic})$ equals one if the population raster cell y belongs to urban centre k of FUA i in country c and zero otherwise. The rest of the terms are already defined in Equations (1) and (14). The decentralisation indicator is based on the use of a *relative* threshold density. The reason for this is that the filtered density in every cell y that belongs to an urban centre, M_y, will by definition exceed the city's average smoothed density, as defined in Equation (14). Therefore, the decentralisation indicator can obtain high (low) values even in an FUA where population density is high (low) everywhere.

At the country level, decentralisation is computed according to the formula shown in Equation (16):

$$D_c = 1 - \left(\underbrace{\sum_k \left(\sum_y I(y, k_c) \cdot M_y \right)}_{\text{total filtered population in urban centres of all FUAs in country c}} \Bigg/ \underbrace{\left(\sum_y I_c(y) \cdot M_y \right)}_{\text{total filtered population in all FUAs of country c}} \right), \tag{16}$$

where I (y, k_c) equals one if the population raster cell y belongs to the urban centre k of any FUA in country c and zero otherwise. The rest of the terms are already defined in Equations (2) and (14).

Notes

1. To compute Equation (7), the GIS software iterates across all cells in the population raster, computing the variance (squared standard deviation) of the population density from the average density of the urban area for all cells belonging to FUA i.
2. The definition of the total area of the fragments differs from the definition of total built-up area as used in the $\overline{P}_{Bi}$ Pindicator, because fragments in which development is less than 723 m^2 (50% of the 1 446 m^2, which is the surface of a land cover cell) are disregarded. This filtering is required so that isolated built-up areas, such as warehouses, remote houses or structures in agricultural land are not considered as fragments. This prevents an inflation of the number of fragments in an FUA.
3. The deployed algorithm is provided by ArcGIS Region Group analysis. It iterates across all cells from the top left to the bottom right of a raster. For each arbitrary cell x, the algorithm checks whether the neighbouring cells of x (horizontally, vertically or diagonally) are already assigned to one or more existing fragments (cell patches). If all the neighbouring cells of x that are already

assigned to a fragment belong to the same fragment F, cell x is also assigned to F. If any of the assigned neighbouring cells of x are found to belong to different fragments, these fragments are merged and cell x is assigned to the new, merged fragment. For instance, if the adjacent to x cells x′ and x″ are found to be assigned to fragments F′ and F″ respectively, fragments F′ and F″ are merged into a new fragment, F‴, that will contain all cells of F′ and F″ and cell x. Finally, if none of the neighbouring cells of x are found to be assigned in a fragment, a new fragment is created and cell x is assigned to it.

4. The distance between any pair of arbitrary cells is measured by the distance between their centroids.

Reference

OECD (2011), "Distribution of population and regional typology", in *OECD Regions at a Glance 2011*, OECD Publishing, Paris, *http://dx.doi.org/10.1787/reg_glance-2011-7-en*.

APPENDIX 3.B

Country sheets

This Appendix presents an overview of the current situation of urban sprawl and its evolution over time for each of the 29 OECD countries considered in the study. The analysis draws on the seven indicators of urban sprawl developed earlier in this chapter. For each country, the Appendix presents: i) a box with basic statistical information and the values of urban sprawl indicators in 2014; ii) a radar chart comparing the country's score in the urban sprawl indicators of 2014 with the average of the 29 countries included in the analysis for that year; iii) three graphs depicting the evolution of different urban sprawl indicators from 1990 until 2014; and iv) a brief discussion of the main findings from the analysis of the indicators.

The radar charts presented in panels a of Figures 3.B.1 to 3.B.29 position each country's score in five sprawl indicators – inverse of average population density, coefficient of variation of population density within urban areas (dispersity), fragmentation of urban fabric, number of peak-density areas (polycentricity), and decentralisation of urban population – *vis-à-vis* the respective cross-country average in 2014. The average of the 29 countries included in the analysis is often referred to as the OECD average. The radar charts are constructed upon five axes, with each axis representing:

$$r_x = \frac{x_c}{\bar{x}_{OECD}} = \frac{x_c}{\frac{1}{29}\sum_q x_q}$$

where x_c is the average value of indicator x for all urban areas in country c, and $\bar{x}_{OECD} = \frac{1}{29}\sum_q x_q$ is the (unweighted) OECD average. The five axes range from the minimum to the maximum value of r_x, with the maximum values denoted on the axes. The value of $\bar{x}_{OECD}$ for each indicator is represented by a red dot. The red dots are connected with red dashed lines, forming a pentagon that illustrates the 29-country average for the five indicators.

The evolution of urban sprawl indicators over the period 1990-2014 is shown in panels b to d of Figures 3.B.1 to 3.B.29. The intertemporal evolution of the five indicators presented in the radar charts is presented in panels b. Instead of changes over time being shown in absolute terms, as in Section 3.4, they are expressed here in percentage changes. Therefore, the red dot which denotes the total percentage change in the period 1990-2014, is usually different from the sum of the individual changes (1990-2000 and 2000-14). The graphs presented in panels c and d show the intertemporal evolution of urban sprawl indicators based on absolute thresholds of population density. These indicators correspond to the percentage of populated urban areas with density levels below 1 500, 2 500 and 3 500 inhabitants per km^2 and the percentage of FUA population residing in these areas.

The data sources used to produce these graphs are the ones presented in Section 3.3, i.e. land-cover data are provided by the Global Human Settlement (GHS) built-up area dataset (Pesaresi et al., 2015), population data by the GHS population grid (European Commission, Joint Research Centre (JRC) and Columbia University, Center for International Earth Science Information Network – CIESIN, 2015) and FUA delimitations by OECD (2012). Data on land area and population at the national level, presented in the top of the boxes for each country are provided by the World Bank (2017).

Australia

Land area (km²):	7 682 300	Mean urban population density (inh./km²):	1 026.1
Population:	23 460 694	Coefficient of variation of urban population density:	1.6
Population density (inhabitants per km²):	3.1	Average number of fragments per km² of urban area	8.8
Number of functional urban areas:	18	Average number of centres per urban area	2.8
Fraction of population residing in FUAs:	78.1%	Percentage of urban population residing outside urban centres	27.6%

Figure 3.B.1. **Sprawl indicators Australia**

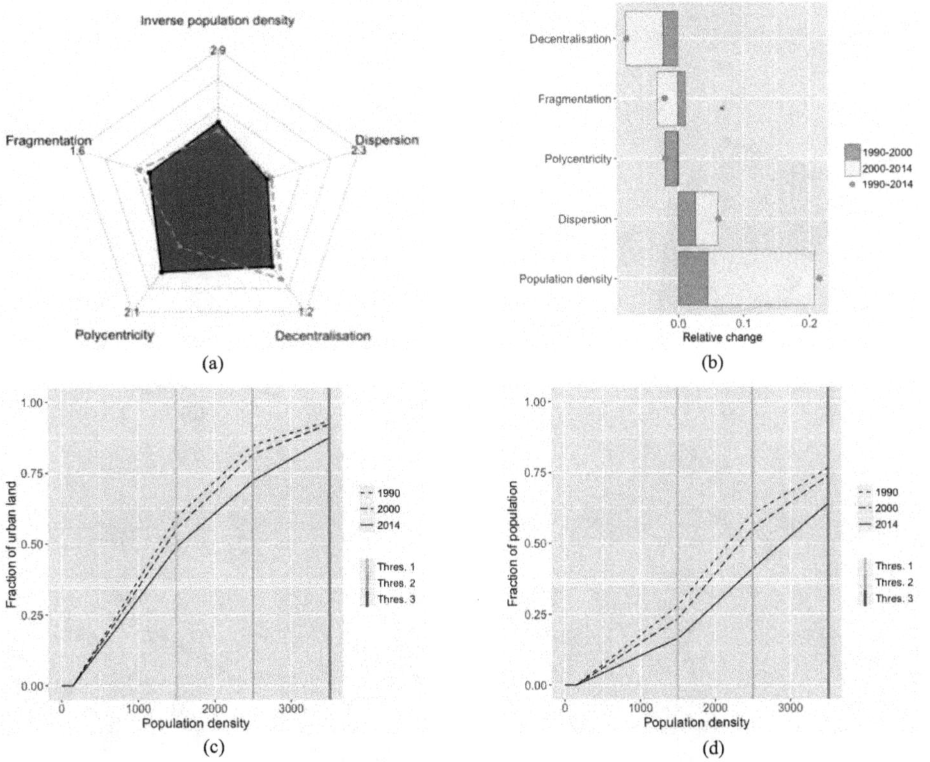

Notes: Thres. 1 denotes a population density of 1 500 inhabitants/km², Thres. 2 a population density of 2 500 inhabitants/km² and Thres. 3 a population density of 3 500 inhabitants/km².

Source: Own calculations, based on GHS built-area data (Pesaresi et al., 2015), GHS population data (European Commission, Joint Research Centre (JRC) and Columbia University, Center for International Earth Science Information Network – CIESIN, 2015) and FUA delimitations (OECD, 2012).

The basic sprawl indicators of Australian urban areas are currently close to the OECD average, as shown in panel a. An exception is the polycentricity index which is 40% higher than the OECD average.

Panel b, which shows the evolution of indicators, reveals that Australian cities have undergone a densification process during the period 1990-2014. That process was especially manifested in the period from 2000 onwards: the urban areas of the country in 2014 were, on average, 16% denser than in 2000. This reveals that the footprint of urban areas has grown substantially slower than the urban population.

A similar trend is revealed by the changes occurring in the entire distribution of population density across urban space. During the period 1990-2014, the percentage of urban land with population density in the range of 150-1 500 inhabitants/km² has steadily decreased from 59% to below 50%. That change was accompanied by a substantial increase in the percentage of urban land with density between 1 500 and 2 500 inhabitants/km² as shown in panel c. The changes in the allocation of urban land are coupled with a similar change in the allocation of population across areas of different density levels, as shown in panel d.

At the same time, panel b suggests that there are signs that centralisation processes have been at play, as the changes in the decentralisation index have been negative for the two sub-periods of study. The evolution of the fragmentation index reveals that Australian urban areas have become slightly more contiguous in the period 2000-14, reversing a modest trend to the opposite direction in the previous period.

Austria

Land area (km²):	82 523	Mean urban population density (inh./km²):	937.9
Population:	8 541 575	Coefficient of variation of urban population density:	1.8
Population density (inhabitants per km²):	103.5	Average number of fragments per km² of urban area	14.0
Number of functional urban areas:	6	Average number of centres per urban area	2.7
Fraction of population residing in FUAs:	57.7%	Percentage of urban population residing outside urban centres	30.8%

Figure 3.B.2. **Sprawl indicators Austria**

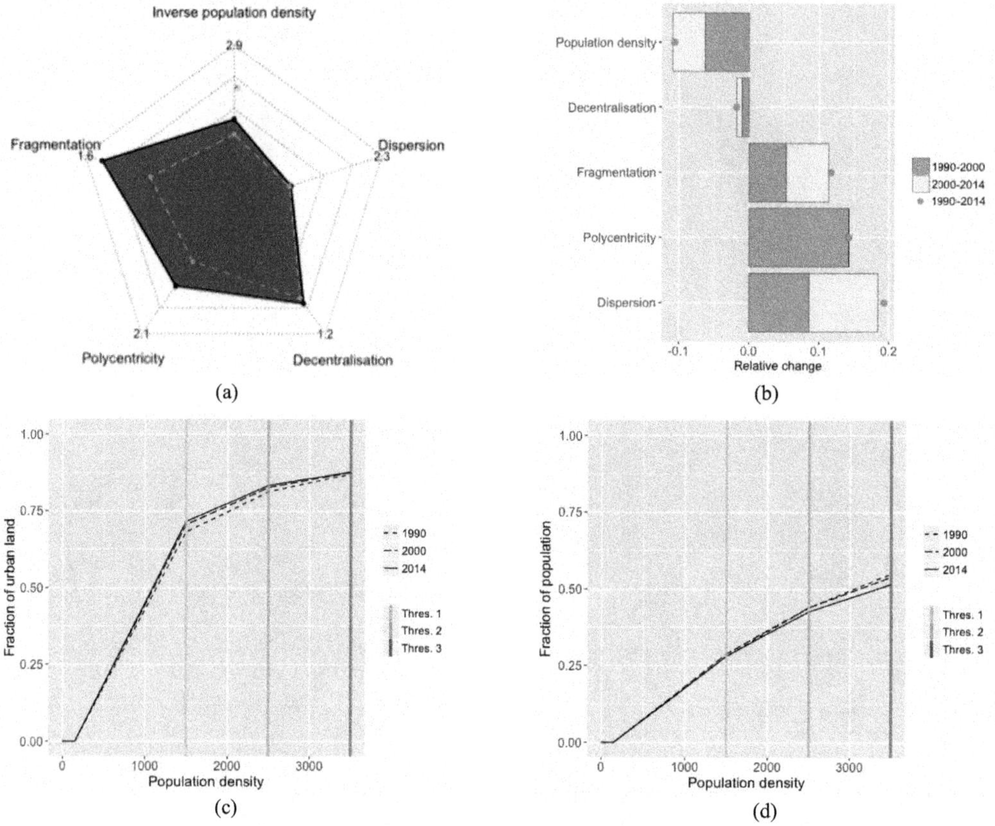

Notes: Thres. 1 denotes a population density of 1 500 inhabitants/km², Thres. 2 a population density of 2 500 inhabitants/km² and Thres. 3 a population density of 3 500 inhabitants/km².

Source: Own calculations, based on GHS built-area data (Pesaresi et al., 2015), GHS population data (European Commission, Joint Research Centre (JRC) and Columbia University, Center for International Earth Science Information Network – CIESIN, 2015) and FUA delimitations (OECD, 2012).

Austrian cities are relatively sprawled, as manifested in all indicators used in this study. Austrian urban areas are approximately 40% more fragmented and polycentric than the average of the countries included in the analysis, as shown in panel a. Their population density also lies below the OECD average.

Urban sprawl has significantly increased since 1990. Average population density in Austrian cities has decreased by around 11% between 1990 and 2014, as shown in panel b. In the same period, the variation of population density across urban space increased by 19% and urban areas became more polycentric (14%) and fragmented (12%).

As depicted in panel c, the share of urban built surfaces hosting population densities within the three examined intervals (150-1 500, 1 500-2 500 and 2 500-3 500 inhabitants per km²) have remained relatively stable over time. A similar pattern is observed for the allocation of population across areas of different density, which is displayed in panel d.

Belgium

Land area (km^2):	30 280	Mean urban population density (inh./km^2):	1 107.2
Population:	11 209 057	Coefficient of variation of urban population density:	1.6
Population density (inhabitants per km^2):	370.2	Average number of fragments per km^2 of urban area	7.6
Number of functional urban areas:	11	Average number of centres per urban area	2.0
Fraction of population residing in FUAs:	60.0%	Percentage of urban population residing outside urban centres	35.0%

Figure 3.B.3. **Sprawl indicators Belgium**

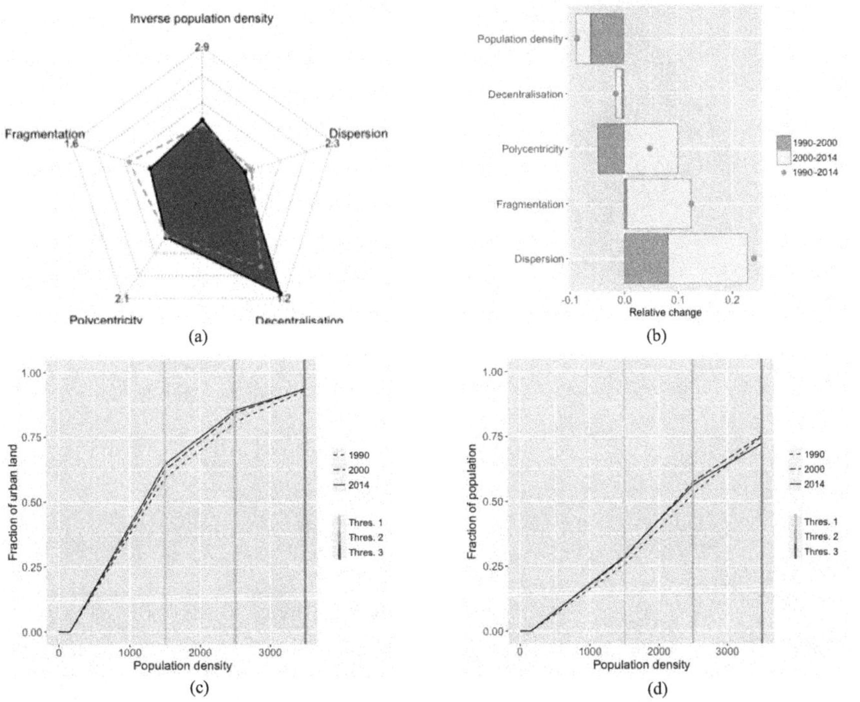

Notes: Thres. 1 denotes a population density of 1 500 inhabitants/km^2, Thres. 2 a population density of 2 500 inhabitants/km^2 and Thres. 3 a population density of 3 500 inhabitants/km^2.
Source: Own calculations, based on GHS built-area data (Pesaresi et al., 2015), GHS population data (European Commission, Joint Research Centre (JRC) and Columbia University, Center for International Earth Science Information Network – CIESIN, 2015) and FUA delimitations (OECD, 2012).

Belgian cities are particularly decentralised, about 17% more than the OECD average, as shown in panel a. Their score in the rest of the indicators is close to the average, with one exception: Belgium's urban areas are about 20% less fragmented. However, fragmentation has been increasing, as illustrated in panel b: between 2000 and 2014 Belgian cities have on average become 12% more fragmented. In addition, the variation of population density (dispersion) has sharply increased since 1990, by 24%. However, in 2014 dispersion still remained slightly below the OECD average.

Belgium's urban areas have become less dense, more fragmented and more polycentric since 1990. Belgium's urban population density has decreased by about 9% since then, while its variation has sharply increased (24%). Especially since 2000, new development has occurred in a more fragmented way and new urban centres have emerged. Fragmentation has increased by 12% and polycentricity by 10% in the period 2000-14.

Panels c and d illustrate the distribution of urban land and population to areas of low-to-moderate density levels (between 150 and 3 500 inhabitants per km^2). Belgium ranks first (together with Luxembourg) among the countries included in the study in the share of urban land allocated to areas of such densities, while second in the share of population residing in them. Since 1990, the share of urban land in areas with density of 150-2 500 inhabitants per km^2 has increased by about 5 percentage points, at the expense of the share of urban land in areas with density between 2 500-3 500 inhabitants per km^2 (panel c). Panel d reveals a similar pattern for the share of urban population residing in areas with density between 150 and 2 500 inhabitants per km^2. However, due to an important decline in the share of urban population living in areas with density of 2 500-3 500 inhabitants per km^2, the percentage of urban population living in areas with low-to-moderate density is lower in 2014 than in 1990.

Canada

Land area (km^2):	9 093 510	Mean urban population density (inh./km^2):	426.4
Population:	35 544 564	Coefficient of variation of urban population density:	3.9
Population density (inhabitants per km^2):	3.9	Average number of fragments per km^2 of urban area	10.0
Number of functional urban areas:	34	Average number of centres per urban area	2.2
Fraction of population residing in FUAs:	73.1%	Percentage of urban population residing outside urban centres	26.8%

Figure 3.B.4. **Sprawl indicators Canada**

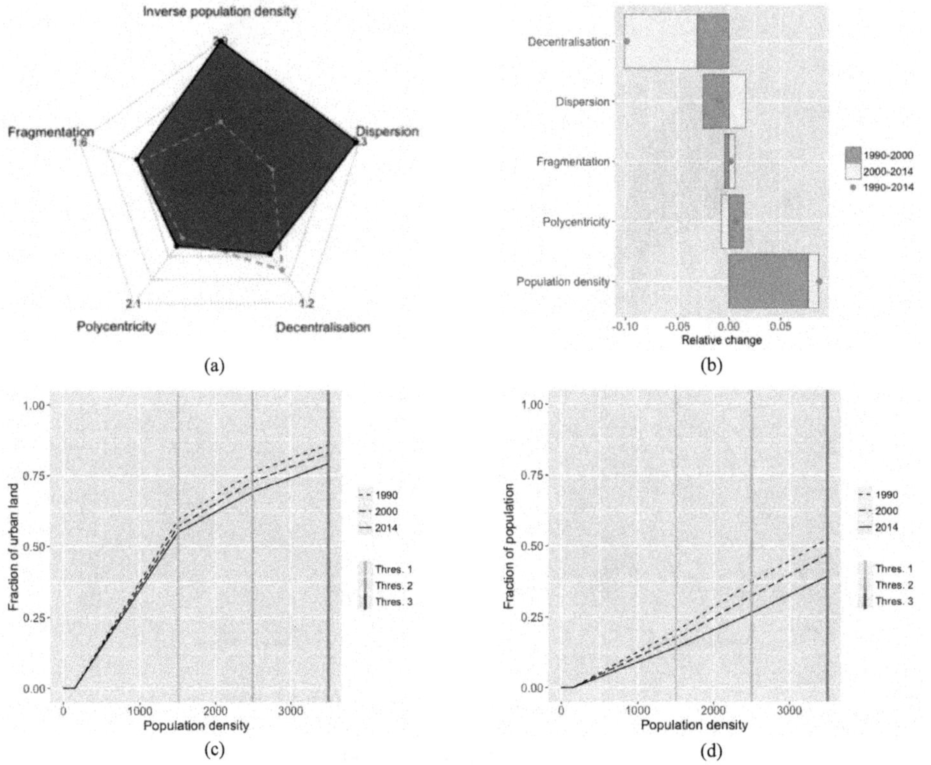

Notes: Thres. 1 denotes a population density of 1 500 inhabitants/km^2, Thres. 2 a population density of 2 500 inhabitants/km^2 and Thres. 3 a population density of 3 500 inhabitants/km^2.
Source: Own calculations, based on GHS built-area data (Pesaresi et al., 2015), GHS population data (European Commission, Joint Research Centre (JRC) and Columbia University, Center for International Earth Science Information Network – CIESIN, 2015) and FUA delimitations (OECD, 2012).

Canada is the country with the lowest urban population density, approximately one third of the OECD average (see panel a). Furthermore, urban population density exhibits the highest variation (dispersion) in the study, about 2.3 times the OECD average.

Population density in Canadian urban areas has significantly increased between 1990 and 2014, recording a total change of 9% (panel b). However, the largest part of this reduction occurred before 2000; population density has only slightly increased since then. In contrast, centralisation forces have been rather strong since 2000: decentralisation has diminished by about 7% in the period 2000-14. In 2014, 27% of FUA population in Canada was residing outside peak-density areas considered as centres, which is below the OECD average.

The changes observed in the distribution of population density across urban space, shown in panel c, reflect the trend of increasing population density. During the period 1990-2014, the percentage of urban land with population density in the range of 150-3 500 inhabitants/km^2 has steadily decreased. This reduction is especially pronounced in density levels above 1 500 inhabitants/km^2. The evolution of the allocation of urban land aligns with the evolution of the allocation of population across areas of different density levels, as shown in panel d.

Chile

Land area (km^2):	743 532	Mean urban population density (inh./km^2):	3 867.5
Population:	17 613 798	Coefficient of variation of urban population density:	1.4
Population density (inhabitants per km^2):	23.7	Average number of fragments per km^2 of urban area	14.2
Number of functional urban areas:	26	Average number of centres per urban area	2.0
Fraction of population residing in FUAs:	74.6%	Percentage of urban population residing outside urban centres	22.0%

Figure 3.B.5. **Sprawl indicators Chile**

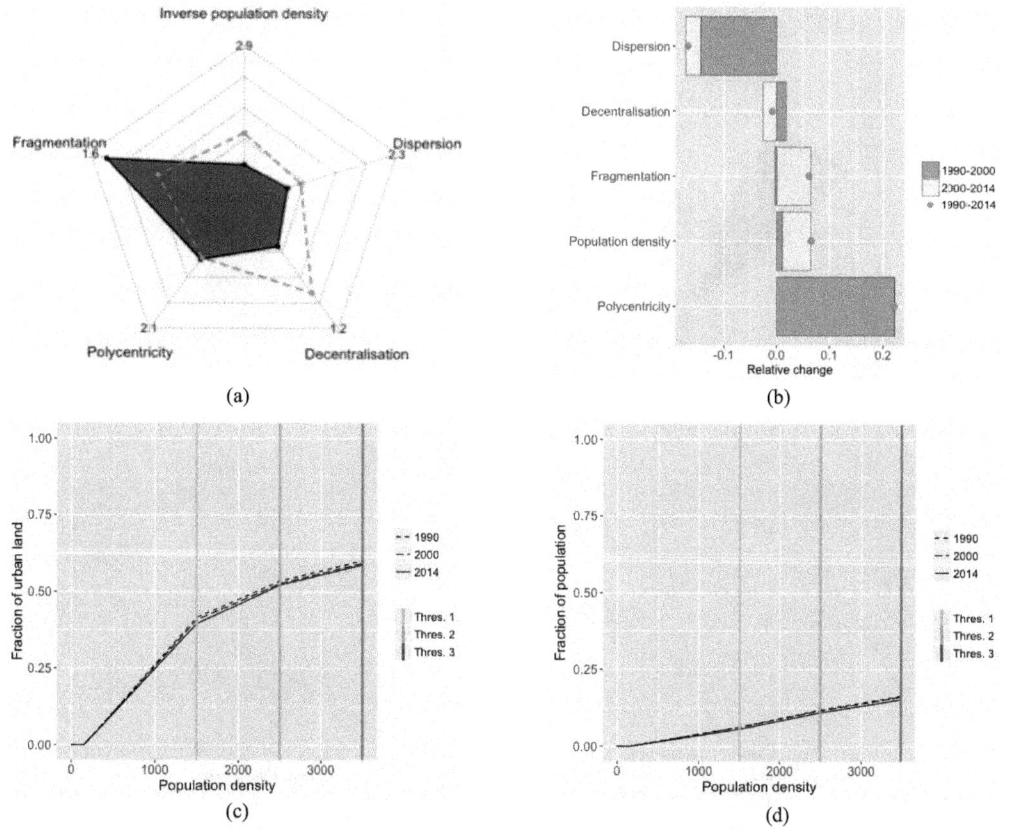

Notes: Thres. 1 denotes a population density of 1 500 inhabitants/km^2, Thres. 2 a population density of 2 500 inhabitants/km^2 and Thres. 3 a population density of 3 500 inhabitants/km^2.

Source: Own calculations, based on GHS built-area data (Pesaresi et al., 2015), GHS population data (European Commission, Joint Research Centre (JRC) and Columbia University, Center for International Earth Science Information Network – CIESIN, 2015) and FUA delimitations (OECD, 2012).

Chilean urban areas are very centralised and dense. They are characterised by high population density that displays little variation (dispersion) within them, and in 2014, 78% of the urban population was residing in areas identified as urban centres (panel a). However, the country's urban areas are about 40% more fragmented than the average country included in the study.

Panel b reveals that average urban population density has increased since 1990 by about 7%, with that change mainly occurring after 2000. Variation of density has also largely decreased: since 2000, it has been reduced by 17%. At the same time, polycentricity has increased by 25% between 1990 and 2000 and has remained stable since then. Chilean urban areas have also become more fragmented, especially in the period following 2000. Overall, it seems that densification has been accompanied by higher fragmentation of urban areas.

As shown in panels c and d, the allocation of land and population to different density levels has remained rather stable during the examined period: areas with density over 3 500 inhabitants per km^2 occupy more than 41% of the urban built environment and accommodate 85% of the urban population.

Czech Republic

Land area (km^2):	77 210	Mean urban population density (inh./km^2):	1 235.6
Population:	10 525 347	Coefficient of variation of urban population density:	1.3
Population density (inhabitants per km^2):	136.3	Average number of fragments per km^2 of urban area	8.4
Number of functional urban areas:	16	Average number of centres per urban area	1.3
Fraction of population residing in FUAs:	48.6%	Percentage of urban population residing outside urban centres	32.7%

Figure 3.B.6. **Sprawl indicators Czech Republic**

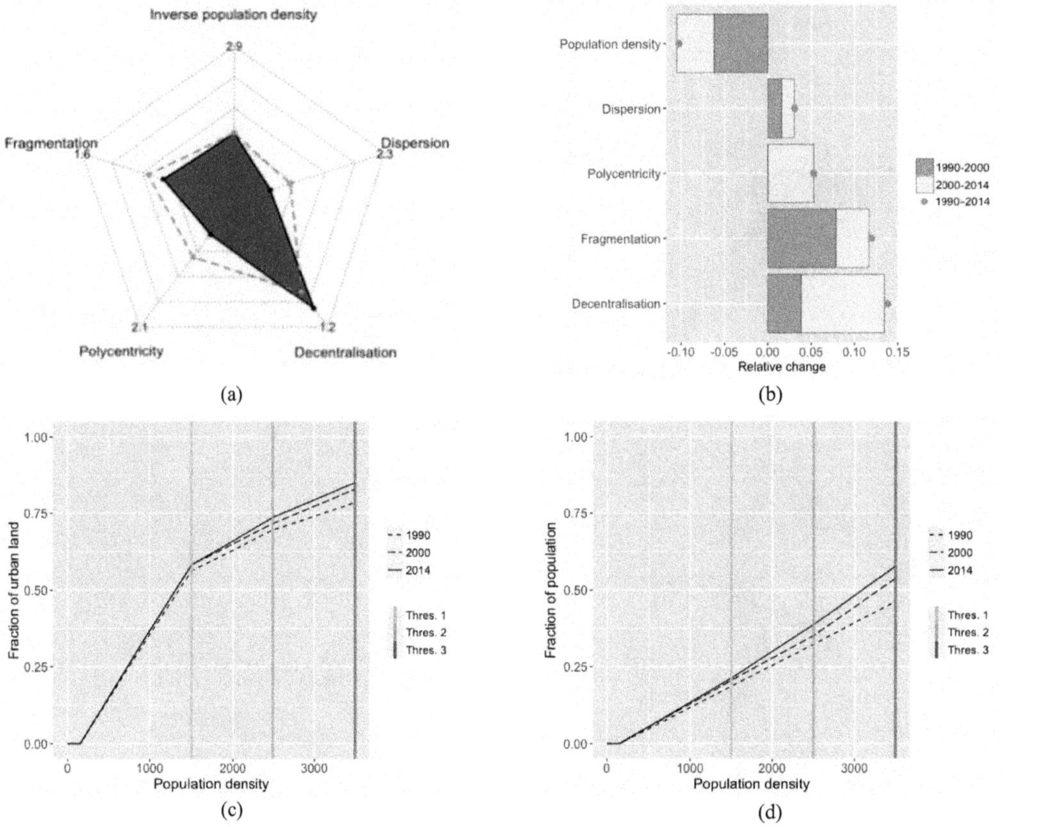

Notes: Thres. 1 denotes a population density of 1 500 inhabitants/km^2, Thres. 2 a population density of 2 500 inhabitants/km^2 and Thres. 3 a population density of 3 500 inhabitants/km^2.
Source: Own calculations, based on GHS built-area data (Pesaresi et al., 2015), GHS population data (European Commission, Joint Research Centre (JRC) and Columbia University, Center for International Earth Science Information Network – CIESIN, 2015) and FUA delimitations (OECD, 2012).

Czech cities are generally less sprawled than the OECD average.

With the exception of decentralisation, Czech Republic lies at the OECD average or below it in all sprawl indicators (panel a). For example, polycentricity in Czech cities is about 1/3 below the OECD average. The decentralisation index is approximately 10% higher than in the average country.

The trends depicted in panel b reveal, however, that Czech cities have been sprawling since 1990. Average population density has decreased by 10%, while fragmentation and decentralisation have increased by 12% and 14% respectively. Decentralisation processes have been more pronounced in the period after 2000, accompanied by an increase in polycentricity. Despite the emergence of more urban centres, a greater number of inhabitants have decided to move outside of them.

The allocation of urban land and population over different density levels, shown in panels c and d, reflects the decrease in population density. Between 1990 and 2014, the fraction of both urban surface and population exposed to very low density levels (150-1 500 inhabitants per km^2) increased by roughly two percentage points.

Denmark

Land area (km²):	42 262	Mean urban population density (inh./km²):	1 226.9
Population:	5 643 475	Coefficient of variation of urban population density:	1.7
Population density (inhabitants per km²):	133.5	Average number of fragments per km² of urban area	8.3
Number of functional urban areas:	5	Average number of centres per urban area	2.3
Fraction of population residing in FUAs:	55.9%	Percentage of urban population residing outside urban centres	32.7%

Figure 3.B.7. **Sprawl indicators Denmark**

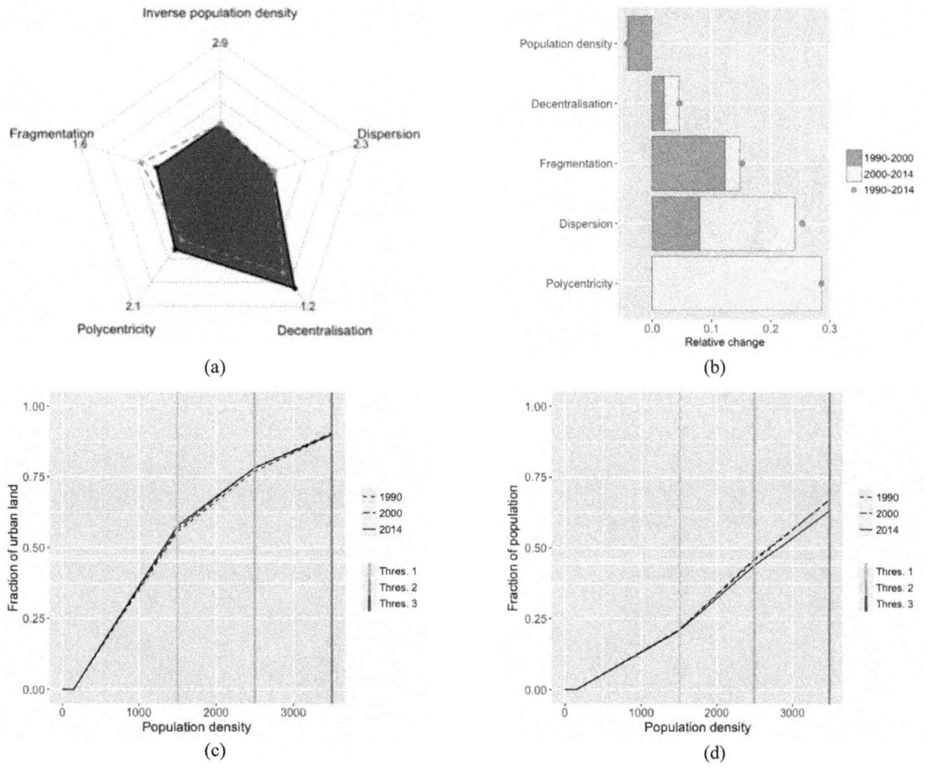

Notes: Thres. 1 denotes a population density of 1 500 inhabitants/km², Thres. 2 a population density of 2 500 inhabitants/km² and Thres. 3 a population density of 3 500 inhabitants/km².
Source: Own calculations, based on GHS built-area data (Pesaresi et al., 2015), GHS population data (European Commission, Joint Research Centre (JRC) and Columbia University, Center for International Earth Science Information Network – CIESIN, 2015) and FUA delimitations (OECD, 2012).

Urban sprawl in Denmark stands relatively close to the OECD average (panel a). Danish urban areas are only slightly more fragmented and somewhat less polycentric and decentralised than cities in the average country.

Panel b shows, however, that Danish cities have sprawled significantly since 1990. They have become 15% more fragmented and the variation (dispersion) of population density within them has increased by 25%. Unlike fragmentation whose increase seems to have slowed down from 2000 onwards, the increase of the variation of density has stepped up. The most prominent indicator change in the period 2000-14 is, however, the increase of polycentricity by 28%. Average population density decreased between 1990 and 2000 but this fall has been halted after 2000.

As depicted in panel c, the share of urban surfaces hosting population densities within the three examined intervals (150-1 500, 1 500-2 500 and 2 500-3 500 inhabitants per km²) have remained relatively stable over time. A similar pattern is observed for the allocation of population across areas with densities between 150-2 500 inhabitants per km², which is displayed in panel d. The fraction of the population residing in areas with densities between 1 500 and 3 500 inhabitants per km² decreased slightly, by 4 percentage points.

Finland

Land area (km^2):	303 890	Mean urban population density (inh./km^2):	1 631.0
Population:	5 461 512	Coefficient of variation of urban population density:	1.4
Population density (inhabitants per km^2):	18.0	Average number of fragments per km^2 of urban area	12.9
Number of functional urban areas:	7	Average number of centres per urban area	1.6
Fraction of population residing in FUAs:	55.3%	Percentage of urban population residing outside urban centres	29.4%

Figure 3.B.8. **Sprawl indicators Finland**

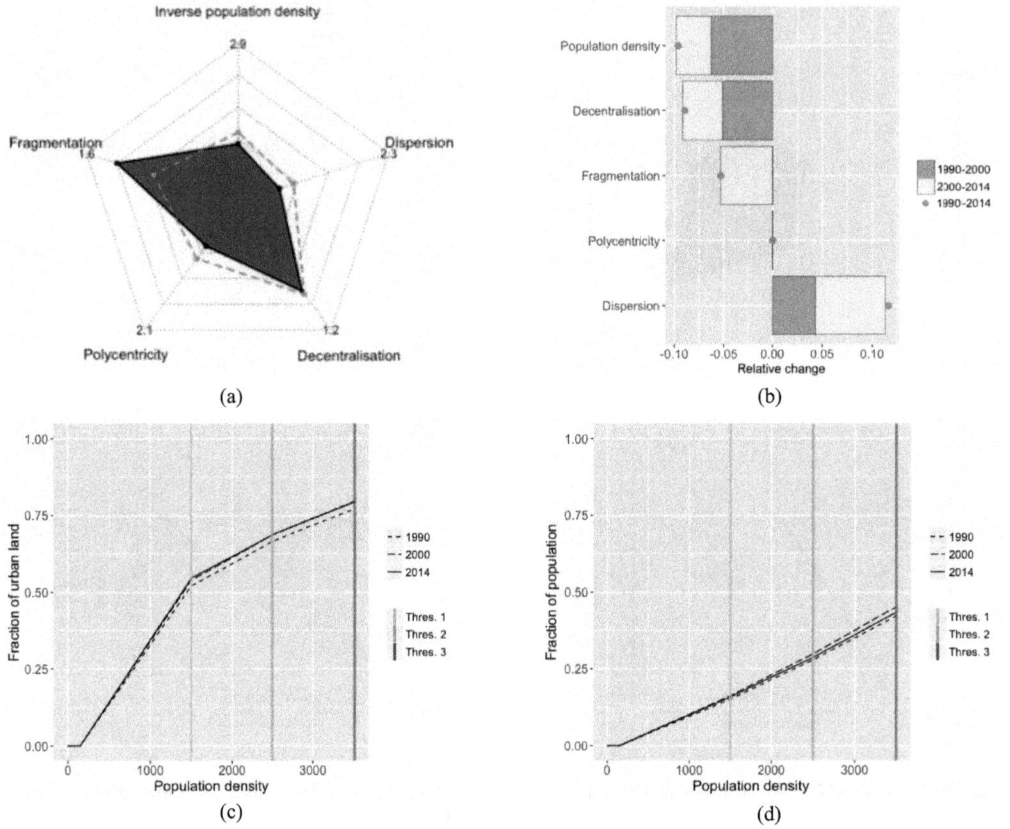

Notes: Thres. 1 denotes a population density of 1 500 inhabitants/km^2, Thres. 2 a population density of 2 500 inhabitants/km^2 and Thres. 3 a population density of 3 500 inhabitants/km^2.
Source: Own calculations, based on GHS built-area data (Pesaresi et al., 2015), GHS population data (European Commission, Joint Research Centre (JRC) and Columbia University, Center for International Earth Science Information Network – CIESIN, 2015) and FUA delimitations (OECD, 2012).

Finnish urban areas are less sprawled than the OECD average. As shown in panel a, they are relatively dense and the variation of urban population density is relatively low. Polycentricity and decentralisation in Finland's cities are also below the cross-country average. The only sprawl dimension along which Finnish urban areas rank higher than the average is fragmentation, by 34%.

Urban sprawl dimensions have evolved in different ways over time (panel b). Since 1990, cities have become about 10% less dense and the variation of density within them has increased by 12%. At the same time, centralisation processes have been into play, leading to a 9% reduction in the decentralisation index. Since 2000, Finnish cities have also become 5% less fragmented.

Both the distribution of urban land and the distribution of population, shown in panels c and d, remained relatively stable over time. The panels reveal a slight increase in the share of urban land and population corresponding to areas with a density between 150 to 3 500 inhabitants per km^2 between 1990 and 2000, followed by a slight decrease between 2000 and 2014.

France

Land area (km²):	547 557	Mean urban population density (inh./km²):	1 122.5
Population:	66 331 957	Coefficient of variation of urban population density:	1.9
Population density (inhabitants per km²):	121.1	Average number of fragments per km² of urban area	10.7
Number of functional urban areas:	83	Average number of centres per urban area	1.7
Fraction of population residing in FUAs:	62.6%	Percentage of urban population residing outside urban centres	30.8%

Figure 3.B.9. **Sprawl indicators France**

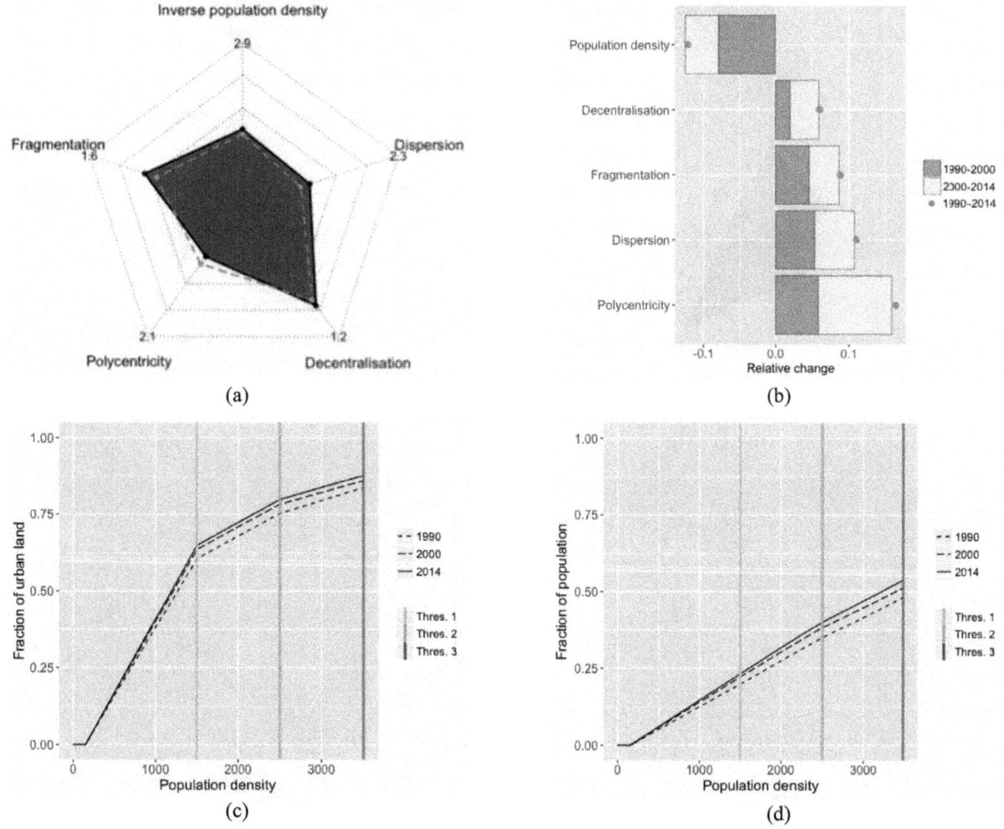

Notes: Thres. 1 denotes a population density of 1 500 inhabitants/km², Thres. 2 a population density of 2 500 inhabitants/km² and Thres. 3 a population density of 3 500 inhabitants/km².
Source: Own calculations, based on GHS built-area data (Pesaresi et al., 2015), GHS population data (European Commission, Joint Research Centre (JRC) and Columbia University, Center for International Earth Science Information Network – CIESIN, 2015) and FUA delimitations (OECD, 2012).

French cities are very close to the cross-country average on all five dimensions of urban sprawl, as shown in panel a.

Panel b shows, however, that French urban areas have noticeably sprawled since 1990. This is manifested in the evolution of all indicators, but the greatest changes (in percentage terms) are observed in population density and polycentricity. French cities have become 12% less dense and 17% more polycentric than they were in 1990. The decrease in population density has been coupled with a 9% increase in fragmentation, which indicates that the urban areas have expanded in a discontinuous way.

Sprawling patterns in France are also revealed by the evolution of the allocation of urban land and population to areas with relatively low density. The distribution of urban land over different urban population density levels, shown in panel c, displays an increase in the portion of urban built areas hosting density levels between 150 and 3 500 inhabitants per km²: from 84% in 1990, the share increased to 88% in 2014. Cumulatively, the share of urban population residing in areas with density levels between 150 and 3 500 inhabitants per km² (panel d) increased by 6 percentage points: from 48% in 1990 to 54% in 2014.

Germany

Land area (km^2):	348 900	Mean urban population density (inh./km^2):	1 419.4
Population:	80 982 500	Coefficient of variation of urban population density:	1.1
Population density (inhabitants per km^2):	232.1	Average number of fragments per km^2 of urban area	6.6
Number of functional urban areas:	109	Average number of centres per urban area	2.0
Fraction of population residing in FUAs:	65.0%	Percentage of urban population residing outside urban centres	33.5%

Figure 3.B.10. **Sprawl indicators Germany**

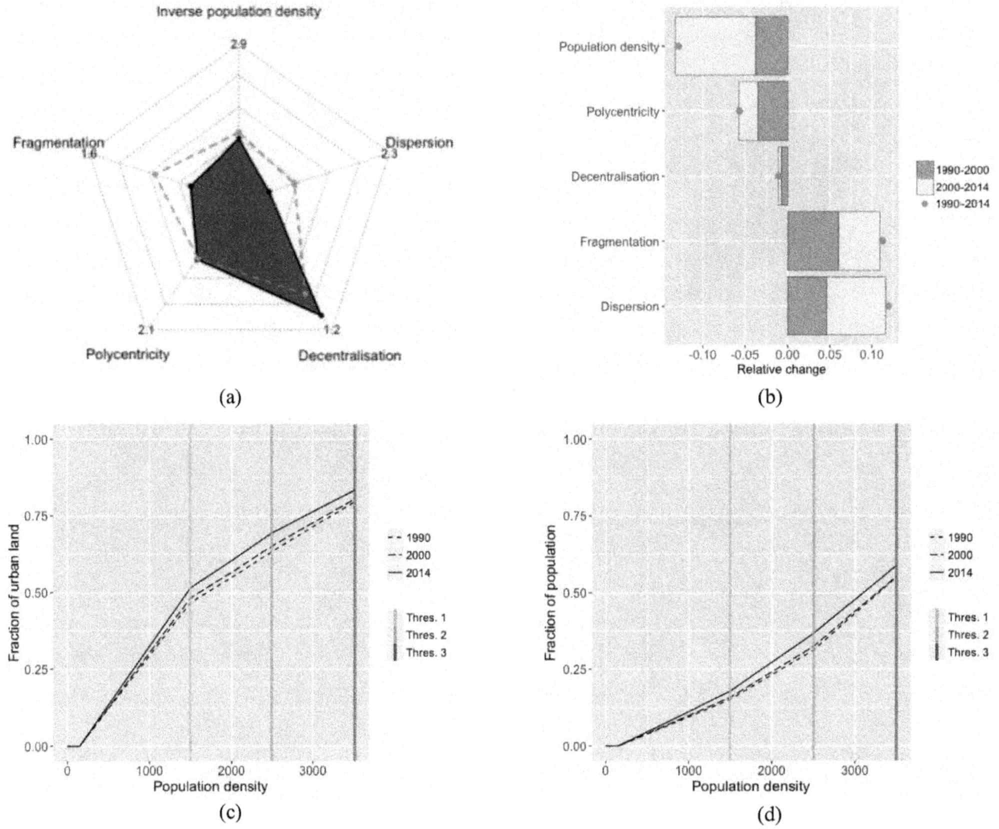

Notes: Thres. 1 denotes a population density of 1 500 inhabitants/km^2, Thres. 2 a population density of 2 500 inhabitants/km^2 and Thres. 3 a population density of 3 500 inhabitants/km^2.
Source: Own calculations, based on GHS built-area data (Pesaresi et al., 2015), GHS population data (European Commission, Joint Research Centre (JRC) and Columbia University, Center for International Earth Science Information Network – CIESIN, 2015) and FUA delimitations (OECD, 2012).

Compared to the OECD average in 2014, German urban areas are more decentralised and contiguous (panel a). Urban population density is slightly above the average and displays a relatively low variation.

Since 1990, Germany has followed a sprawling process (panel b). Between 1990 and 2014, urban population density decreased by about 13%, while its variation (dispersion) increased by 12%. German urban areas have also become 12% more fragmented than they were in 1990.

As shown in panel c, the decrease in population density between 1990 and 2014 has been accompanied by an increase of five percentage points (47% to 52%) in the share of urban land hosting very low population density levels (150-1 500 inhabitants per km^2). The corresponding increase in the share of population, shown in panel d, is three percentage points: from 15% to 18%.

Greece

Land area (km^2):	128 900	Mean urban population density (inh./km^2):	2 719.1
Population:	10 892 413	Coefficient of variation of urban population density:	1.7
Population density (inhabitants per km^2):	84.5	Average number of fragments per km^2 of urban area	9.6
Number of functional urban areas:	9	Average number of centres per urban area	1.0
Fraction of population residing in FUAs:	51.2%	Percentage of urban population residing outside urban centres	18.7%

Figure 3.B.11. **Sprawl indicators Greece**

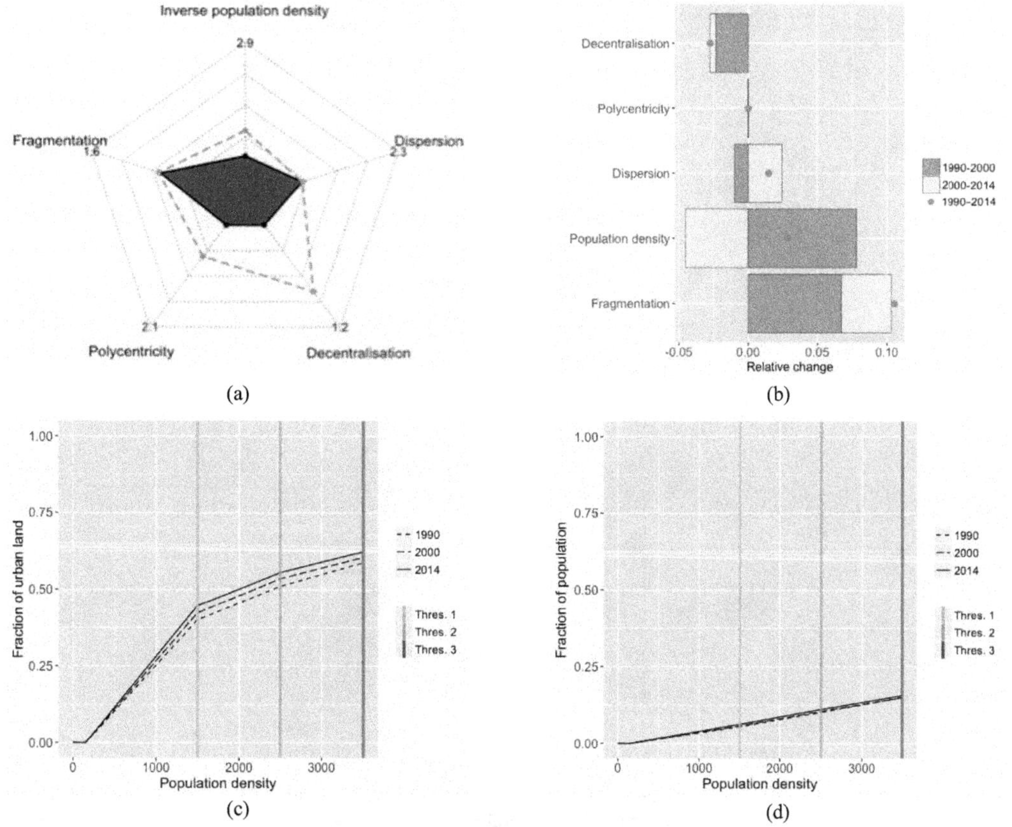

Notes: Thres. 1 denotes a population density of 1 500 inhabitants/km^2, Thres. 2 a population density of 2 500 inhabitants/km^2 and Thres. 3 a population density of 3 500 inhabitants/km^2.

Source: Own calculations, based on GHS built-area data (Pesaresi et al., 2015), GHS population data (European Commission, Joint Research Centre (JRC) and Columbia University, Center for International Earth Science Information Network – CIESIN, 2015) and FUA delimitations (OECD, 2012).

Greek urban areas are among the most compact of those included in the study (panel a). Greece ranks fourth in average urban population density and contains exclusively monocentric urban areas that display the minimum decentralisation recorded in the study. Fragmentation and variation of urban population density (dispersion) are very close to the OECD average values.

As shown in panel b, Greek urban areas have sprawled since 2000. Average urban population density has decreased by about 5% during that period, while its variation has slightly increased. Fragmentation has been rising since 1990, exhibiting an increase of about 11% in the entire period of study.

The distribution of the urban area and the population over different population density levels is shown in panel c and panel d respectively. The percentage of the urban area exposed to densities between 150 and 3 500 people/km^2 increased in both periods of the study, whereas the distribution of the population at those density levels remained rather stable.

Hungary

Land area (km^2):	90 530	Mean urban population density (inh./km^2):	1 263.2
Population:	9 866 468	Coefficient of variation of urban population density:	1.5
Population density (inhabitants per km^2):	109.0	Average number of fragments per km^2 of urban area	9.6
Number of functional urban areas:	10	Average number of centres per urban area	1.3
Fraction of population residing in FUAs:	51.5%	Percentage of urban population residing outside urban centres	31.5%

Figure 3.B.12. **Sprawl indicators Hungary**

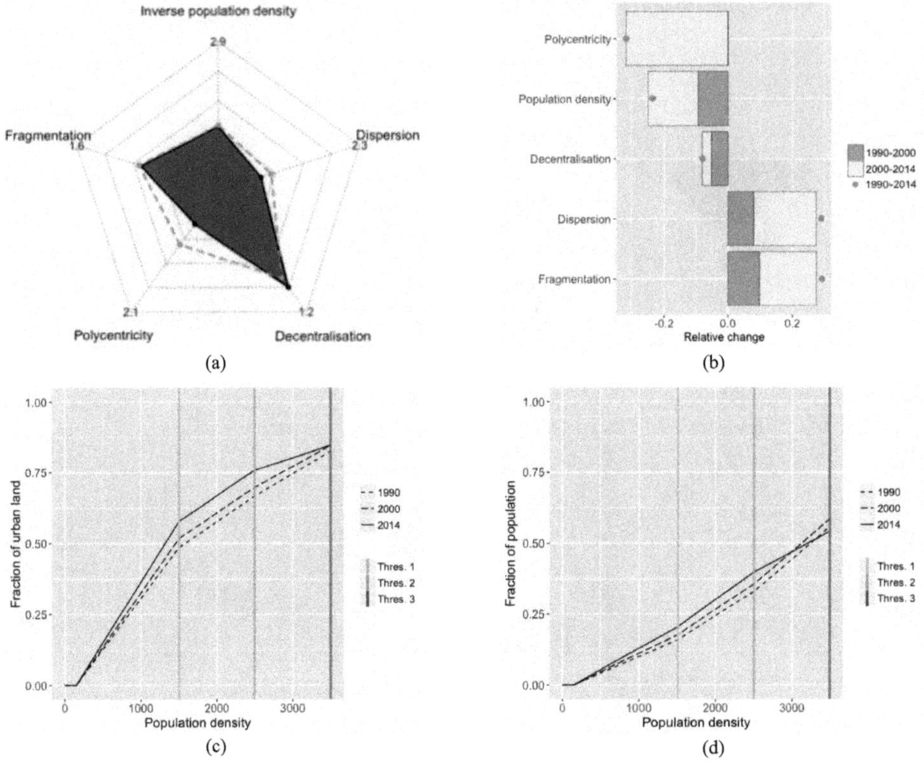

Notes: Thres. 1 denotes a population density of 1 500 inhabitants/km^2, Thres. 2 a population density of 2 500 inhabitants/km^2 and Thres. 3 a population density of 3 500 inhabitants/km^2.
Source: Own calculations, based on GHS built-area data (Pesaresi et al., 2015), GHS population data (European Commission, Joint Research Centre (JRC) and Columbia University, Center for International Earth Science Information Network – CIESIN, 2015) and FUA delimitations (OECD, 2012).

Hungarian cities are close to the OECD average in most urban sprawl indicators, with the exception of decentralisation and polycentricity. They are 33% less polycentric and 7% more decentralised than the average country, as shown in panel a.

Panel b shows that while Hungarian cities have become less dense and more fragmented since 1990, they have also become less polycentric and decentralised. Urban population density fell by 24% in the examined period, with the largest part of this change occurring from 2000 onwards. Since that year, the number of urban centres has also decreased by 32%, the largest decrease in the polycentricity index recorded in this study. On the other hand, the variation of urban population density and fragmentation have significantly increased since 1990, by about 29%.

One of the drivers of the reduction of average population density is the increase in the share of urban surfaces hosting very low densities (150-1 500 inhabitants per km^2) by 9 percentage points (panel c). In contrast, the share of urban surface corresponding to population densities between 2 500 and 3 500 inhabitants per km^2 was reduced in the examined period. This has been accompanied by a decline in the share of population residing in areas with such densities (panel d). The share of urban population living in areas with density below 3 500 inhabitants per km^2 was lower in 2014 than in 1990.

Ireland

Land area (km^2):	68 890	Mean urban population density (inh./km^2):	1 384.6
Population:	4 617 225	Coefficient of variation of urban population density:	1.7
Population density (inhabitants per km^2):	67.0	Average number of fragments per km^2 of urban area	10.5
Number of functional urban areas:	5	Average number of centres per urban area	2.2
Fraction of population residing in FUAs:	55.1%	Percentage of urban population residing outside urban centres	31.2%

Figure 3.B.13. **Sprawl indicators Ireland**

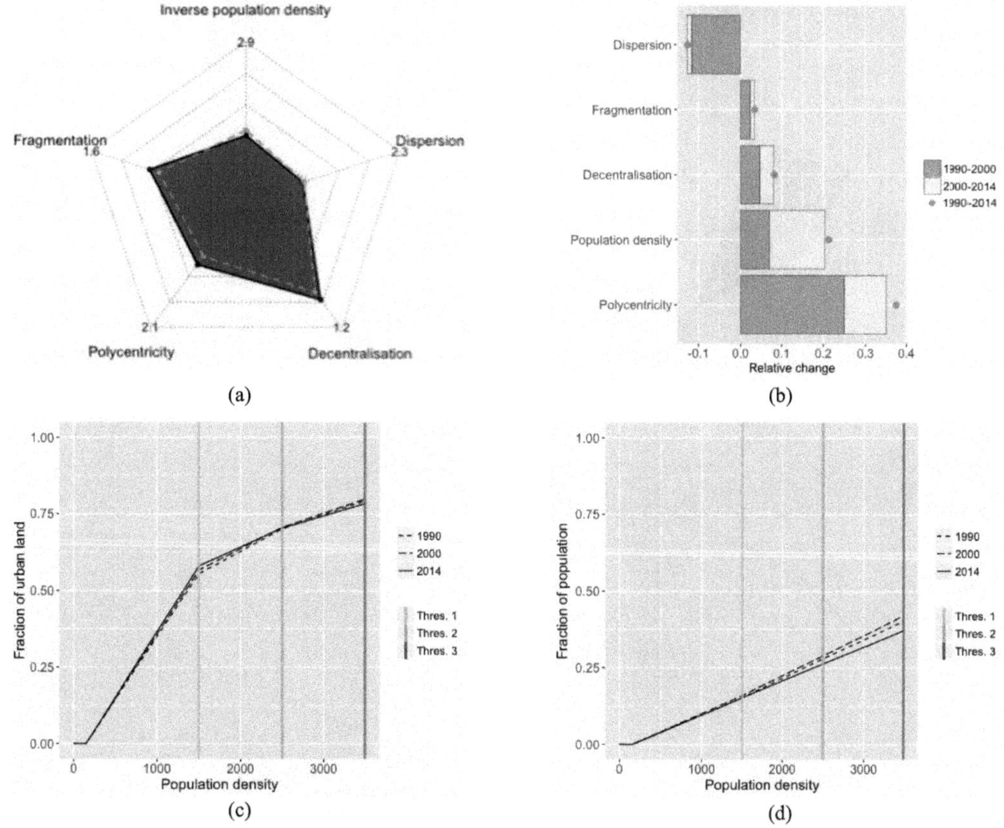

Notes: Thres. 1 denotes a population density of 1 500 inhabitants/km^2, Thres. 2 a population density of 2 500 inhabitants/km^2 and Thres. 3 a population density of 3 500 inhabitants/km^2.

Source: Own calculations, based on GHS built-area data (Pesaresi et al., 2015), GHS population data (European Commission, Joint Research Centre (JRC) and Columbia University, Center for International Earth Science Information Network – CIESIN, 2015) and FUA delimitations (OECD, 2012).

Irish urban areas were, in 2014, close to the OECD average in all five sprawl dimensions shown in panel a.

The trends depicted in panel b, however, reveal a less typical pattern. Ireland experienced a 21% increase in population density between 1990 and 2014, but new development was realised in a polycentric and decentralised fashion: urban areas became 38% more polycentric and 8% more decentralised. This is the largest increase in the polycentricity index recorded in the study.

Despite the large increase in average population density, the share of areas hosting densities between 150 and 3 500 inhabitants per km^2 remained rather stable (panel c). At the same time, the share of population living in areas of such densities has slightly decreased (panel d). This is mainly driven by a small reduction in the share of population residing in densities between 1 500 and 2 500 inhabitants per km^2.

Italy

Land area (km^2):	294 140	Mean urban population density (inh./km^2):	1 778.1
Population:	60 789 140	Coefficient of variation of urban population density:	1.2
Population density (inhabitants per km^2):	206.7	Average number of fragments per km^2 of urban area	8.6
Number of functional urban areas:	74	Average number of centres per urban area	1.8
Fraction of population residing in FUAs:	50.4%	Percentage of urban population residing outside urban centres	32.3%

Figure 3.B.14. **Sprawl indicators Italy**

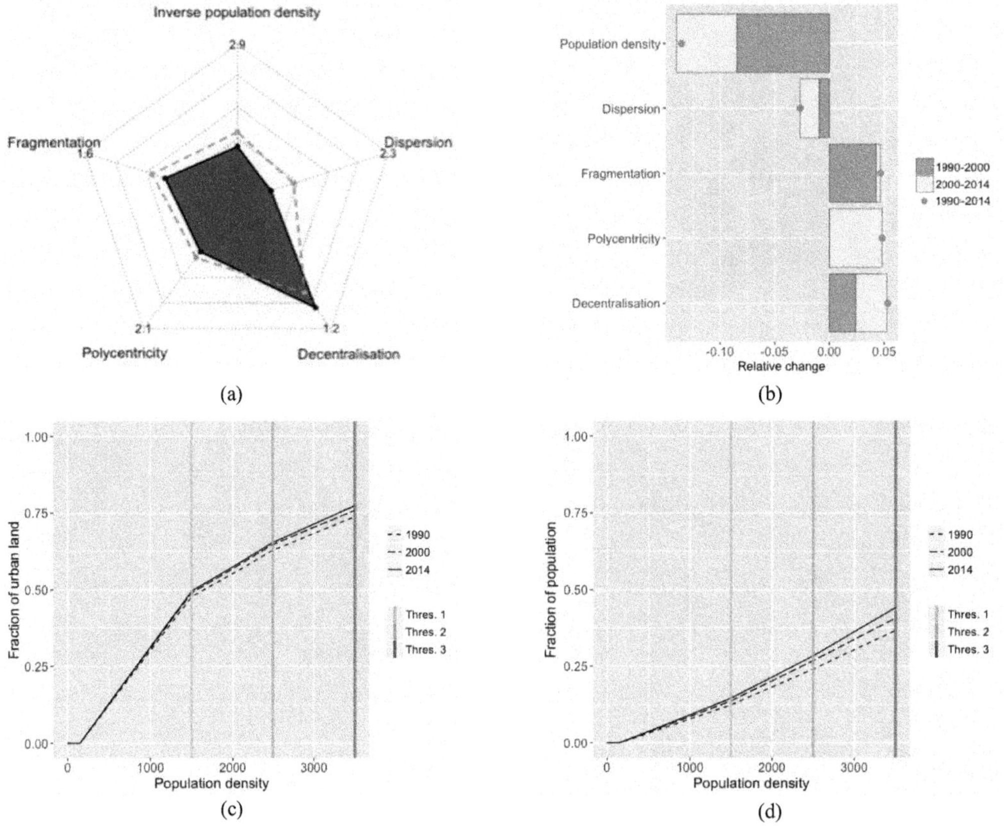

Notes: Thres. 1 denotes a population density of 1 500 inhabitants/km^2, Thres. 2 a population density of 2 500 inhabitants/km^2 and Thres. 3 a population density of 3 500 inhabitants/km^2.

Source: Own calculations, based on GHS built-area data (Pesaresi et al., 2015), GHS population data (European Commission, Joint Research Centre (JRC) and Columbia University, Center for International Earth Science Information Network – CIESIN, 2015) and FUA delimitations (OECD, 2012).

Urban sprawl in Italy is below the OECD average with respect to multiple dimensions. The only exception is decentralisation, where Italian cities lie considerably above the OECD average (panel a).

Italy's urban population density has decreased by 14% since 1990, as shown in panel b. Despite that decline, Italy's average urban population density was still above the OECD average, by 30%, in 2014. In addition to being less dense, new development was realised in a fragmented and decentralised way, with both indicators increasing by 5% between 1990 and 2014.

Panel c reveals that the large reduction of average population density has not been accompanied by an equally pronounced increase in the share of urban land hosting surfaces with density between 150 and 3 500 inhabitants/km^2. While that share has only grown by 3 percentage points, the share of urban population residing in these areas has increased from 37% in 1990 to 44% in 2014 (panel d).

Japan

Land area (km^2):	364 560	Mean urban population density (inh./km^2):	2 965.1
Population:	127 276 000	Coefficient of variation of urban population density:	1.1
Population density (inhabitants per km^2):	349.1	Average number of fragments per km^2 of urban area	4.9
Number of functional urban areas:	76	Average number of centres per urban area	1.7
Fraction of population residing in FUAs:	77.0%	Percentage of urban population residing outside urban centres	26.1%

Figure 3.B.15. **Sprawl indicators Japan**

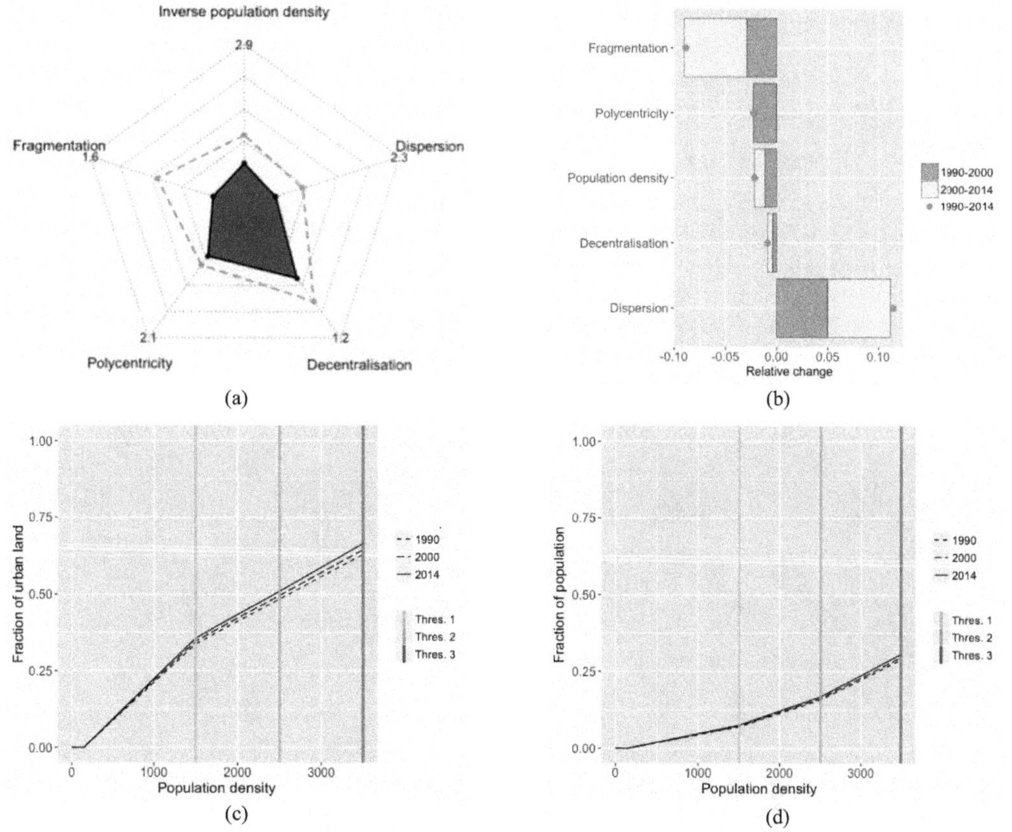

Notes: Thres. 1 denotes a population density of 1 500 inhabitants/km^2, Thres. 2 a population density of 2 500 inhabitants/km^2 and Thres. 3 a population density of 3 500 inhabitants/km^2.
Source: Own calculations, based on GHS built-area data (Pesaresi et al., 2015), GHS population data (European Commission, Joint Research Centre (JRC) and Columbia University, Center for International Earth Science Information Network – CIESIN, 2015) and FUA delimitations (OECD, 2012).

Japanese cities are compact, dense and centralised. They score relatively low in all dimensions of urban sprawl, as shown in panel a. Urban population density lies far above the OECD average and displays the lowest variation (dispersion) across the OECD countries. Japanese urban areas are the most contiguous, with only 4.9 fragments per km^2 of built area.

The evolution of these sprawl indicators over time is displayed in panel b. Indicators changed only modestly between 1990 and 2014, with two exceptions. Despite variation of population density being relatively low in 2014, it has increased by approximately 12% since 1990. On the other hand, urban areas in Japan became substantially more contiguous (by about 9%) in the examined period, with the largest part of this change taking place from 2000 onwards.

As can be seen from panel c, the share of urban developed surfaces hosting population densities within the three proposed intervals (150-1 500, 1 500-2 500 and 2 500-3 500 inhabitants per km^2) has remained relatively stable over time. A similar pattern is observed for the allocation of population across areas of different density, which is displayed in panel d.

Korea

Land area (km²):	97 480	Mean urban population density (inh./km²):	6 682.8
Population:	50 746 659	Coefficient of variation of urban population density:	2.0
Population density (inhabitants per km²):	513.7	Average number of fragments per km² of urban area	8.8
Number of functional urban areas:	45	Average number of centres per urban area	1.3
Fraction of population residing in FUAs:	84.1%	Percentage of urban population residing outside urban centres	22.0%

Figure 3.B.16. **Sprawl indicators Korea**

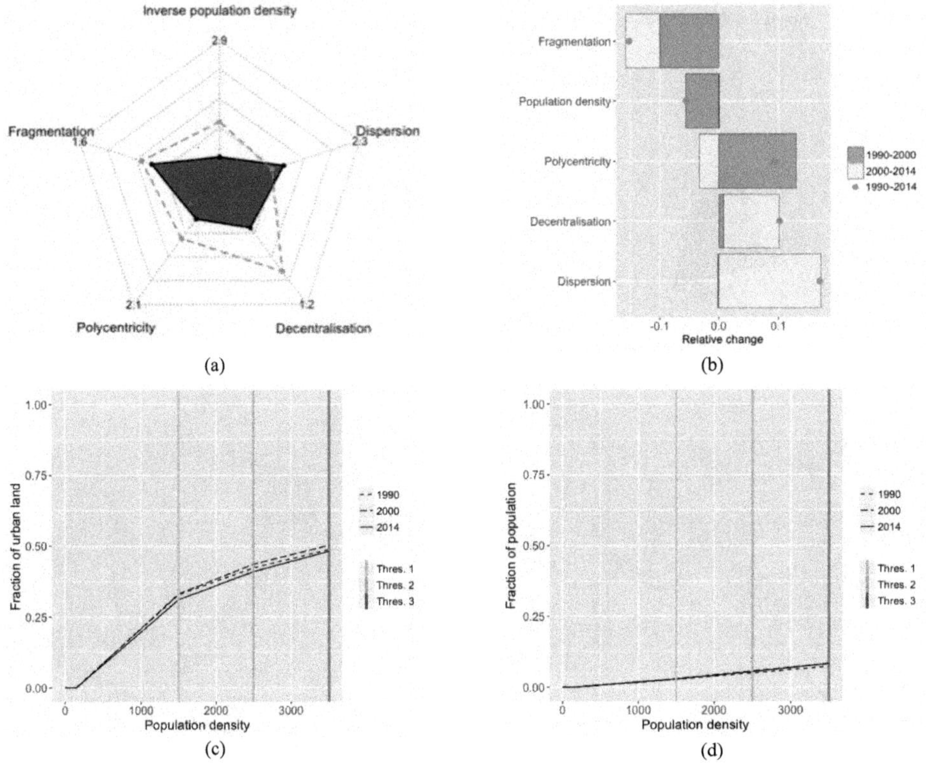

Notes: Thres. 1 denotes a population density of 1 500 inhabitants/km², Thres. 2 a population density of 2 500 inhabitants/km² and Thres. 3 a population density of 3 500 inhabitants/km².

Source: Own calculations, based on GHS built-area data (Pesaresi et al., 2015), GHS population data (European Commission, Joint Research Centre (JRC) and Columbia University, Center for International Earth Science Information Network – CIESIN, 2015) and FUA delimitations (OECD, 2012).

Korean urban areas are the densest among the 29 OECD countries considered in the study: their population density is 82% higher than the OECD average. Urban fabric in the country is relatively contiguous and residential locations particularly centralised. As shown in panel a, Korean cities score relatively low in all indicators except for dispersion, which lies 17% above the OECD average.

Korean urban areas used to be even denser and centralised in the past (panel b), as average population density decreased by 6% between 1990 and 2000 and decentralisation increased by 10% between 2000 and 2014. Since 2000, there has also been a significant (17%) increase in the variation (dispersion) of urban population density. On the other hand, urban fabric in Korea has become considerably (15%) more contiguous than it was in 1990.

The dominant urban development pattern in Korea is reflected in panel c and panel d, which show the distribution of the urban built surface and urban population across three different segments of population density. Among the examined countries, cities in Korea are characterised by the lowest share of urban land hosting residential areas of density between 150 and 3 500 inhabitants per km² (48%) and the lowest percentage of population residing in them (8%). That pattern is very similar when areas of very low density (between 150-1 500 inhabitants per km²) are considered instead. The evolution of the two distributions has remained relatively stable over time.

Luxembourg

Land area (km^2):	2 590	Mean urban population density (inh./km^2):	965.1
Population:	556 319	Coefficient of variation of urban population density:	1.3
Population density (inhabitants per km^2):	214.8	Average number of fragments per km^2 of urban area	8.3
Number of functional urban areas:	1	Average number of centres per urban area	4.0
Fraction of population residing in FUAs:	89.9%	Percentage of urban population residing outside urban centres	35.0%

Figure 3.B.17. **Sprawl indicators Luxembourg**

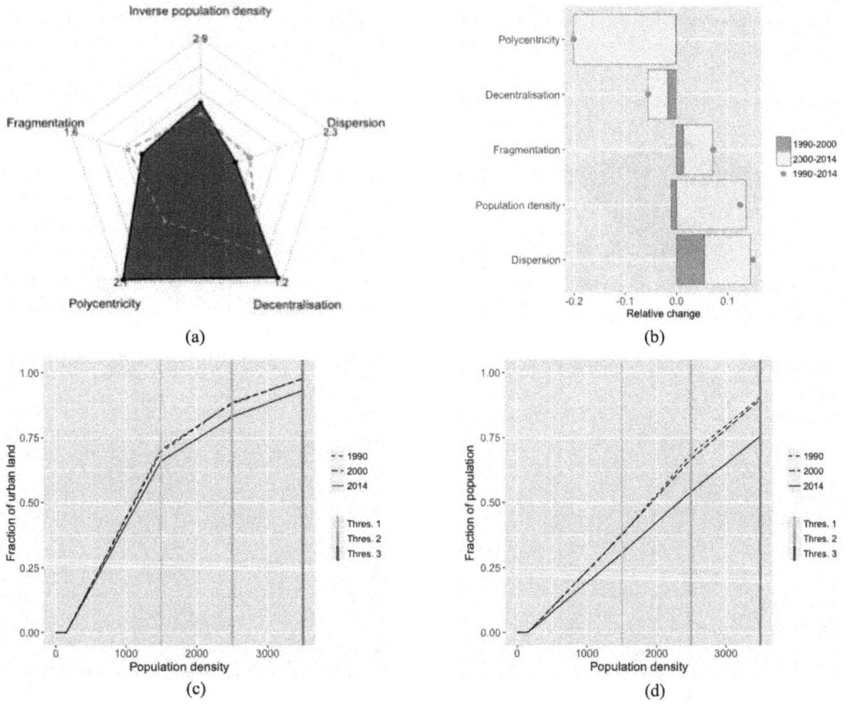

Notes: Thres. 1 denotes a population density of 1 500 inhabitants/km^2, Thres. 2 a population density of 2 500 inhabitants/km^2 and Thres. 3 a population density of 3 500 inhabitants/km^2.
Source: Own calculations, based on GHS built-area data (Pesaresi et al., 2015), GHS population data (European Commission, Joint Research Centre (JRC) and Columbia University, Center for International Earth Science Information Network – CIESIN, 2015) and FUA delimitations (OECD, 2012).

Luxembourg comprises only one functional urban area that occupies a large part (82%) of the country's surface. As shown in panel a, that urban area is relatively contiguous and its average population density lies 28% lower than the OECD average. The sole FUA of the country is more decentralised (17%) and contains twice as many urban centres as the average OECD urban area does. The value of the polycentricity indicator is the largest recorded in the study.

Luxembourg's urban area has become significantly denser, less polycentric and more centralised since 2000, as shown in panel b. Population density has increased by approximately 15%, polycentricity has declined by 20% and decentralisation by 4%. However, new development has occurred in a rather fragmented way, as indicated by the 6% increase in fragmentation since 2000. Since 1990, the variation of urban population density (dispersion) in Luxembourg has increased by 15%. Even then, however, variation remained low compared to other countries included in the study.

Among the OECD countries included in the analysis, Luxembourg has the highest share of urban land and urban population allocated to areas of low to moderate density, i.e. between 150 and 3 500 inhabitants per km^2. As shown in panel c, the share of urban built surfaces hosting residential areas of densities between 150 and 3 500 inhabitants per km^2 decreased by about 5 percentage points between 1990 and 2014. That change was accompanied by a sharp reduction in the percentage of population residing in such density levels by about 15 percentage points, as panel d suggests. Most of this reduction is due to the decline of the share of population residing in areas between 1 500 and 2 500 inhabitants per km^2.

Mexico

Land area (km^2):	1 943 950	Mean urban population density (inh./km^2):	1 291.7
Population:	124 221 600	Coefficient of variation urban population density:	3.2
Population density (inhabitants per km^2):	63.9	Average number of fragments per km^2 of urban area	11.2
Number of functional urban areas:	77	Average number of centres per urban area	1.5
Fraction of population residing in FUAs:	62.9%	Percentage of urban population residing outside urban centres	22.2%

Figure 3.B.18. **Sprawl indicators Mexico**

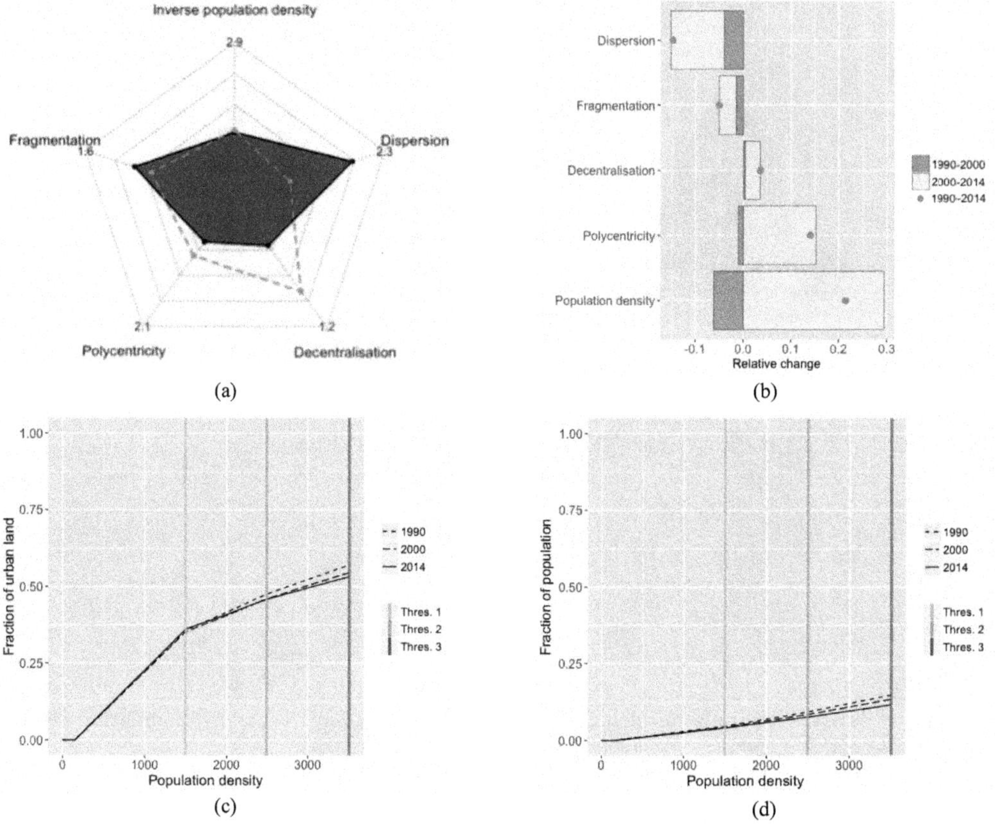

Notes: Thres. 1 denotes a population density of 1 500 inhabitants/km^2, Thres. 2 a population density of 2 500 inhabitants/km^2 and Thres. 3 a population density of 3 500 inhabitants/km^2.

Source: Own calculations, based on GHS built-area data (Pesaresi et al., 2015), GHS population data (European Commission, Joint Research Centre (JRC) and Columbia University, Center for International Earth Science Information Network – CIESIN, 2015) and FUA delimitations (OECD, 2012).

Mexican cities are more fragmented than the average of the countries included in the study, but also less polycentric and decentralised (panel a). While their population density lies close to the OECD average, it varies across urban space much more (86%) than the OECD average.

Since 2000, Mexican cities have become much denser and more polycentric, while the variation of density within them has decreased (panel b). Population density has increased by 29% and polycentricity by 15%, while the variation of population density has declined by about 11%. During the same period (2000-14), fragmentation has declined by approximately 4%.

The share of urban developed surfaces hosting residential areas of population density between 150 and 3 500 inhabitants per km^2 has decreased by approximately four percentage points: from 57% in 1990 to 53% in 2014 (panel c). The largest part of this change is due to a decline in the share of urban land hosting density levels between 2 500 and 3 500 inhabitants per km^2. This implies that some of these areas have densified and crossed the threshold of 3 500 inhabitants per km^2 during the time period covered in the study. A similar pattern is observed with respect to the share of urban population residing in density levels between 2 500 and 3 500 inhabitants per km^2 (panel d).

Netherlands

Land area (km²):	33 690	Mean urban population density (inh./km²):	1 375.0
Population:	16 865 008	Coefficient of variation urban population density:	1.2
Population density (inhabitants per km²):	500.6	Average number of fragments per km² of urban area	7.4
Number of functional urban areas:	35	Average number of centres per urban area	2.0
Fraction of population residing in FUAs:	73.7%	Percentage of urban population residing outside urban centres	31.8%

Figure 3.B.19. **Sprawl indicators Netherlands**

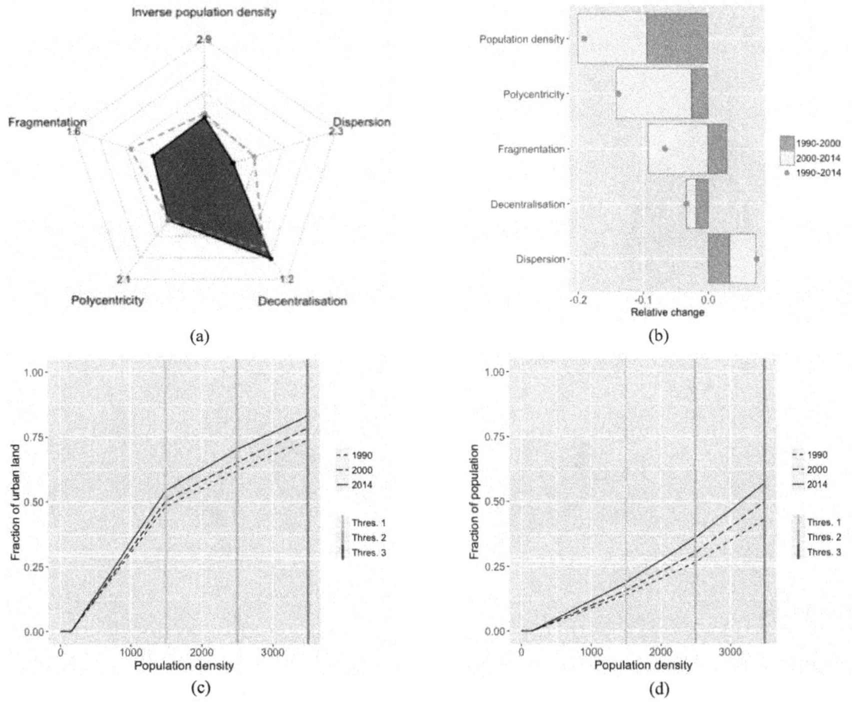

Notes: Thres. 1 denotes a population density of 1 500 inhabitants/km², Thres. 2 a population density of 2 500 inhabitants/km² and Thres. 3 a population density of 3 500 inhabitants/km².
Source: Own calculations, based on GHS built-area data (Pesaresi et al., 2015), GHS population data (European Commission, Joint Research Centre (JRC) and Columbia University, Center for International Earth Science Information Network – CIESIN, 2015) and FUA delimitations (OECD, 2012).

Dutch urban areas are less fragmented, but also more decentralised than the OECD average (panel a). The variation of population density (dispersion) across urban space in the Netherlands lies far below the respective OECD average.

The Netherlands has experienced a suburbanisation process since 1990, mainly manifested in a 19% reduction of the population density (panel b). New developments seem, however, to have been constructed in a more contiguous manner; this is reflected in a 9% reduction of the fragmentation index in the period between 2000 and 2014. During the same period, the number of urban centres declined by 14%, whereas the variation of population density increased by about 4%.

The sharp decrease in population density is reflected in the changes occurred in the way urban land is allocated across different density levels (panel c). The share of urban built surface hosting residential areas of very low population density (150-1 500 inhabitants per km²) increased gradually from 48% in 1990 to 54% in 2014. The respective increase in the share of land hosting density of 1 500-2 500 and 2 500-3 500 inhabitants per km² is substantially smaller. This suggests that new development of very low density is the main driver behind the fall of average population density in Dutch urban areas. Panel d displays the evolution of the allocation of population across the three different density segments considered in the study. The share of population living in areas of density between 150 and 3 500 inhabitants per km² has sharply increased in the examined period, from 43% in 1990 to 57% in 2014.

Norway

Land area (km²):	365 245	Mean urban population density (inh./km²):	1 273.5
Population:	5 137 232	Coefficient of variation urban population density:	1.6
Population density (inhabitants per km²):	14.1	Average number of fragments per km² of urban area	10.9
Number of functional urban areas:	6	Average number of centres per urban area	1.8
Fraction of population residing in FUAs:	47.0%	Percentage of urban population residing outside urban centres	32.1%

Figure 3.B.20. **Sprawl indicators Norway**

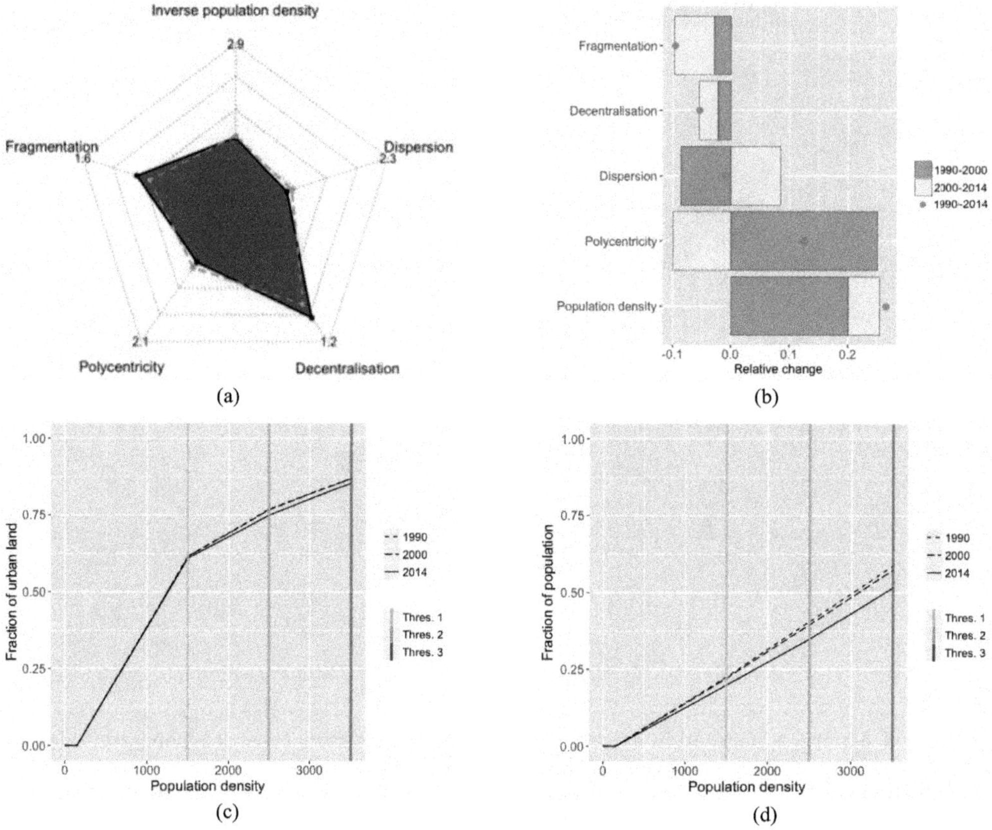

Notes: Thres. 1 denotes a population density of 1 500 inhabitants/km², Thres. 2 a population density of 2 500 inhabitants/km² and Thres. 3 a population density of 3 500 inhabitants/km².
Source: Own calculations, based on GHS built-area data (Pesaresi et al., 2015), GHS population data (European Commission, Joint Research Centre (JRC) and Columbia University, Center for International Earth Science Information Network – CIESIN, 2015) and FUA delimitations (OECD, 2012).

Most of the sprawl indicators values for Norwegian cities lie close to the OECD average (panel a). Urban areas in Norway are slightly more fragmented and decentralised than the OECD average while the variation of population density (dispersion) and the polycentricity index values are slightly below the average.

Among the 29 countries included in the study, Norway experienced the largest increase in population density between 1990 and 2014, as during that period Norwegian urban areas densified by 26%. During the same period, urban areas developed in a relatively more contiguous and centralised way, as fragmentation decreased by 10% and decentralisation by 5%.

As it can be seen from panel c, the share of urban built surfaces hosting population densities between 1 500 and 2 500 inhabitants per km² decreased slightly over time. A similar, but relatively stronger, pattern is observed for the allocation of population across areas of different density, which is displayed in panel d. The share of population residing in areas of densities between 150 and 3 500 inhabitants per km² has declined from 59% in 1990 to 52% in 2014. Most of this decline has occurred in areas of densities of 1 500-2 500 inhabitants per km².

Poland

Land area (km^2):	312 679	Mean urban population density (inh./km^2):	1 453.8
Population:	38 011 735	Coefficient of variation urban population density:	1.5
Population density (inhabitants per km^2):	124.1	Average number of fragments per km^2 of urban area	12.4
Number of functional urban areas:	58	Average number of centres per urban area	1.6
Fraction of population residing in FUAs:	53.9%	Percentage of urban population residing outside urban centres	30.6%

Figure 3.B.21. **Sprawl indicators Poland**

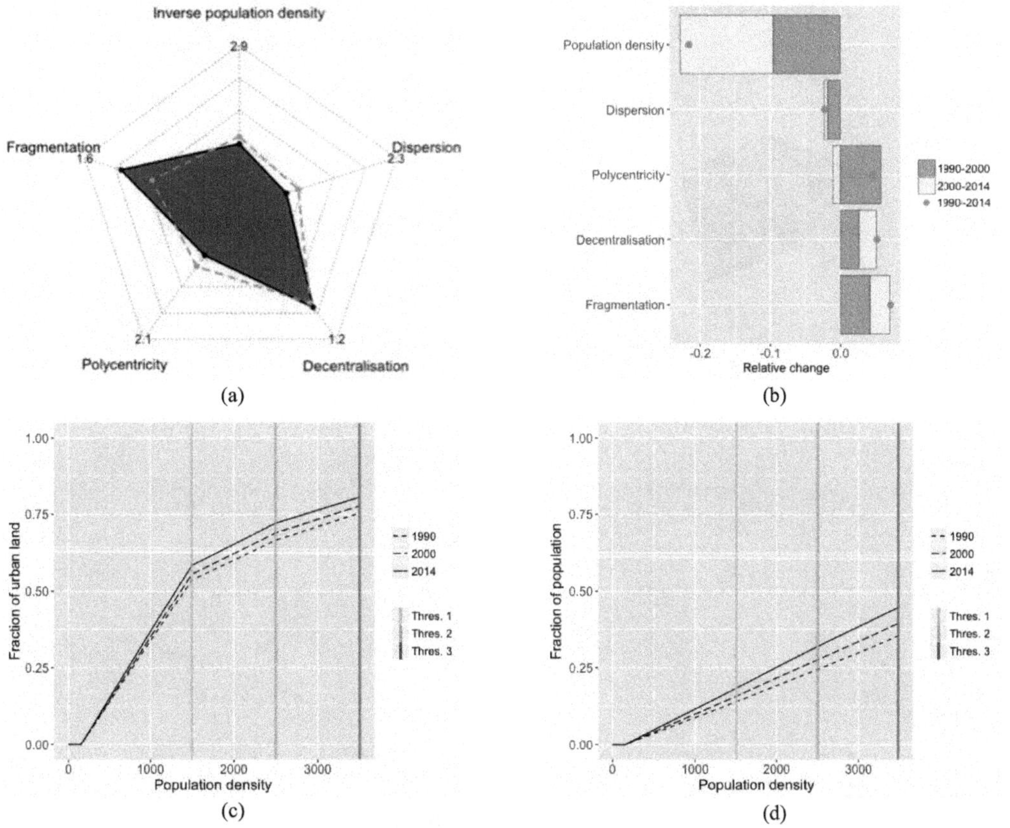

Notes: Thres. 1 denotes a population density of 1 500 inhabitants/km^2, Thres. 2 a population density of 2 500 inhabitants/km^2 and Thres. 3 a population density of 3 500 inhabitants/km^2.
Source: Own calculations, based on GHS built-area data (Pesaresi et al., 2015), GHS population data (European Commission, Joint Research Centre (JRC) and Columbia University, Center for International Earth Science Information Network – CIESIN, 2015) and FUA delimitations (OECD, 2012).

Polish urban areas are denser, less polycentric and more fragmented than the OECD average (panel a). Population density displays a variation (dispersion) that is 20% lower than the OECD average.

The most prominent trend in the evolution of urban sprawl in Poland is the sharp reduction of population density between 1990 and 2014 (panel b). The latter has declined by 21%, with the largest part of this reduction occurring in the period between 2000 and 2014. The reduction of average population density was accompanied by a 7% increase in fragmentation and a 5% increase in decentralisation.

The distribution of urban land and population over different density levels, shown in panel c and panel d, reflects the decrease in average population density. Between 1990 and 2014, the share of built surfaces hosting areas of low-to-moderate population density (between 150 and 3 500 inhabitants per km^2) increased by 6 percentage points: from 75% in 1990 to 81% in 2014 (panel c). During the same period, the share of population residing in areas of such densities increased from 35% to 45% (panel d). Population increased particularly in areas of low density, i.e. between 150 and 2 500 inhabitants per km^2.

Portugal

Land area (km^2):	91 605	Mean urban population density (inh./km^2):	1 284.5
Population:	10 401 062	Coefficient of variation of urban population density:	2.4
Population density (inhabitants per km^2):	113.5	Average number of fragments per km^2 of urban area	10.4
Number of functional urban areas:	13	Average number of centres per urban area	1.6
Fraction of population residing in FUAs:	54.1%	Percentage of urban population residing outside urban centres	27.6%

Figure 3.B.22. **Sprawl indicators Portugal**

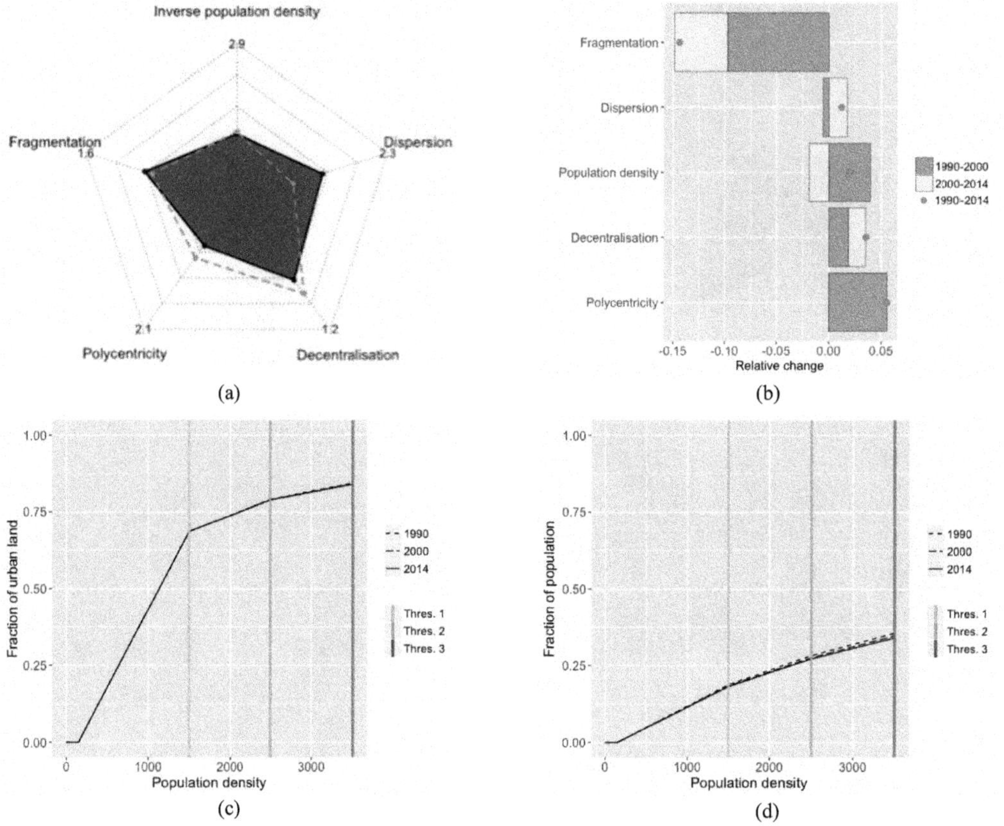

Notes: Thres. 1 denotes a population density of 1 500 inhabitants/km^2, Thres. 2 a population density of 2 500 inhabitants/km^2 and Thres. 3 a population density of 3 500 inhabitants/km^2.
Source: Own calculations, based on GHS built-area data (Pesaresi et al., 2015), GHS population data (European Commission, Joint Research Centre (JRC) and Columbia University, Center for International Earth Science Information Network – CIESIN, 2015) and FUA delimitations (OECD, 2012).

Portuguese cities are relatively centralised and their population density lies close to the OECD average (panel a). However, population density exhibits a large variation across the urban fabric. This is reflected in the dispersion indicator that lies 40% above the OECD average. Portuguese urban areas tend to be monocentric, while the fragmentation index lies very close to the OECD average.

The evolution of urban sprawl indicator between 1990 and 2014 does not reveal major changes, with the exception of a 14% reduction in fragmentation (panel b). Furthermore, some new urban centres emerged in Portuguese urban areas between 1990 and 2000.

The fraction of urban land occupied by low density areas (150-3 500 inhabitants per km^2) has remained relatively stable in the period 1990-2014, as panel c suggests. A similar trend is also observed in the evolution of the fraction of population residing in those areas, as shown in panel d.

Slovak Republic

Land area (km^2):	48 086	Mean urban population density (inh./km^2):	961.5
Population:	5 418 649	Coefficient of variation of urban population density:	1.5
Population density (inhabitants per km^2):	112.7	Average number of fragments per km^2 of urban area	8.3
Number of functional urban areas:	8	Average number of centres per urban area	1.9
Fraction of population residing in FUAs:	37.4%	Percentage of urban population residing outside urban centres	35.0%

Figure 3.B.23. **Sprawl indicators Slovak Republic**

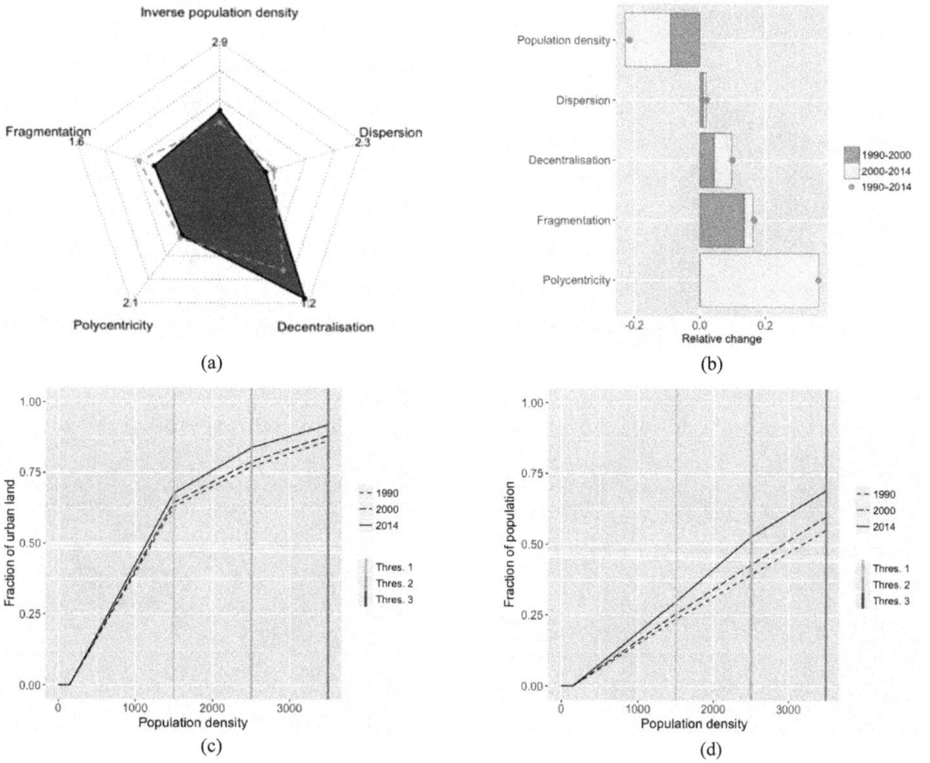

Notes: Thres. 1 denotes a population density of 1 500 inhabitants/km^2, Thres. 2 a population density of 2 500 inhabitants/km^2 and Thres. 3 a population density of 3 500 inhabitants/km^2.
Source: Own calculations, based on GHS built-area data (Pesaresi et al., 2015), GHS population data (European Commission, Joint Research Centre (JRC) and Columbia University, Center for International Earth Science Information Network – CIESIN, 2015) and FUA delimitations (OECD, 2012).

Slovak cities are decentralised and less dense than the OECD average, but they also exhibit a lower fragmentation of the urban fabric (panel a). Per capita land consumption (inverse of population density) in Slovak Republic's eight functional urban areas is 29% higher than the OECD average; the variation of urban population density (dispersion) is 11% lower than the corresponding OECD average.

Since 1990, Slovak urban areas have sprawled substantially. As shown in panel b, average population density has declined by 22%, while decentralisation and fragmentation have increased by 10% and 17% respectively. New urban centres have emerged between 2000 and 2014, when polycentricity increased by 36%.

The decreasing average population density has been coupled with sharp changes in the way urban surfaces and population are allocated across different population density segments. Between 1990 and 2014, the share of built surfaces hosting areas of low population density (between 150 and 3 500 inhabitants per km^2) increased considerably: from 86% in 1990 to 92% in 2014 (panel c). This is the third highest value of the indicator recorded in the study for that year. The share of population residing in areas of low population density increased by 14 percentage points in the examined period: from 55% in 1990 to 69% in 2014 (panel d).

Slovenia

Land area (km^2):	20 140	Mean urban population density (inh./km^2):	776.3
Population:	2 061 980	Coefficient of variation of urban population density:	1.6
Population density (inhabitants per km^2):	102.4	Average number of fragments per km^2 of urban area	15.2
Number of functional urban areas:	2	Average number of centres per urban area	2.0
Fraction of population residing in FUAs:	40.9%	Percentage of urban population residing outside urban centres	36.6%

Figure 3.B.24. **Sprawl indicators Slovenia**

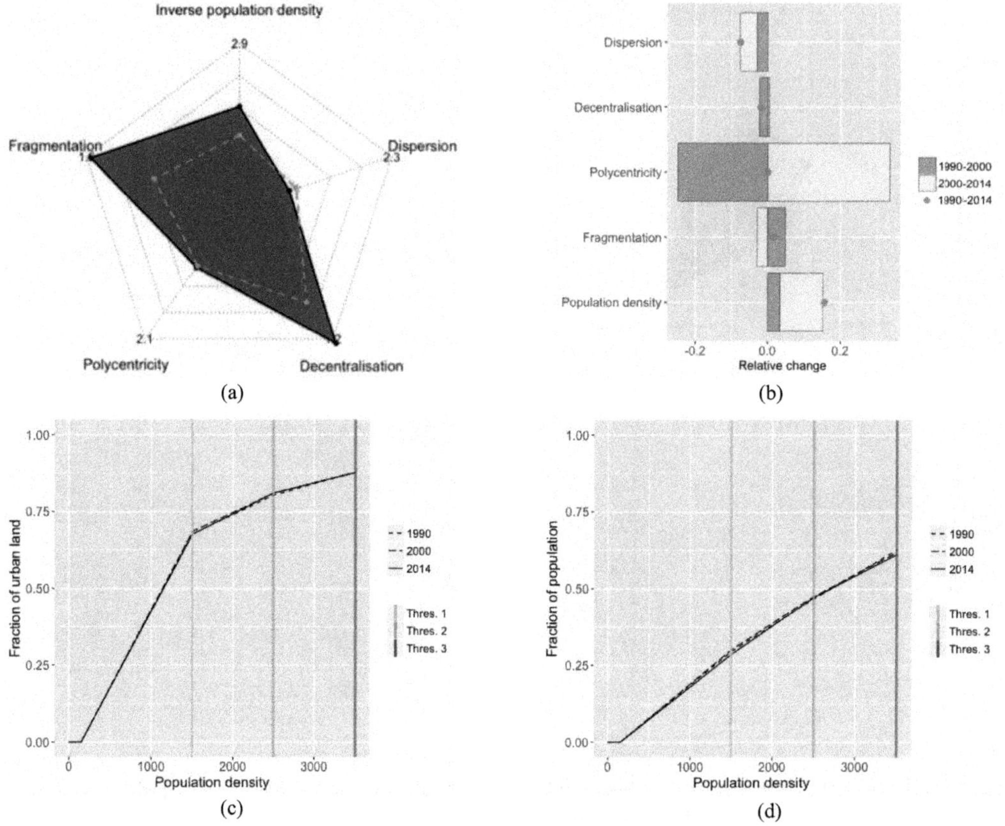

Notes: Thres. 1 denotes a population density of 1 500 inhabitants/km^2, Thres. 2 a population density of 2 500 inhabitants/km^2 and Thres. 3 a population density of 3 500 inhabitants/km^2.

Source: Own calculations, based on GHS built-area data (Pesaresi et al., 2015), GHS population data (European Commission, Joint Research Centre (JRC) and Columbia University, Center for International Earth Science Information Network – CIESIN, 2015) and FUA delimitations (OECD, 2012).

Slovenia's two functional urban areas, Ljubljana and Maribor, are relatively sprawled. They are very decentralised, fragmented and sparsely populated (panel a). The country average of fragmentation and decentralisation are the highest recorded in the study, 54% and 22% higher than the OECD average respectively. Average urban population density is also low, less than half of the average OECD country.

Evolution of sprawl over time shows, however, some slightly encouraging trends. Between 1990 and 2014, Slovenian urban areas have densified by about 16%, as shown in panel b. Cities have also become somewhat less decentralised in that period, while variation of urban population density (dispersion) has declined by about 8%.

Panel c and panel d show that the way urban built surfaces and population are distributed across different population density segments has remained relatively stable since 1990. The densification observed in the examined period has not been translated in a noticeable reduction of the share of urban land and population in areas of low-to-moderate density (between 150-3 500 inhabitants per km^2).

Spain

Land area (km^2):	500 210	Mean urban population density (inh./km^2):	1 898.3
Population:	46 480 882	Coefficient of variation of urban population density:	1.8
Population density (inhabitants per km^2):	92.9	Average number of fragments per km^2 of urban area	12.5
Number of functional urban areas:	76	Average number of centres per urban area	1.4
Fraction of population residing in FUAs:	66.1%	Percentage of urban population residing outside urban centres	26.5%

Figure 3.B.25. **Sprawl indicators Spain**

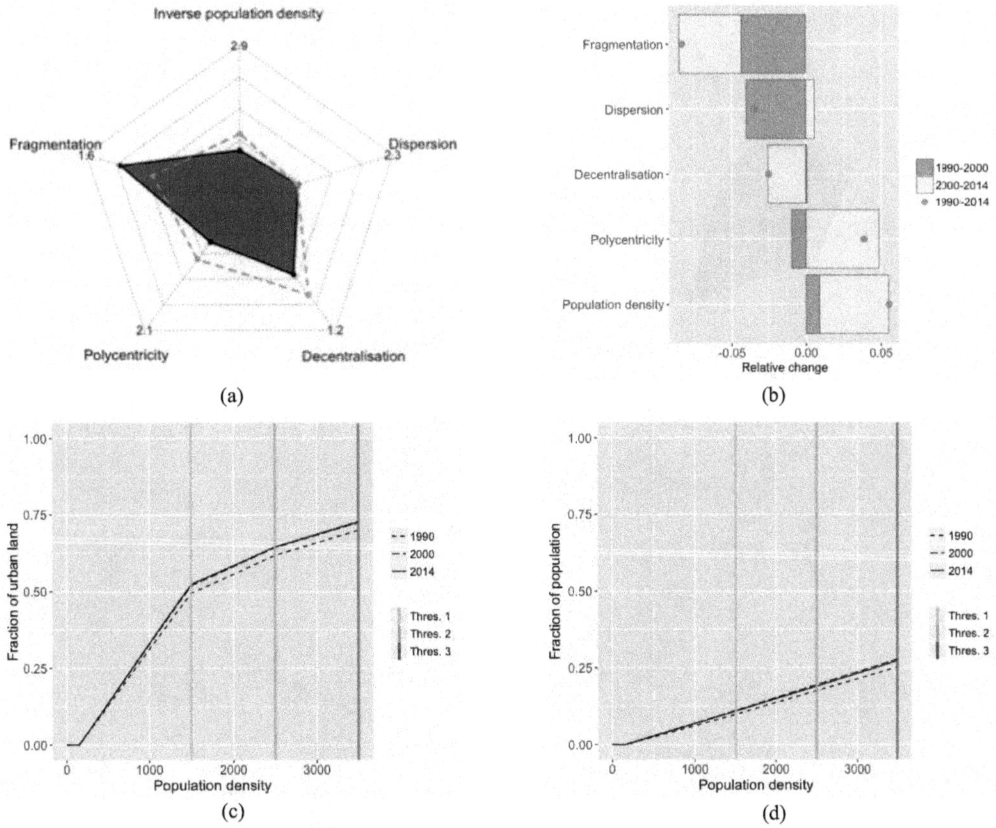

Notes: Thres. 1 denotes a population density of 1 500 inhabitants/km^2, Thres. 2 a population density of 2 500 inhabitants/km^2 and Thres. 3 a population density of 3 500 inhabitants/km^2.

Source: Own calculations, based on GHS built-area data (Pesaresi et al., 2015), GHS population data (European Commission, Joint Research Centre (JRC) and Columbia University, Center for International Earth Science Information Network – CIESIN, 2015) and FUA delimitations (OECD, 2012).

Spanish urban areas are rather dense and centralised, have relatively fewer centres and are more fragmented than the OECD average (panel a). Land consumed per person in urban areas is 35% lower than the OECD average, while polycentricity and decentralisation are below cross-country averages by 27% and 12% respectively. On the other hand, urban fabric in Spanish cities is more fragmented than the OECD average.

Since 1990, Spanish cities have become denser, less fragmented and less decentralised (panel b). Population density has increased by 6% in the examined period, with most of this change occurring after 2000, while fragmentation has decreased by 8%. The number of urban centres has increased slightly (3%) since 2000.

The distributions of urban land and population over different density levels, shown in panels c and d, reflect that the increase in average population density between 1990 and 2014 has been accompanied by a parallel process of suburbanisation. The share of urban built surface and urban population in areas with densities of 150-3 500 inhabitants per km^2 slightly increased (by 2-3 percentage points) in that period.

Sweden

Land area (km^2):	407 310	Mean urban population density (inh./km^2):	1 548.7
Population:	9 696 110	Coefficient of variation of urban population density:	1.4
Population density (inhabitants per km^2):	23.8	Average number of fragments per km^2 of urban area	9.9
Number of functional urban areas:	12	Average number of centres per urban area	2.3
Fraction of population residing in FUAs:	56.3%	Percentage of urban population residing outside urban centres	32.0%

Figure 3.B.26. **Sprawl indicators Sweden**

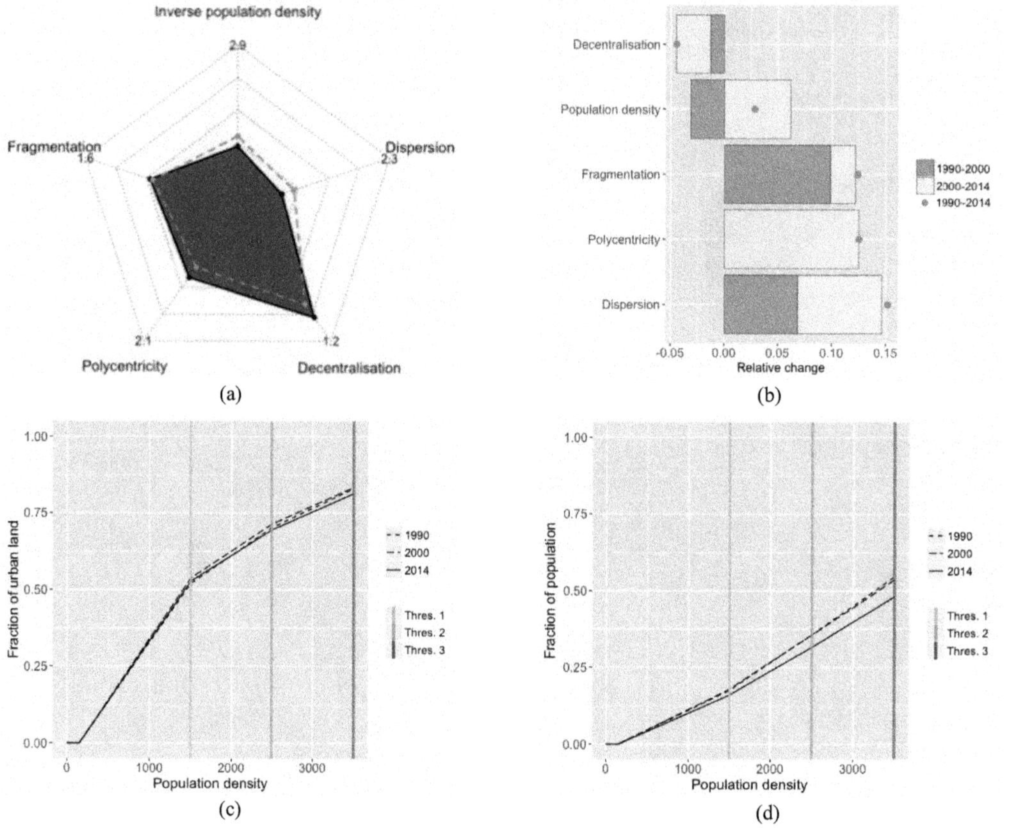

Notes: Thres. 1 denotes a population density of 1 500 inhabitants/km^2, Thres. 2 a population density of 2 500 inhabitants/km^2 and Thres. 3 a population density of 3 500 inhabitants/km^2.

Source: Own calculations, based on GHS built-area data (Pesaresi et al., 2015), GHS population data (European Commission, Joint Research Centre (JRC) and Columbia University, Center for International Earth Science Information Network – CIESIN, 2015) and FUA delimitations (OECD, 2012).

Swedish urban areas are denser than the OECD average. They are also rather polycentric and decentralised (panel a). The variation of population density within Swedish cities (dispersion) is smaller than the OECD average.

In 2014 Swedish cities were more fragmented, centralised and polycentric than they were in 1990 (panel b). In the examined period (1990-2014), fragmentation of urban fabric and the variation of urban population density (dispersion) increased by 12% and 15% respectively. New urban centres have emerged in Swedish cities since 2000, increasing polycentricity by about 13%. On the other hand, decentralisation declined by 4% between 1990 and 2014 and population density increased by 6% between 2000 and 2014.

Panel c and panel d summarise the way urban surfaces and population are distributed across different population density segments. During the period 1990-2014, the percentage of urban population residing in areas where population density is relatively low (i.e. 150-3 500 inhabitants per km^2) has decreased by 7 percentage points (panel d). The share of urban surfaces hosting residential areas of such density levels exhibit a much smaller decrease of 2 percentage points in the same period (panel c).

Switzerland

Land area (km^2):	39 516	Mean urban population density (inh./km^2):	1 692.0
Population:	8 188 649	Coefficient of variation of urban population density:	1.3
Population density (inhabitants per km^2):	207.2	Average number of fragments per km^2 of urban area	7.9
Number of functional urban areas:	10	Average number of centres per urban area	2.1
Fraction of population residing in FUAs:	57.1%	Percentage of urban population residing outside urban centres	34.0%

Figure 3.B.27. **Sprawl indicators Switzerland**

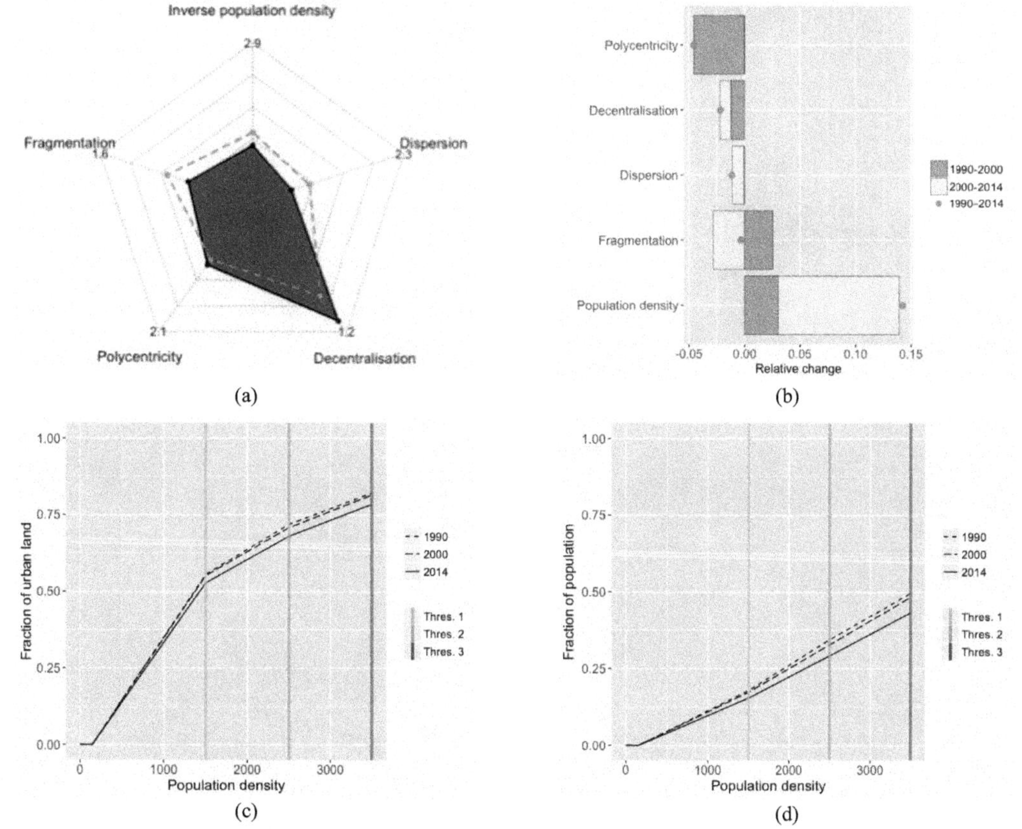

Notes: Thres. 1 denotes a population density of 1 500 inhabitants/km^2, Thres. 2 a population density of 2 500 inhabitants/km^2 and Thres. 3 a population density of 3 500 inhabitants/km^2.

Source: Own calculations, based on GHS built-area data (Pesaresi et al., 2015), GHS population data (European Commission, Joint Research Centre (JRC) and Columbia University, Center for International Earth Science Information Network – CIESIN, 2015) and FUA delimitations (OECD, 2012).

Swiss urban areas are relatively dense and developed on a rather contiguous urban fabric (panel a). However, they are also more decentralised and polycentric than the OECD average. Fragmentation is considerably lower than the average of the countries included in the analysis, while urban population density also exhibits a variation (dispersion) which is 24% lower than the corresponding average.

The main features of the evolution of urban sprawl since 1990 are a sharp increase of population density and a small reduction of polycentricity (panel b). Population density has increased by 14% since 1990 and by 11% since 2000, while polycentricity declined by about 5% between 1990 and 2000.

The increase in average density is also reflected in the distribution of the urban area and population over different density levels, shown in panel c and d. The share of urban population residing in areas of density between 150 and 3 500 inhabitants per km^2 decreased by about 7 percentage points between 1990 and 2014 (panel d). Over the same period, the share of urban surfaces hosting residential areas of density between 150 and 3 500 inhabitants per km^2 decreased by approximately 4 percentage points (panel c).

United Kingdom

Land area (km²):	241 930	Mean urban population density (inh./km²):	2 059.0
Population:	64 613 160	Coefficient of variation of urban population density:	1.5
Population density (inhabitants per km²):	267.1	Average number of fragments per km² of urban area	5.0
Number of functional urban areas:	101	Average number of centres per urban area	2.0
Fraction of population residing in FUAs:	73.5%	Percentage of urban population residing outside urban centres	28.1%

Figure 3.B.28. **Sprawl indicators United Kingdom**

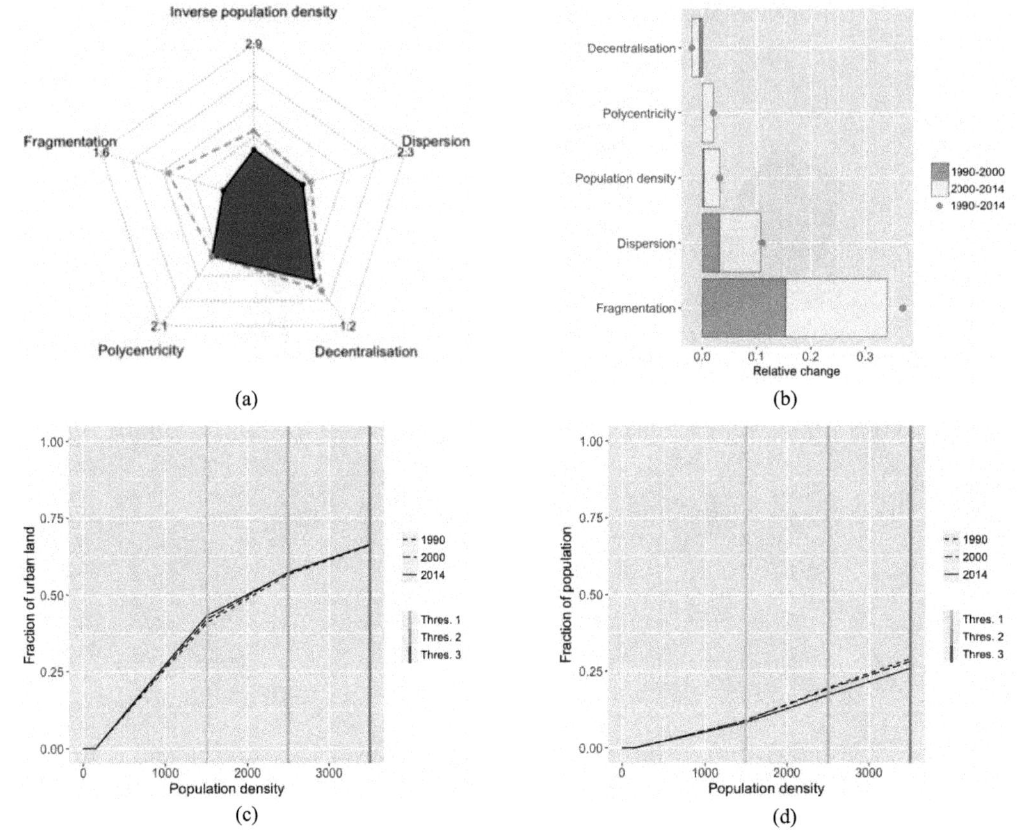

Notes: Thres. 1 denotes a population density of 1 500 inhabitants/km², Thres. 2 a population density of 2 500 inhabitants/km² and Thres. 3 a population density of 3 500 inhabitants/km².

Source: Own calculations, based on GHS built-area data (Pesaresi et al., 2015), GHS population data (European Commission, Joint Research Centre (JRC) and Columbia University, Center for International Earth Science Information Network – CIESIN, 2015) and FUA delimitations (OECD, 2012).

The urban areas of the United Kingdom are relatively dense, compact and centralised. Urban population density is much higher than the OECD average and exhibits a rather low variation across urban space. Urban fabric is particularly contiguous, as it contains just five fragments per km², i.e. half of the OECD average (panel a).

Since 1990, British urban areas have become much more fragmented, but also slightly denser, as shown in panel b. United Kingdom's urban areas underwent the largest total increase in fragmentation observed in the study, with urban areas becoming 37% more fragmented. Variation of population density within urban areas (dispersion) has also increased by 11% since 1990.

As can be seen from panel c, the share of urban built surfaces hosting population densities within the three examined intervals (150-1 500, 1 500-2 500 and 2 500-3 500 inhabitants per km²) has remained relatively stable over time. The share of urban population residing in areas of such densities has declined by 3 percentage points since 1990, mainly due a reduction of the share of population living in areas of density between 1 500 and 2 500 inhabitants per km² (panel d).

United States

Land area (km^2):	9 147 420	Mean urban population density (inh./km^2):	561.5
Population:	318 563 456	Coefficient of variation of urban population density:	2.8
Population density (inhabitants per km^2):	34.8	Average number of fragments per km^2 of urban area	8.8
Number of functional urban areas:	262	Average number of centres per urban area	2.7
Fraction of population residing in FUAs:	68.0%	Percentage of urban population residing outside urban centres	31.8%

Figure 3.B.29. **Sprawl indicators United States**

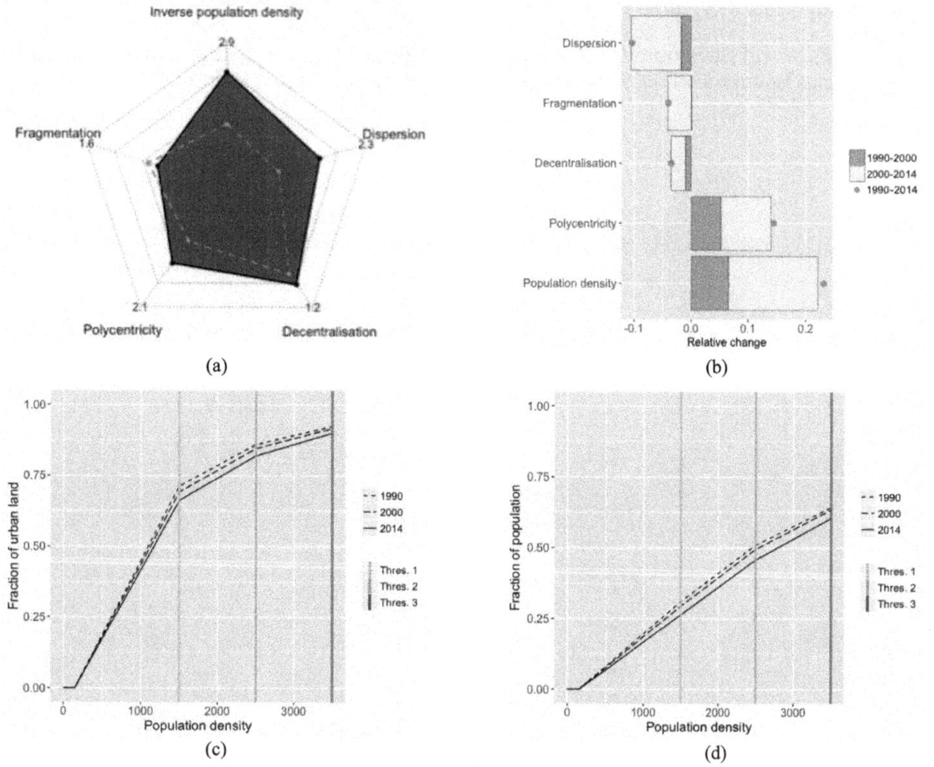

Notes: Thres. 1 denotes a population density of 1 500 inhabitants/km^2, Thres. 2 a population density of 2 500 inhabitants/km^2 and Thres. 3 a population density of 3 500 inhabitants/km^2.
Source: Own calculations, based on GHS built-area data (Pesaresi et al., 2015), GHS population data (European Commission, Joint Research Centre (JRC) and Columbia University, Center for International Earth Science Information Network – CIESIN, 2015) and FUA delimitations (OECD, 2012).

United States' urban areas are sparsely populated, polycentric and rather decentralised, but also less fragmented than the average of the countries included in this analysis (panel a). Population density is on average very low and varies widely across a relatively contiguous urban fabric. The country also contains the most polycentric urban areas identified in this study: Washington and New York.

Since 1990, cities of the United States have significantly densified and have become less fragmented and decentralised (panel b). Population density has increased by 23% since 1990, with most of this change taking place after 2000. At the same time, the variation of urban population density across urban space (dispersion) has declined by about 10%. Several new centres have also emerged within urban areas since 1990, leading to a 14% increase in polycentricity.

The densification process identified above is also reflected in a reduction of the share of urban land and population allocated to areas of low density. The distribution of urban land across different density levels, displayed in panel c, shows that the share of very low density areas (150-1 500 inhabitants per km^2) in total urban built area decreased by about 5 percentage points between 1990 and 2014. The respective decline in the share of urban land allocated to areas of density between 150 and 3 500 inhabitants per km^2 was, however, much smaller: from 92% in 1990 to 90% in 2014. At the same time, the share of population residing in those areas decreased slightly from 64% in 1990 to 60% in 2014, as panel d suggests.

References

European Commission, Joint Research Centre (JRC) and Columbia University, Center for International Earth Science Information Network – CIESIN (2015), "GHS population grid, derived from GPW4, multitemporal (1975, 1990, 2000, 2015)" (database), European Commission, Joint Research Centre (JRC), *http://data.europa.eu/89h/jrc-ghsl-ghs_pop_gpw4_globe_r2015a.*

OECD (2012), *Redefining "Urban": A New Way to Measure Metropolitan Areas*, OECD Publishing, Paris, *http://dx.doi.org/10.1787/9789264174108-en.*

Pesaresi, M. et al. (2015), "GHS built-up grid, derived from Landsat, multitemporal (1975, 1990, 2000, 2014)" (database), European Commission, Joint Research Centre (JRC), *http://data.europa.eu/89h/jrc-ghsl-ghs_built_ldsmt_globe_r2015b.*

World Bank (2017), World Development Indicators (database), World Bank, *http://databank.worldbank.org/data/reports.aspx?source=world-development-indicators* (accessed 24 November 2017).

PART II

Consequences of urban sprawl and implications for policy makers

PART II

Chapter 4

Causes and consequences of urban sprawl

This chapter provides an extensive review of the main drivers of urban sprawl, as well as of its impacts on the environment, economy and society. The chapter discusses economic, geographic, technological and policy drivers of urban sprawl, including household preferences, developers' expectations, and stringent land-use policies. It also investigates a set of potential environmental effects of urban sprawl comprising: i) increases in emissions from more extensive car use; ii) changes in energy needs and emissions associated with residential heating; iii) losses of periurban arable land and their further effect on food prices; iv) losses of biodiversity and environmental amenities; v) degradation of water resources; and vi) changes in microclimate. The potential effects of urban sprawl on land and housing prices, public finance, and on human health, are also reviewed.

4.1. Introduction

This chapter provides an extensive literature review focusing on the drivers and the effects of urban sprawl, as the latter was defined in Chapter 2. Section 4.2 draws from a voluminous body of literature that spans several scientific disciplines (economics, biology, hydrology, environmental and agricultural sciences), to summarise the various drivers of the phenomenon. It pays special attention to the preference-driven causes of urban sprawl, as well as to other forces (such as speculation and expectations) that contribute to a growth pattern that may appear as sprawling in the short run, but constitutes a temporary stage in the long-run development of a compact city. In addition, a series of policy interventions that may give rise to more sprawled urban environments are analysed and illustrated graphically. The chapter also examines the role of path dependence, historical drivers, the technological progress in car manufacturing and other factors that reduced the private costs of automobile use and commuting.

Similarly, Section 4.3 reviews the multiple impacts of urban sprawl on the environment, economy and society. The review examines the various sprawl dimensions presented in Chapter 2 in conjunction with a series of environmental variables: greenhouse gas emissions, local air quality, the relative scarcity of periurban arable land, a series of hydrological functions, biodiversity, water quality, urban heat islands and the resilience to climate change. It also examines the links between these sprawl dimensions and the social cost of providing a series of local public services such as public transport and fresh water. The discussion of consequences abstains from an emotionally-charged indictment of sprawl; instead, it investigates the internal and external validity of numerous studies, some of which provide contradictory evidence. Accounting for the various methodological limitations, the chapter highlights that, while many of the concerns raised are sensible, many others lack substantial evidence-based support. Finally, the chapter identifies concerns that may refer to effects erroneously attributed to urban sprawl; instead, these effects stem from other forms of urban development, or urbanisation *per se*. That distinction may be important for the development of interventions that target urban sprawl, rather than urbanisation (whose economic importance has been examined in Chapter 1). A series of such interventions will be provided in Chapter 5.

4.2. Urban sprawl drivers

Several studies have explored the nature of urban sprawl and the potential reasons for its occurrence in different contexts (Anas, Arnott and Small, 1998; Brueckner, 2000; Brueckner, 2001; Burchfield et al., 2006; Deng et al., 2008; Glaeser and Kahn, 2004; Nechyba and Walsh, 2004; Oueslati, Alvanides and Garrod, 2015; Patacchini and Zenou, 2009). Different factors are often identified as the main drivers of urban sprawl. These factors include population growth, the rise in household incomes, individual preferences favouring low-density development, complex historical processes that gradually enhanced such preferences, physical constraints on development continuity and structural density, the significant technological progress in car manufacturing and several other factors that contributed to a general decline of commuting costs. Box 4.1 discusses the determinants of urban sprawl in the context of monocentric cities. Policy-related factors include persistently low prices on car use, massive and unbalanced investment in highway capacity and a series of land-use regulations, such as maximum building height restrictions, that are known to keep population density in levels lower than those that would prevail otherwise. The above drivers are investigated in detail in the following subsections.

Box 4.1. **The determinants of urban sprawl in monocentric cities: some empirical evidence**

When it comes to urban expansion, the monocentric city model (Alonso, 1964; Mills, 1981; Muth, 1961; Wheaton, 1974) is the cornerstone of urban economics. The model provides a set of testable hypotheses which can be evaluated using empirical methods. First, an increase in the urban population increases demand for housing and is expected to increase the urban footprint. Second, households demand more floor space as income grows, as housing is a normal good. In turn, the increased demand for floor space leads to an extended city with a lower population density. Third, a decrease in generalised commuting costs increases the disposable income at all locations. This boosts demand for floor space and willingness to reside far from one's workplace, and eventually leads to a city with lower population density. Changes in commuting costs can occur through changes in the pecuniary costs of transport (fuel prices, public transport fares, car ownership costs, parking fees, road taxes, etc.) or through adjustments in the required travel time (wider roads, faster transport modes, etc.). Fourth, a reduction in the opportunity cost of land, i.e. the financial return from land uses other than development, such as farming, causes cities to expand and lowers the overall population density.

Several studies have tested the empirical validity of the monocentric city model. In the context of the United States, income, population and agricultural rent have been shown to be significant determinants of the total land uptake of an urban area (Brueckner and Fansler, 1983; McGrath, 2005; Song and Zenou, 2006). On the other hand, commuting costs had an ambiguous effect, which varied with the proxies used to measure them. Income growth has also been shown to have a major influence in the People's Republic of China's urban expansion (Deng et al., 2008; Shanzi, Song and Ming, 2009). In the European context, Oueslati, Alvanides and Garrod (2015) consider two indices of urban sprawl that reflect changes in artificial area and urban fragmentation. They find that the fundamental conclusions of the monocentric model are valid for both indices. The monocentric city model was found to explain satisfactorily the total footprint of a city, but had limited power to predict the extent to which urban fabric will be fragmented. Urban planning policies, land availability and physical geography constraints are particularly strong predictors of fragmentation, along with other factors that discourage infill development between fragments.

Sources: Alonso, 1964; Brueckner and Fansler, 1983; Deng et al., 2008; McGrath, 2005; Mills, 1981; Muth, 1961; Oueslati, Alvanides and Garrod, 2015; Shanzi, Song and Ming, 2009; Song and Zenou, 2006; Wheaton, 1974.

Preferences and pull effects

Many households are willing to pay for attributes that often characterise low-density areas. For example, proximity to open spaces and natural amenities, lower noise levels, better air quality, longer exposure to sunlight and local visibility are acting as attractors to these households, which boost the demand for housing in relatively remote areas. Gordon and Richardson (1997) claim that the preference for low density is the main driver of urban sprawl. They invoke the National Housing Surveys performed by the Federal Home Mortgage Association (1994) to argue that the observed low density in the US is preference-driven. Turner (2005) investigates the choice of residential location taking into account the willingness to pay for proximity to open spaces. He shows that, if open space is highly valued, development in remote areas with access to plenty of open space may take place before development of areas that are closer to the city centre. Therefore, part of the observed vacant land and fragmentation within urban areas may be a result of individual preferences.

The *pull effect* exerted by suburban natural amenities on household location decisions encourages the development of areas formerly occupied by farmers (Cavailhès et al., 2004; Coisnon, Oueslati and Salanié, 2014; Ready and Abdalla, 2005; Roe, Irwin and Morrow-Jones, 2004). Using stated preference data from the United States, Roe, Irwin and Morrow-Jones (2004) find that rural-urban fringe areas that are located within a certain distance from urban centres and are abundant in farmland could attract residential development. Therefore, efforts to preserve small parcels of farmland may induce further residential growth in areas of high accessibility. Land conservation policies aiming at preserving landscape and natural amenities have been shown to indirectly encourage the development of surrounding parcels of land (Geniaux, Ay and Napoleone, 2011; Irwin and Bockstael, 2004). Therefore, pull effects tend to increase the percentage of urban footprint hosting low-density development and the share of urban population residing in low-density areas.

Historical drivers and path dependence

Are there any historical drivers behind the formation of preferences for living in low-density areas? If housing type preferences in OECD countries have remained stable during the twentieth century, the vast suburbanisation observed during its second half has been driven by economic progress, rising incomes and s fall in the real costs of car use. If, on the other hand, preferences have changed substantially towards living in low-density areas, urban sprawl would emerge, at least to some extent, even in absence of the economic progress and population growth that followed the Second World War. Due to a large number of methodological constraints, empirical analysis has not managed to answer that important question thus far. However, historical arguments can still offer some useful insights.

Path dependence is a key driver of urban sprawl. Urban systems evolve through path dependent processes, thus history plays an important role: past policy choices and major events do not only determine the current state of a city but also the set of responses that are currently available to policy makers. For example, stringent building height restrictions implemented decades ago in many cities have led them to an urban form with very low density levels. Such land-use policies usually have effects persisting for many decades, as changing development patterns in existing urban environments is particularly challenging. If path dependence is strong, a sprawled urban area has, to a large extent, evolved in that way because the initial conditions or policy framework (e.g. stringent building height restrictions) were favouring sprawled development patterns. Through time, policy-making that failed to account for the long-run social cost of urban sprawl may have reinforced those conditions.

Expectations and speculation

Expectations for the evolution of land and housing prices may play a crucial role in the pattern of urban fabric expansion over time. Development of seemingly profitable vacant land parcels may be postponed when three contributing factors co-exist. First, the development types that maximise the present value of profits in the short and long term are different, due to e.g. expectations for population or economic growth. Second, the long-run development type is not profitable in the short run, i.e. revenues fall short of costs. Finally, conversion costs are high enough to rule out a development plan in which the short-run profit-maximising type is developed and maintained, with a view to being demolished and replaced by the other type in the longer run.

The three conditions are illustrated with an example in Figure 4.1. For example, the two development types can be considered to be a multi-story building (solid lines) and a construction of low structural density (dashed lines), such as attached family housing. The curves show that the current demand for floor space in multi-family housing types at the beginning (year 0) is too weak to generate substantial profits from development in the short run. However, developers are expecting this to change in the long run (e.g. fifteen years later); population growth and improvements in accessibility (for instance due to anticipated infrastructure investments) often underlie such expectations. On the other hand, developing single-family housing can yield immediate profits. However, these profits are substantially smaller than those yielded by the multi-family development type when considered in a longer horizon. If the short-run profits from development of single-family housing, represented by the shaded areas in Figure 4.1, fall short of the conversion costs (i.e. from single- to multi-family housing), land will stay vacant in the short run.

Figure 4.1. **Alternative development options for a land parcel**

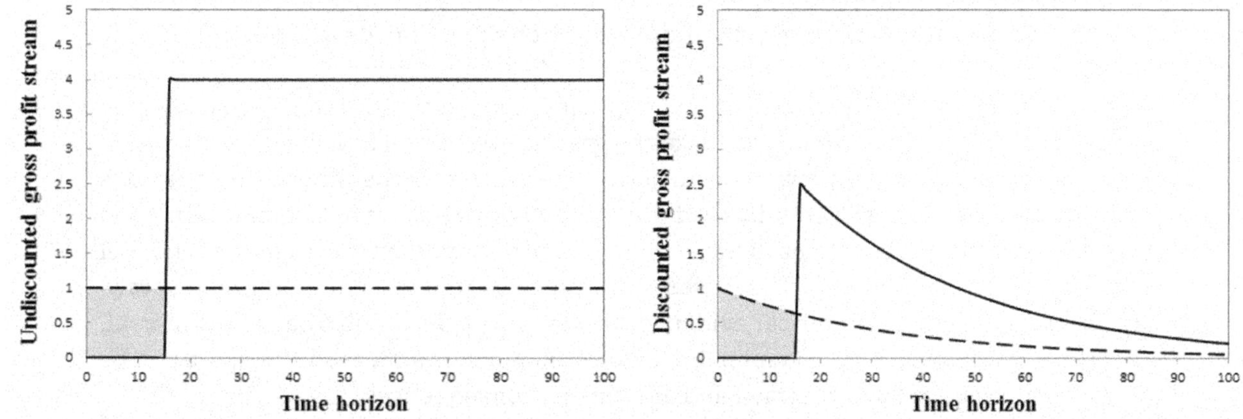

Notes: The left panel displays the undiscounted streams of profit net of capital costs, but not land rents, for the investment in two different buildings: a constant low return option (building type A, dashed line) and an option with a high future return (building type B, solid line). The right panel shows the present value of each stream in a time horizon of hundred years using an annual discount rate of 5%. The total present value of the latter option, i.e. the area under the solid curve, outweighs the total present value of the former option, i.e. the area under the dashed curve. Therefore, in the long run (years 15-100), building B will occupy the land parcel. If the conversion costs exceed the short-run total present value of developing building type A, i.e. the area below the dashed curve for the first 15 years, the land parcel will remain undeveloped in the short run (years 0-15).

Meanwhile, the more accurately investors anticipate future profitability, the more they drive current demand up, raising the prices of those vacant land parcels even in the short run. This narrative explains a phenomenon observed in many modern urban areas: even in their interior, a substantial portion of developable land remains vacant while at the same time its price is high. A relevant stream of literature in urban economics provides various reasons why it may be efficient to postpone development of certain parcels in the interior of an urban area, so that they can be developed in a way that better suits future needs (Braid, 1988, 1991; Brueckner and von Rabenau, 1981; Clawson, 1962; Fujita, 1976; Mills, 1981; Ohls and Pines, 1975; Turnbull, 1988). This suggests that a fragmented development pattern may, to some extent, constitute a natural step in an economically efficient long-run process of urban land transformation.

Technological progress in car manufacturing

Part of the urban expansion can be explained by technological advances in car manufacturing, and the production of cheaper, faster, safer, more reliable, more comfortable and more fuel efficient cars (see also Glaeser and Kahn, 2004). Technological progress and economic growth have made cars affordable by a large share of the population in OECD countries. In turn, lower costs of car ownership and use translated into willingness to accept larger commuting distances, i.e. willingness to live further away from work. Driving distances that seemed restrictive gradually became reasonable. The outcome was that previously remote land plots became accessible to the majority of households. Simultaneously, in many places of the world the institutional framework did not account for these changes (see also the discussion below about the policy-induced drivers of sprawl). That resulted in relatively affordable periurban land prices and massive supply of accessible land readily available for residential consumption, a combination which promoted low density development. In summary, technological progress in car manufacturing contributes to lower average population densities and an increase in the share of urban footprint hosting very low density levels.

Policies encouraging car use

Car use has not only been promoted by technological developments in car manufacturing: it has also been encouraged by policies subsidising car use or failing to price its external costs. The absence of road pricing, the neglect of the external costs of on-street parking, and persistently low taxes on gasoline and diesel have kept the pecuniary cost of vehicle use artificially low in the majority of countries. At the same time, enormous public and private investments in road – mainly highway – capacity expansion have resulted in significant reductions in travel time, as well as increased travel comfort and fuel efficiency. The consequences of improved road transport infrastructure on urban sprawl have been validated by empirical evidence (Garcia-López, Holl and Viladecans-Marsal, 2015; Su and DeSalvo, 2008). Chapter 5 discusses how policies on road transport can be transformed to control urban sprawl and alleviate its consequences.

Land-use policy drivers

Understanding the functions of land-use regulatory mechanisms is key to understanding the causes of urban sprawl. This subsection investigates the effects of three types of policy interventions that affect directly the sprawl dimensions described in Chapter 2. Building height regulations, urban containment policies and taxation of property and land are long known to influence long-run development patterns. The subsection also explains why these policy mechanisms are rigid and persistent over time.

Building height restrictions

Maximum building height restrictions contribute to the development of cities with a larger urban footprint compared to the one that would occur if they evolved without them (Bertaud and Brueckner, 2005). In general, a uniform-in-space building height restriction (e.g. 30 metres of height across the city) translates into lower average population density, although it may also (indirectly) influence the two density allocation indicators developed in the report: the percentage of urban land hosting low density levels (land-to-density allocation function) and the share of population residing in low density areas (population-to-density allocation function). Figure 4.2 illustrates the hypothetical evolution of an urban area under two different scenarios. The left panel displays the floor-to-area ratio in a city that has evolved with (dashed curves) or without (solid curves) a maximum building height regulation that is uniform across space. The right panel presents population density under the two scenarios. To keep things simple, it is assumed that the hypothetical restriction is uniform across space.

Figure 4.2. **The long-run effect of a uniform building height restriction on city shape and population density**

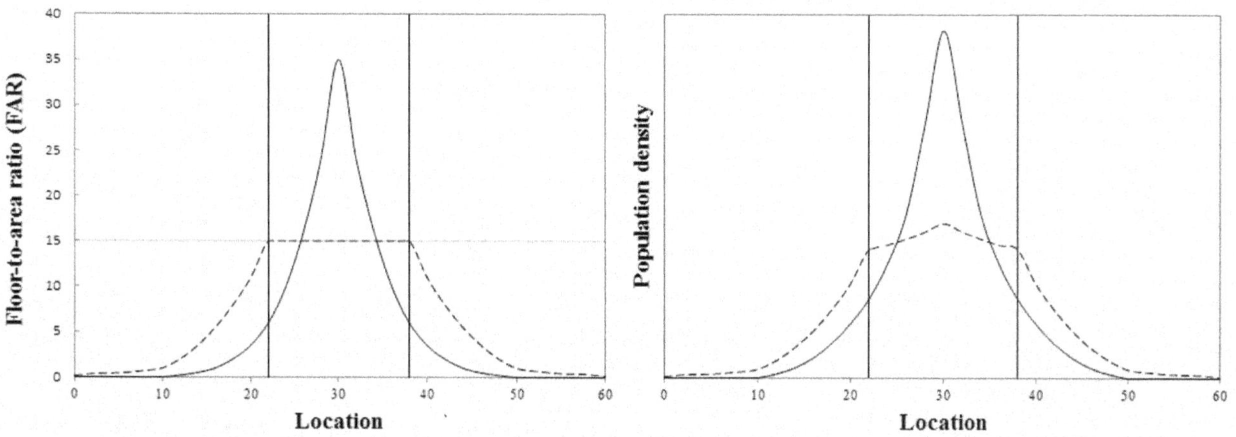

Notes: Solid lines represent the urban area that has evolved without any maximum restriction on building height; dashed lines represent the urban area that has evolved with a maximum floor-to-area ratio of fifteen floors (horizontal dashed line in left panel). The vertical lines designate the boundaries of the area directly affected by the restriction.

A stringent building height restriction, such as the one depicted in Figure 4.2, will result in an urban area with a larger footprint and a different allocation of floor space and population. The environmental and economic effects of this are analysed in Section 4.3.

Urban containment policies and leapfrogging

Urban containment policies, such as urban growth boundaries and greenbelts, have been proposed as a remedy to the uncontrolled expansion of urban footprint. Whether such boundaries improve environmental conditions and the extent to which they affect housing prices are questions that spawned important policy debates that are summarised in Chapter 5. Instead, what is emphasised here is that part of the observed fragmentation in an urban area and a tendency towards low-density development may be attributed to the use of urban growth boundaries and other zoning policies that prevent development in designated areas. *Leapfrogging* is a common response to such regulations. It is characterised by scattered, low-density development beyond the buffer zones designed to restrain the footprint of an urban area. The time needed for leapfrog development to occur depends on various factors, such as the width of the buffer zone, the pace of technical progress and the growth rates of population and income.

Figure 4.3 illustrates an example of the short- and long-run effect of a ten kilometre buffer zone that is initially designed to restrain the urban area to its current footprint. The

Figure 4.3. **The short- and long-run effect of a 10-km-wide buffer zone acting as an urban growth boundary**

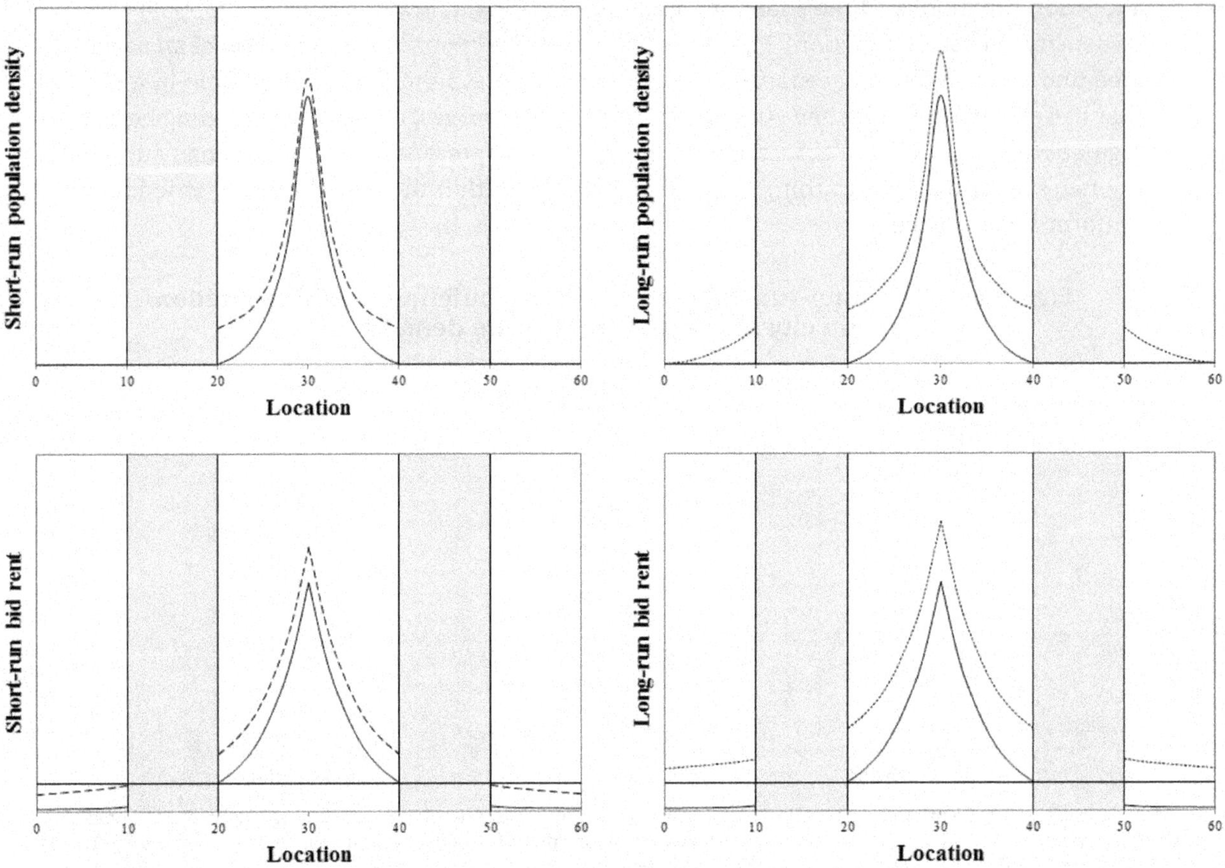

Notes: Solid curves represent the current state of an urban area; long-dashed curves represent the state of the urban area at the end of the short-run; short-dashed curves represent the state of the urban area in the long-run. The shadowed area represents a 10 km buffer zone that in the short-run acts as an urban growth boundary designed to restrain the urban area to its current footprint, i.e. a 20 km diameter circle (locations 20-40). Upper panels display population densities. Lower panels display land rents. The horizontal solid line represents the opportunity cost of land (i.e. agricultural rent).

upper left panel of the picture shows that, in the short run, population growth is accommodated exclusively by densification of the existing urban area (infill development). The extent to which this policy backfires through higher housing prices depends on the ability of developers to substitute capital for land by raising higher buildings. The lower left panel of Figure 4.3 shows the developers' willingness to pay at the moment of the urban growth boundary introduction (solid curve) and at the end of the short run (dashed curve). The increased demand for floor space causes upward pressures on land prices within the existing urban area, but these pressures may not be strong enough to generate leapfrog development: in the lower left panel the willingness to pay to use the land for development falls short of the willingness to pay for alternative land uses (e.g. agriculture) in remote areas.

However, in the long-run income grows substantially and transport costs fall. Then, the return from developing remote areas exceeds the return from alternative land uses and leapfrog development emerges. This way, an initially effective anti-sprawl policy converts into a policy that generates urban sprawl, as the latter was defined in Chapter 2.

Property and land tax

Property taxes, i.e. recurrent *ad valorem* taxes on immovable property, are the most widely used price instrument applied to land use. In most cities, property taxes are levied at equal rates on land and capital improvements, i.e. buildings and other structures constructed on it (Bird and Slack, 2004; Brueckner and Kim, 2003). The long-run effect of property taxation on city size has been a debated issue in the relevant literature (Arnott and MacKinnon, 1977; Brueckner, 2001; Brueckner and Kim, 2003; Carlton, 1981; LeRoy, 1976; Song and Zenou, 2006; Sullivan, 1984, 1985).

Property taxes affect urban sprawl through at least two channels. First, a property tax increases the cost of property ownership. In the long run, this provides incentives for the construction of smaller dwellings, as households will respond to the increased housing costs by substituting away from the consumption of residential floor space. In turn, smaller residences imply that the same population can, *ceteris paribus*, be accommodated in a city of smaller footprint. This affects negatively both the average population density and the two density allocation indicators (land-to-density allocation, population-to-density allocation) in a city. Second, the property tax will exert a downward pressure on land prices, but not on the capital costs of construction and maintenance, which are not determined within city boundaries. This may cause the development of lower buildings, a force that affects the aforementioned indicators in the opposite way. Therefore, whether property taxation impedes or fuels the spatial expansion of cities depends on which of the two effects is stronger (Brueckner and Kim, 2003).

The two possible outcomes described above are depicted in Figure 4.4. The left panel represents the case in which the first effect described in the previous paragraph dominates, i.e. the property tax eventually leads to a smaller city size. In contrast, the right panel illustrates the case where the second effect prevails, shorter buildings are constructed, and a more dispersed urban form emerges.

Figure 4.4. **Different long-term effects of a property tax on city size**

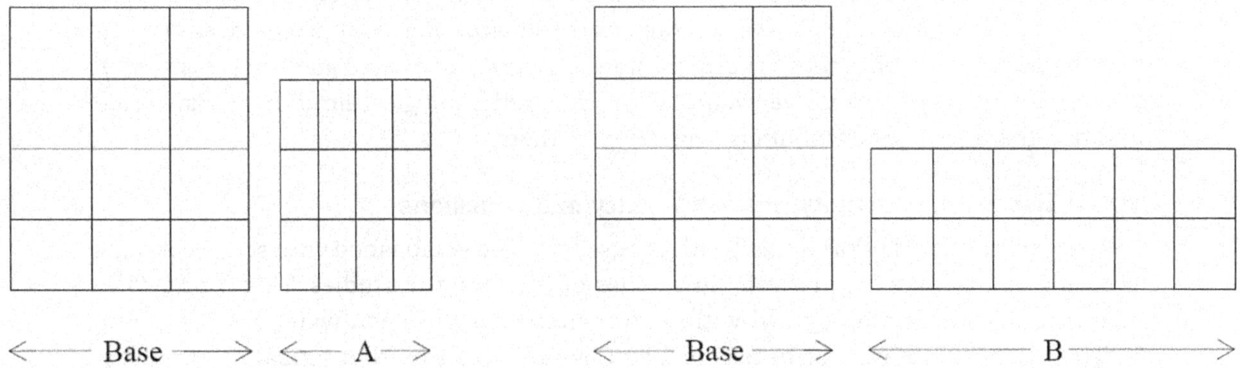

Notes: Horizontal arrows represent the size of the urban footprint under different outcomes. *Base*: absence of property tax; *A*: property tax imposed, residence-size effect prevails; *B*: property tax imposed, tax-on-improvements effect prevails.

Land-use policies have long-term effects

The policies mentioned in the previous subsections are, for several reasons, rigid and persistent over time. First, it might be difficult to adjust land-use regulations since current homeowners have strong incentives to lobby for building height restrictions, as well as zoning (Fischel, 2001; Schuetz, 2009). These regulations have been shown to increase housing prices in certain contexts and are, therefore, likely to remain intact over time (see e.g. Ihlanfeldt, 2007). Another reason for which building height regulations, zoning and urban growth boundaries are persistent is that adjusting them may be impossible in an already formed urban landscape and network. For example, it is impossible to introduce an urban growth boundary in the interior of a city or a maximum building height restriction below the one observed in a specific location. The former policy reform would outlaw existing private property located outside the boundary; the latter would impose a heavy financial cost associated with demolition and reconstruction.

Similarly, immovable property taxation has been established in many OECD countries as a standard way to raise public revenue. Property taxes might in theory be easier to adjust, but in practice this is much more complicated, especially if the adjustment is justified on criteria not related to revenue-raising. Chapter 5 will highlight the importance of adjusting fiscal instruments to account for environmental objectives.

Physical geography

Unsuitable physical terrain (e.g. mountains, rivers, coastlines) may prohibit contiguous development. Furthermore, geological factors posing disaster risks, such as proximity to volcanoes or exposure to earthquakes, may limit population density by imposing safety ceilings in floor-to-area ratios, lot sizes, etc. For instance, Saiz (2010) shows that physical geography is a key factor in the contemporary urban development of the United States. Land constraints, such as steep-sloped terrain and water bodies (lakes, wetlands, oceans), decrease the housing supply elasticity. This effect of geography is both direct, i.e. via reductions in the amount of land available, and indirect, i.e. via increased land values and higher incentives for land-use regulations.

4.3. Effects of urban sprawl

The primary objective of this section is to provide an objective discussion of the potential environmental and economic effects of the various sprawl characteristics (discussed in Chapter 2) while abstaining from the adoption of a prejudiced view of urban sprawl. Such an analysis should avoid confusing the environmental consequences of other forms of urbanisation with those of urban sprawl. It should also avoid adopting anti-sprawl arguments without an extensive evaluation of the methodological limitations that could condition the scientific contributions that support them.

Spatial dispersion of activity, car dependency and emissions

The association of urban sprawl with car use has been established with socioeconomic modelling and validated empirically in a series of econometric studies. This contrasts to the relationships of urban sprawl with land scarcity, pressures on water resources and biodiversity, which have not been supported equally well by theoretical or empirical evidence. These relationships are discussed in detail later in this section.

The environmental relevance of the link between urban sprawl and private vehicle use is crucial, as vehicle kilometres translate into air pollution and greenhouse gas emissions. Theoretical work highlights two main channels through which urban development may translate to more vehicle kilometres and thus emissions: i) through changes in the spatial dispersion of residences, jobs and other key locations (e.g. malls, schools); and ii) through changes in the modal split, i.e. the share of each transport mode in the total number of kilometres travelled. The former channel determines the distances to be covered in daily activities such as commuting and shopping, whereas the latter determines whether these distances will be covered by public transport or private vehicles. The two channels are interrelated, but the analysis that follows investigates them separately for expositional convenience.

Urban economic theory (Alonso, 1964; Muth, 1969) provides the basic intuition on the relationship between city size, population density and vehicle kilometres travelled. The main theoretical insights are illustrated in the left panel of Figure 4.5, which displays two cities of equal population. This population is, however, distributed very differently around a central business district (CBD), where all jobs are located. With job location fixed, the relatively less compact city will generate more vehicle kilometres, and therefore more emissions, as commuting distances grow.

Figure 4.5. **Population and job density in compact and polycentric cities**

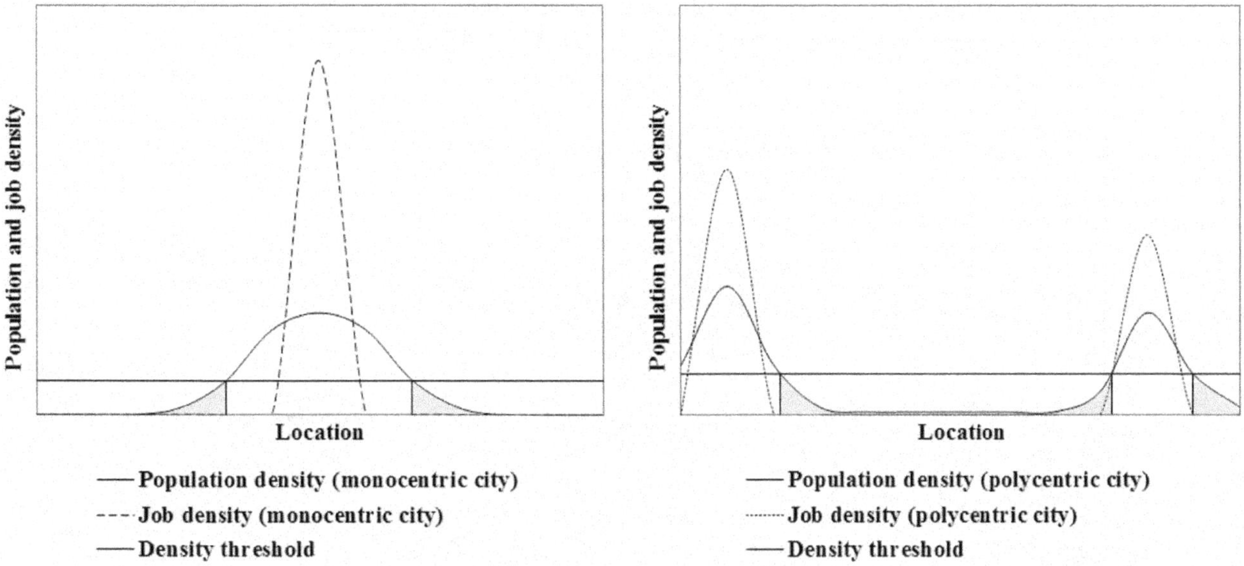

Notes: Solid curves display the population density around the central business districts of a monocentric (left panel) and a bicentric (right panel) urban area. Dashed curves represent job concentration around business districts. The threshold population densities determine the limits of public transport coverage in the two cases. Shaded areas provide a rough representation of the car-dependent parts of population.

The above primary effect may be reinforced or weakened when some of the determinants of modal split are taken into account. First, public transport in low-density areas will be provided at lower service frequency rates. Typically this occurs to curb the large deficits that result from the low occupancy of public transport modes in suburban areas. In turn, lower frequency of service induces more people to switch from public transport to private vehicles. Thus, less compact cities may generate more vehicle kilometres not only because distances between points of interest are larger, but also because the dependence on private modes of transport is higher. This is illustrated in Figure 4.5, in which the most car-dependent fractions of the population are represented by the shaded areas of the residential density distributions. These groups reside in areas where population density is below a threshold level (horizontal line) that ensures frequent provision of service without large deficits.

Second, the dispersion of key points of daily activity, such as jobs, schools, malls and public services, is an important determinant of the effects of urban sprawl on private vehicle kilometres. Figure 4.5 illustrates a case in which the vehicle kilometres generated in a contiguous urban area with two distinct employment hubs (right panel) may not differ substantially from those generated in a city with a unique central business district. The figure reveals that the average land uptake per person is not necessarily a good predictor of the vehicle kilometres travelled in an urban area. The average land uptake is roughly double in the city displayed on the right panel. However, the local distribution of population around the two employment hubs in the polycentric case mimics the population distribution of a monocentric city. Furthermore, the distribution is such that only a small minority of the most car-dependent fractions of the population reside in distances that induce long commutes. As is the case with all urban sprawl dimensions, polycentricity indices are insufficient predictors of private vehicle use.

The relationship between urban sprawl and emissions has been established in empirical studies that use highly informative data sets and state-of-the-art statistical methods. Such studies (see below and Table 4.1) shed light on the observed correlation between urban form patterns and the use of private vehicles, from which emissions can be estimated with the use of conversion coefficients.

Table 4.1. **Summary of studies on transport mode choice and urban form**

Contribution	Type	Main findings
Cervero (2002)	Case study (Montgomery county, US)	The probability of using public transport choice increases with residential density and mixed land use at the origin of the commuting trip.
Kenworthy and Laube (1996)	International cross-country comparative study (39 cities in 15 countries)	Non-linear (negative) relationship between annual vehicle kilometres travelled and average population density. Non-linear (positive) relationship between public transport trips per capita and average population density.
Bento et al. (2003, 2005)	Cross-city study in the US (114 urban areas)	The probability of traveling by car increases with population centrality.

A well-known study on the relationship between urban development characteristics and greenhouse gas emissions has been conducted by Glaeser and Kahn (2010). The authors combine data on gasoline consumption, energy use in public transport, heating expenditure of households, prices of fuel and oil, and carbon intensity of the power generation sector in different areas of the United States. The study finds a strong negative relationship between CO_2 emissions and the stringency of land-use controls. The findings also indicate that the metropolitan areas with the lowest per-household emissions are those which are most restrictive towards new development.

Bento et al. (2003, 2005) investigate the effects of city shape, public transport supply, and the spatial distribution of population, jobs and residences on mode choice and distances travelled by motor vehicles in 114 US urban areas. In doing so, they control for demographic characteristics, such as age, gender and household size, weather conditions, city-specific gasoline prices, urban morphology and the characteristics of public transport supply. Their findings can be summarised as follows. First, the probability of walking or cycling to work increases as population becomes more centralised and the allocation of land between jobs and residences more balanced. Second, increasing rail route miles by 1% can increase the share of people using rail to commute by at least 2.9%. The corresponding number for bus route miles is 0.4%. Finally, increasing the amount of land allocated to highways, moving away from mixed land use, and allowing the city shape to be more elliptical rather than radial all significantly increase vehicle miles travelled.

Kahn (2000) shows that households located at the city centre drive 17-43% less than seemingly identical households (in terms of lot size and income) located in the suburbs. Furthermore, he finds that the non-linear relationship between per capita energy use in transport and population density proposed in earlier studies (Newman and Kenworthy, 1989) is robust even after controlling for unobserved city, region and household characteristics. Hankley and Marshall (2010) find that comprehensive compact development could reduce cumulative emissions in the United States by up to 3.2 Gt CO_2 equivalent, or 15-20% of the projected cumulative emissions in the period between 2000 and 2020.

Urban sprawl and local public finance

Figures 4.5 and 4.6 illustrate how a lower population density may translate into car dependency and, by extension, to emissions. However, the impacts of low population density also expand to the economic sphere. Public services in low-density areas are often provided with substantial subsidies that could be significantly smaller, or even completely avoided, in compact development settings. Figure 4.6 shows this for the case of public transport provision in monocentric cities. The trade-off between quality of service and economic efficiency becomes clearer with a graphical analysis of two extreme examples of how public transport could be provided to the population group that resides in low-density areas of a highly sprawled urban area. The population distribution in that area (city A) is represented by the solid curve; the size of the affected population group is represented by the shaded area below that curve.

Figure 4.6. **Commuting distances and car dependency in two monocentric cities**

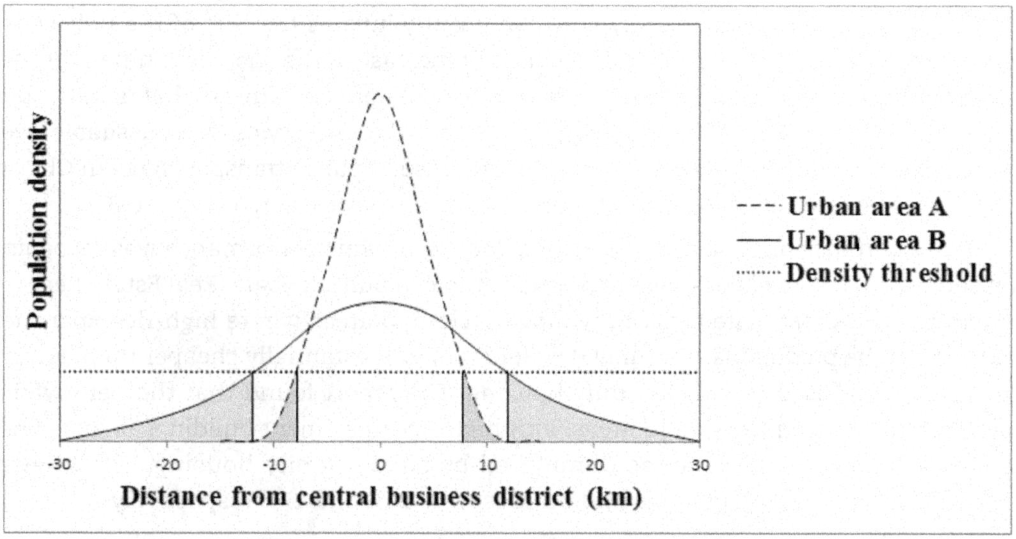

Notes: The two curves display the population density around the central business district of a monocentric city with high (solid curve) and low (dashed curve) land uptake per person. The density threshold determines the limits of public transport coverage. Shaded areas provide a rough representation of the car-dependent parts of population.

In the first extreme case, that population group could be served with the same route frequency with which downtown areas are served, ensuring this way that waiting times are roughly equalised across the city. Car dependency is then eliminated (without this implying that car use will necessarily be reduced) with a substantial economic cost, as low-occupancy rates imply a large deficit in the public transport operator's budget. In the other extreme, that population group is not served at all by public transport. Then, operator deficits are eliminated but the absence of public transport leaves car as the only mode to cover the long-distance trips from the urban fringe to the central business district. This policy option is environmentally detrimental and may also bear a significant distributional impact that renders it politically unpopular.

Actual policies lie between these two extreme cases, with the levels of suburban coverage and public transport subsidies ranging widely across metropolitan areas of OECD countries. Public transport subsidies show a sharp upward trend with time. Taylor et al. (2009) show that the inflation-adjusted increase in local, state and federal public transit subsidies between 1990 and 2003 in the United States was about 51%. At the same time, the per capita ridership remained at historically low levels, with public transport serving only 2.1% of all trips recorded in 2001. Savage (2004) provides a historical analysis of the Chicago Transit Authority's deficits based on times series data from 1948 to 1997. During that period, the annual operating surplus of USD 48 million recorded in 1948 (adjusted for 1997 prices) gradually turned into an annual operating deficit of USD 543 million in 1997. The study finds that the relocation of homes and jobs – that mainly occurred in the decade following the Second World War – reduced annual revenues by USD 399 million. Together with the fact that average occupancy rates for both bus and rail in 1997 were only half of what they were in 1948, the findings indicate that urban sprawl has been one of the leading drivers of the current deficit.

Similar reasoning carries over to a wide array of public services and facilities whose provision is characterised by economies of density: road cleaning and maintenance services, garbage collection and disposal, sewerage and water provision, police and fire protection, libraries and maintenance of parks and other recreational areas. Low population density does not allow such economies of density and significantly inflates the cost of the provision of public services per user. As density may be hard to increase in the short run, time-persistent budget deficits may occur. Such deficits call for consolidation programmes that raise the price of public transport or reduce the frequency and quality of these services to undesirable levels. For example, the annual welfare loss from the increase of public transport fares in Chicago, Illinois, has been estimated to be around USD 82 million (Savage and Schupp, 1997).

The importance of population density to local economic performance was recognised long before urban sprawl became an important topic in public debate. Real Estate Research Corporation (1974) estimated that providing services to areas where high-rise apartment buildings are the predominant form of development is substantially cheaper than doing so in areas characterised by single-family housing. The report found that the per dwelling capital cost of school provision in areas with high-rise apartment buildings is just 30% of the corresponding costs in areas dominated by single-family housing. The relevant numbers for the provision of roads and utilities were 26% and 17% respectively.

Speir and Stephenson (2002) simulate the capital and energy costs of providing water and sewer services under sixty scenarios of growth of a hypothetical town of 30 000 inhabitants. The scenarios differ with respect to the lot size and fragmentation in the areas that are planned to be developed. Provision costs are found to be much more responsive to the average lot size than to the fragmentation of urban fabric. Larger lots imply that the total length of mains required for serving dwellings within newly developed urban fragments increases. In contrast, fragmentation inflates provision costs only by increasing the required length of mains so that fragments are connected to each other. As the distance between fragments diminishes, the extra cost introduced by fragmentation *per se* sharply decreases. Similar reasoning holds for other relevant public services such as electric power and gas supply.

Table 4.2 provides a brief, non-exhaustive, overview of the literature investigating the relationship between urban form and costs of public service provision. The econometric study by Hortas-Rico and Solé-Ollé (2010) disentangled the effect of low-density development from other determinants of municipal expenditure in Spain. The study covers six expenditure types (basic infrastructure and transport, community facilities, local police, housing and community development, culture and sports, and general administration) that represent 70% of total local spending. They show that low-density development leads to greater provision costs in all spending categories considered, apart from housing, and basic infrastructure and transport.

Table 4.2. **Summary of the relevant literature on urban form and cost of providing public services**

Contribution	Type	Main findings
Carruthers and Ulfarsson (2003, 2008)	E	Significant economies of density in capital facilities.
Duncan and Associates (1989)	E	Water provision costs in compact development are 60% of those in spread-out patterns.
Frank (1989)	E	Sewer costs in compact development are 66% of those in spread-out patterns.
Hortas-Rico and Solé-Ollé (2010)	E	Low-density development patterns inflate the provision costs of several local services.
RERC (1974)	S	The cost of providing schools, roads and utilities under high density may be 17-30% of provision costs under low density.
Savage (2004)	T,E	Factors that drive residential and job dispersion underlay more that 73% of Chicago Transit Authority's annual operating deficit.
Speir and Stephenson (2002)	S	Elasticity of water supply and sewer costs with respect to lot size: 0.2-0.4. Elasticity of water supply and sewer costs with respect to fragmentation (number of patches of artificial surface in the urban area): 0.03-0.06.

Notes: S: Simulation study; E: Econometric study; T: Theoretical study. RERC: Real Estate Research Corporation.

Another strand of literature has argued that the cost savings from economies of density are limited: densification decreases the per capita cost of service provision as long as population density lies below a threshold. For instance, Ladd (1992, 1994) analysed the spending profile of 247 large US counties that in 1985 accounted for 59% of the U.S. population. Her findings suggest that a substantial fraction of the analysed counties had a level of density lying above the implied cost-minimizing level. However, her findings should be interpreted with caution due to multiple methodological limitations.

Sprawl and consumption of energy from stationary sources

As it is the case with vehicle-kilometres travelled, consumption of energy from stationary sources can be translated into emissions if the energy efficiency of the technology used for space and water heating in different building types and the emission intensity (greenhouse gases, air pollutants) of the energy sources used for this purpose in a given geographical region are known. Suburban residences are on average larger and therefore consume more energy, and detached housing is ceteris paribus less energy efficient than multi-household buildings. Table 4.3 presents a decomposition of the total energy consumption of the residential and commercial sector by end-use in the United States, the European Union and Canada. The data show that up to 85% of the total energy consumption originates from end-uses that may be indirectly related to urban form.

Table 4.3. **Residential and commercial primary energy consumption, decomposed by end-use**

Country	Year	Space heating	Space cooling	Water heating	Lighting
		Residential energy use decomposition			
US(i)	1997	35%	8%	14%	6%
EU(ii)	1998	57%	N.A.	25%	11%
Canada(ii)	2003	60%	1%	21%	5%
		Commercial energy use decomposition			
US(i)	1997	13%	7%	6%	25%
EU(ii)	1998	52%	4%	9%	14%
Canada(ii)	2000	54%	6%	7%	13%

Notes: Data sources: (i) Koomey et al. (2000) and (ii) Ürge-Vorsatz et al. (2007).

Temperature in the interior of residential buildings may be sensitive to different local conditions and interactions. Such possibly determining conditions include the degree to which a building is detached from buildings in its close neighbourhood, the entire building morphology at the block and neighbourhood level, and the proximity to trees, plants and roads.

Unlike the links between urban sprawl and travel demand, however, the link between urban form and energy consumption has been poorly explored in the literature. Does lower residential density translate into significantly lower lighting needs? Are energy needs for space heating higher in the suburbs compared to high-density areas? Are buildings in areas characterised by high fragmentation harder to warm up or cool down? Does heating require significantly more energy in areas dominated by detached housing? Does a low floor-to-area ratio imply extra energy needs for space and water heating? Do denser urban forms entail higher energy needs for cooling? Filling these knowledge gaps could have important policy implications, since a significant fraction of the total GHG emissions may be attributed to residential heating and cooling. Unfortunately, the existing knowledge on these issues is limited.

Research on the impact of urban sprawl on residential energy use is at embryonic stage, with the proposed effects reflecting speculations and intuition, rather than well-established evidence. In one of the few empirical studies of this subject, Kahn (2000) fails to confirm the hypothesis that suburban dwellings consume more energy for residential purposes, such as heating and cooling. After controlling for important determinants, such as the household's annual exposure to very high or low temperatures, its size and income, energy consumption differences between low-density suburbs and high-density urban cores are found to be negligible. However, this finding reflects the fact that important factors such as the insulation technology of the building and local development patterns are unobserved. Therefore, results may just reflect the fact that a detached development pattern in the suburbs is offset by a superior insulation technology characterising contemporary dwellings, which are more likely to be located in the suburbs. Therefore, future studies should attempt to measure important determinants of temperatures in the interior of buildings.

Earlier studies found that consumption of energy from stationary sources is significantly lower in areas of higher density. For instance, the study by Real Estate Research Corporation (1974) suggested that apartments in high-rise buildings consume only 44% of the energy single family-households do. Future research should provide a better understanding of the degree to which these differences can be attributed to local development patterns and the degree to which they simply reflect the fact that single-family housing units are on average much larger than high-rise apartments and are usually occupied by residents with higher income.

Loss of periurban arable land and environmental amenities

Agricultural land has declined, on average, by 4% in OECD countries over the past two decades and this decline is projected to continue (OECD, 2009). The effect of urban expansion on agriculture has always been at the heart of the debate on sustainable land-use patterns. There are at least three major concerns over the continuing urban sprawl and farmland loss. First, the conversion of the most fertile farmland to development reduces agricultural productivity, which decreases food supply in the short run and threatens food security in the long run. Second, urban sprawl reduces amenities and quality of life in rural communities. In many places, urban sprawl has encroached into communities to such an extent that the communities themselves have been lost (Wu, Fisher and Pascual, 2011). Third, farmland loss may have a detrimental effect on agricultural infrastructure. With farmland loss, the local agricultural support sector, such as input suppliers or output processors, may go out of business because of insufficient demand for their output or insufficient supply of input for their production (Lynch and Carpenter, 2003; Wu, Fisher and Pascual, 2011). In addition, land-use conflicts, such as urban residents' complaints about noise and odour from agricultural production, will likely increase as more farmland is converted to development. Such land-use conflicts may lead to more stringent land-use regulation that restricts traditional farming practices (Lisansky, 1986). Consequently, agricultural economies may shrink in the short run and become unviable in the long run.

The uncontrolled expansion of urban areas has been argued to consume the most fertile parts of arable land. This concern is based on the idea that cities emerge from the evolution of smaller settlements initially hosting populations living from agriculture (Wilson and Chakraborty, 2013). Eigenbrod et al. (2011) model the change in urban land cover in Britain based on a projected population increase of 16% by 2031 under two development scenarios: i) a densification scenario, in which existing suburban housing is converted to dense urban housing, and ii) a sprawl scenario, in which housing demands in the study horizon are met by creating new dwellings in pre-defined undeveloped areas at the existing density observed in suburbs. In the latter scenario, densification of suburbs occurs only when no more space is available. In that context, they investigate the effects upon flood mitigation, agricultural production and carbon sequestration. Their simulation shows that losses of agricultural production are over three times higher in the sprawl scenario compared to the densification scenario.

There are serious counter-arguments, however, to the concerns about the loss of farmland and possible increases in food scarcity due to urban expansion. First, cities occupy only a small fraction of the total land area in a global scale, so urban expansion per se does not seem to pose a real threat for future food supply. At the world scale, for example, Alcamo et al. (2005) projected agricultural land to increase by 10-20% between 2000 and 2050. Fischel (1985) showed that even if the entire US population lived at suburban sprawl densities of 0.25 acres per person, just 3% of the total land area of the forty eight contiguous states would be utilised.

Another counter-argument neglected in some other reports on urban sprawl (e.g. EEA, 2016) is that the methods employed in many simulation studies, including the one by Eigenbrod et al. (2011), fail to account for the effects of urban sprawl on agricultural land prices. Accounting for those effects reveals that urban sprawl is not very likely to cause food scarcity. If food production declined sharply due to urban expansion, food produced in periurban areas could be substituted by imports of food produced elsewhere. If substitution was relatively cheap, cities would expand in an uncurbed way (as the upper panels of Figure 4.7 suggest) but food scarcity would not be an issue. On the other hand, if food produced in periurban areas were costly to substitute, the financial return from cultivating periurban areas would increase sharply (as the lower panels of Figure 4.7 suggest) preventing urban sprawl from being realised in the first place. Thus, uncurbed urban sprawl scenarios are inconsistent with a sharp increase in food prices (Brueckner, 2000), because market price setting mechanisms act as automatic stabilisers that prevent possible effects of urban sprawl on food scarcity. The above arguments suggest that the scenario displayed in the upper panels of Figure 4.7 is probably a better representation of reality.

Figure 4.7. **Changes in urban footprint and arable land under two mutually exclusive scenarios**

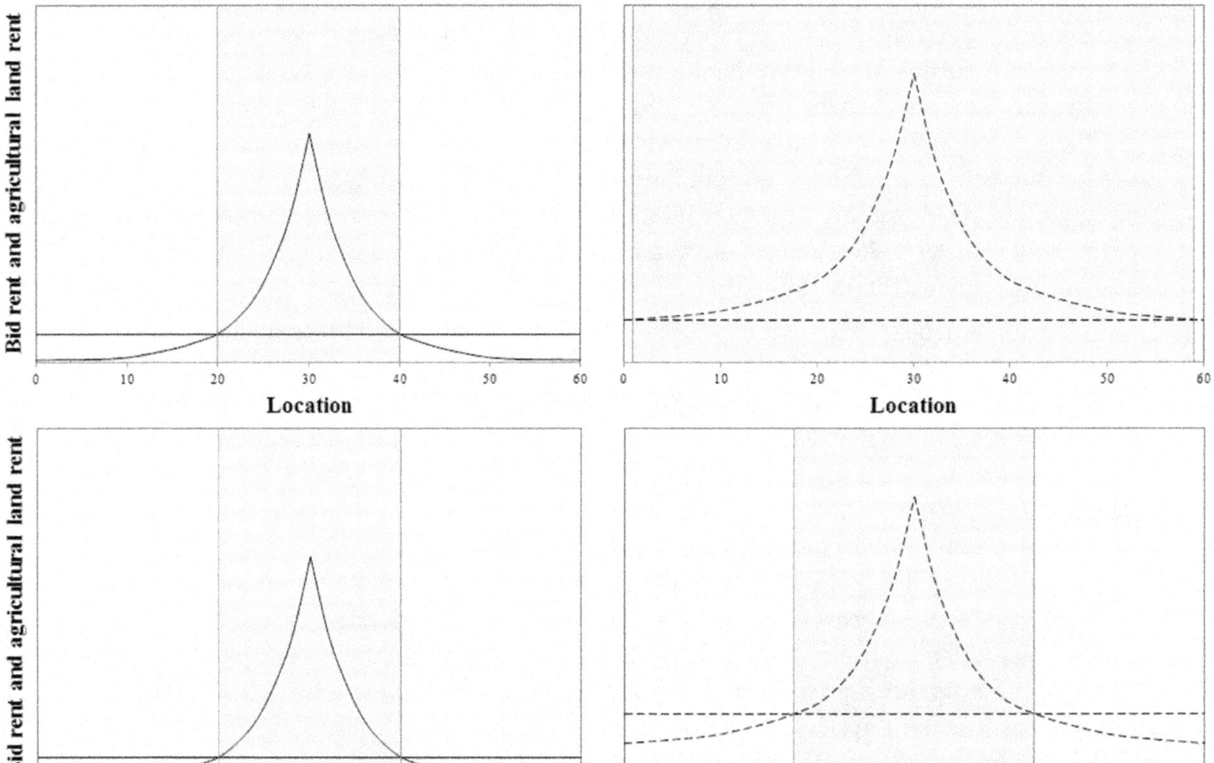

Notes: The figure displays the effect of a major shock in the demand for floor space on the allocation of land between residential development and agriculture when the price elasticity of food supply is high (left panels) and low (left panels). Solid curves: initial willingness to pay for a unit of land surface for development (initial bid rents); dashed curves: final willingness to pay for a unit of land surface for development (final bid rents); Solid lines: initial financial return from cultivating land (initial opportunity cost of land or agricultural rent); Dashed lines: final financial return from cultivating land (final opportunity cost of land or agricultural rent). Shaded areas: land allocated to development; non-shaded areas: land allocated to agriculture. Vertical lines: city boundaries.

The current literature lacks reliable studies on the pressures exerted by urban development on food prices. Future efforts should take into explicit account the fertility rate in periurban areas, the competition for land between the agricultural and the development sector, the import price of food substitutes from the international markets and the trade agreements between countries.

Urban expansion may be socially inefficient not only for reasons related to the negative externalities of residential development, such as congestion and pollution, but also for reasons related to the foregone positive externalities generated from alternative land uses in periurban areas, such as forestry or agriculture. Forests and cultivated areas are hubs of wildlife, perform functions related to air quality and carbon sequestration, prevent surface runoff and soil erosion, and provide amenities or other public environmental attributes. Figure 4.8 displays two different allocations of land between residential development and an alternative land use that generates positive externalities, such as periurban forestry. Under free market conditions, displayed in the left panel, city limits are determined through the equalisation of marginal private benefits of the two land use types. That is, locations in which land rents (solid curve) exceed the private return from forestry (dashed line) are conceded for development and *vice versa*.

Figure 4.8. **Free-market and socially optimal allocation of periurban land**

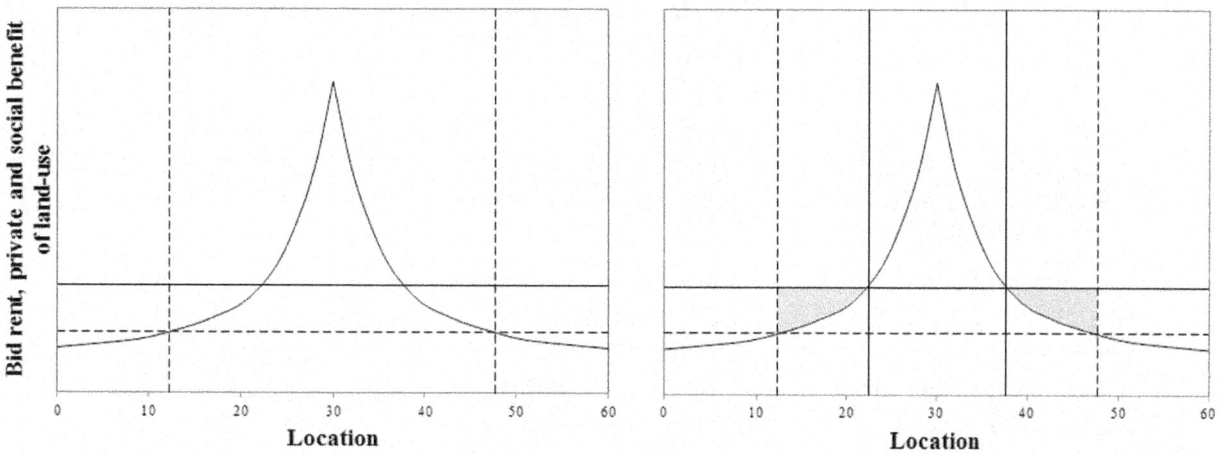

Notes: The figure displays land-use allocation under two alternative regimes. Left panel: free-market conditions; right panel: socially optimal conditions; horizontal dashed line: private return of alternative land-use (e.g. forestry); horizontal solid line: marginal social value of alternative land-use; vertical dashed lines: city limits under free-market conditions; vertical solid lines: city limits under socially optimal conditions; solid curve: return from residential development of land. The vertical distance between the two horizontal lines represents the marginal external benefit of the alternative land use. Shaded areas: total social benefit from containing city size to its socially-optimal level.

The above allocation is not socially optimal, because it fails to take into account that every square metre of land developed at the city fringe removes a square meter of forest land that provides useful environmental functions and amenities. Such services provided by forests are valued positively by a major part of the public, but no market mechanism exists for them. Furthermore, the scarcity of periurban forests in many OECD urban areas – in over 40% of them forests account for less than 10% of their total surface – indicates that the external social benefits of them may be substantial. To obtain the socially desirable city size, policy makers may use market mechanisms, such as taxing periurban development, or regulatory instruments (e.g. greenbelts). Policy-makers should, however, ensure that the selected instruments are designed in a way that deters leapfrog development. The shaded areas in the right panel of Figure 4.8 represent the welfare gains from containing urban expansion. This is the difference between the aggregate social value of the land being protected and the aggregate willingness to pay by developers for the same land.

Hydrological effects

Soil performs important filtering and runoff-regulating functions that may be impaired by land development. Local water balance is affected by sealing surfaces for development purposes. Surface sealing leads to a rise in water run-off on impervious surfaces, which results in a reduction in *groundwater recharge* and a decline in effective *evapotranspiration* (see also Haase and Nuissl, 2007).[1] Haase (2009) highlights the need to identify the exact channels through which development affects the above functions. Both contributions analyse the impact of urban land-use change and development on the urban water balance for a 130-year period in the German city of Leipzig. Poelmans, van Rompaey and Batelaan (2010) compile land cover maps of the highly urbanised region of Flanders – Brussels to simulate twelve urban expansion scenarios for the future (2025 and 2050). These scenarios are an input to a spatially distributed water balance model that assesses the impact on surface run-off, evapotranspiration and groundwater recharge.

Development density and lot size may have an important effect on groundwater levels in the presence of domestic wells. Rayne and Bradbury (2011) used models for groundwater flow to test the impact of suburban development on groundwater levels and discharge to streams. In their simulations they use lot sizes of ca. 4 000, 12 000 and 20 000 m^2 with one domestic well per lot that pumps water from shallow aquifers. They showed that pumping had little impact on water levels and groundwater discharge to streams, provided that the developed area was of moderate size. However, domestic wells had the potential to impact local groundwater levels and baseflows in township-wide development scenarios of ca. 4 000 m^2, where drawdowns beneath developed areas ranged from 0.3 to 5.5 metres, and baseflow reductions ranged from 20 to 40%.

Urban expansion has been blamed for increasing flood risk (Semadeni-Davies et al., 2008). That study simulates forward climate change scenarios characterised by different precipitation rates and various urbanisation patterns to show how urban expansion may be related to drainage. Several studies discuss or simulate the link between land-use change and flood risk (Bhaduri et al., 2001; Rose and Peters, 2001; Bronstert, Niehoff and Bürger, 2002; Hundecha and Bardossy, 2004; Tang et al. 2005; Liu et al., 2006; McColl and Aggett, 2007). All the aforementioned contributions model land-use change; however, the underlying settings do not take into explicit account the critical differences between urbanisation, urban expansion and urban sprawl.

There also appears to be a link between the fraction of land covered by impervious surfaces and the quality of drinking water. The United States Environmental Protection Agency (EPA) has highlighted that water run-off from impervious surfaces may be a threat to water quality due to washed-off contaminants carried directly or indirectly into waterways or the groundwater (United States Environmental Protection Agency, 1994). Berke et al. (2003) compared fifty matched pairs of new urban and conventional developments in five U.S. states to highlight that conventional low-density developments create larger impervious surfaces that generate more runoff than compact developments. Schueler (1994) estimated that compact development can reduce imperviousness by 10-50%, depending on the average lot size and road network. This reduction stems from the large surfaces that have to be tied-down to roads and parking lots under low-density development patterns. Foster, Morris and Chilton (1999) discuss the impact of rapid urbanisation on water quality.

Effects on biodiversity

Suburban areas often display a relatively high diversity of flora and fauna. The natural habitats at the urban fringe are usually occupied by native species: plants, animals, such as mesopredator mammals, as well as ground-foraging, omnivorous and frugivorous birds. Such species may utilise gardens, forest fragments and other habitats available in suburban areas (McKinney, 2006).

As it is the case with hydrological effects, a part of the existing literature confuses the impact of a fragmented, low-density development pattern with the general effects of urban expansion. Alberti (2005) reviews the empirical evidence of the effects of urban expansion on biodiversity. In that review, it is shown that most of the current knowledge stems from studies that use correlations of aggregate measures of urbanisation, rather than detailed urban form metrics, with environmental performance indicators (including biodiversity). While generic urban expansion affects biodiversity in a clearer manner, the impact of fragmented, low-density development on it is more complex. What is reviewed below is a stream of literature that is more precise when it comes to the effects of specific urban development patterns on biodiversity.

McKinney (2008) reviews 105 studies on the correlation between urbanisation, suburbanisation and biodiversity, focusing on mammals, reptiles, amphibians, invertebrates and plants. For all groups, species richness tends to be reduced in areas with extreme urbanisation, i.e. urban core areas. However, the findings in moderate levels of urbanisation, i.e. suburban areas, vary significantly among groups of species. Most of the studies (65%) indicate that moderate suburbanisation is statistically associated with increased plant biodiversity. The corresponding percentage of studies showing a positive association of low density and biodiversity is substantially smaller in the case of invertebrates (30%) and very small in the case of non-avian vertebrates (12%).

Results from such correlation-based studies must be interpreted with caution for two reasons. First, the issue of reverse causality should be taken into account. People may be more willing to suburbanise areas characterised by rich initial biodiversity conditions. This is reflected in the findings of a voluminous literature, which indicates that the willingness to pay for residential space in locations closer to natural amenities may be high (see e.g. Gibbons, Mourato and Resende, 2014; Mahan, Polasky and Adams, 2000). Failing to account for the fact that specific areas are characterised by low-density development partially because of their biodiversity may result in biased conclusions. A more reliable empirical strategy would involve the repeated measurement of biodiversity indicators at fixed locations and their association with changes in urban form characteristics occurring earlier in time.

At the same time, studies should also focus on disentangling the effect of intentional or unintentional import of animals and plants by suburban households from the evolution of native biodiversity. McKinney (2006) goes as far as claiming that the import effect may be strong enough to fully offset the biodiversity loss in the surrounding landscape, but this argumentation involves questionable assumptions regarding the substitutability between native and invasive species. In fact, invasive species have been shown to have detrimental effects on the evolution of native species (see e.g. Karousakis et al., 2012).

Suburbanisation has been blamed for disrupting periurban ecological corridors that connect different complex ecosystems. A series of studies highlight the potential consequences of *habitat fragmentation* in different contexts. Soule (1991) conducted a case study in 37 isolated canyons in San Diego, California. That study showed a statistical relationship between habitat fragmentation and the extinction of native birds, with the author concluding that the provision of corridors linking habitat patches may be essential to maintain the balance of wildlife. The field of island biogeography established the principle of *inverse size*, according to which the rate of species extinction in an isolated patch of habitat is inversely related to its size (MacArthur and Wilson, 1967).

Simulation models provide further insights on how habitat fragmentation may trigger or accelerate the extinction of particular species. Fahring and Merriam (1985) constructed a model to simulate populations in a series of interconnected habitat patches. The model was applied to white-footed mice (*Peromyscus Leucopus*) inhabiting patches of forest in an agricultural landscape. It predicted that mouse populations in isolated woodlots would have lower growth rates and be more prone to extinction than those in connected woodlots. Fahring and Paloheimo (1988) developed a detailed simulation model of the movement behaviour of adult female cabbage butterflies (*Pieris rapae*) in patchy habitats. The purpose of this study was to examine the effect of the spatial arrangement of host-plant patches on the local abundance of the butterfly. The results suggested that the effect of the spatial arrangement of habitat patches on local population size also depends on the distances between patches.

Howe (1984) surveyed forest islands, i.e. small isolated forest patches of areas between 0.1 and 7.0 hectares, in eastern New South Wales (Australia) and southern Wisconsin (United States) between 1977 and 1981. Woodlands in both regions were cleared extensively during the century before the study was conducted. The study examined how fragmentation of forest habitat affected the composition and dynamics of local bird populations. Species in forest islands were compared with a control group of species residing at the edge of a large, continuous forest. The study suggested that the disruption of continuous tracts may affect not only bird populations in the interior of the forest island, but also those residing along or near the edge.

Lynch and Whigham (1984) conducted surveys to estimate the abundance and diversity of birds in relation to the size, spatial arrangement and characteristics of 270 forest patches in the state of Maryland (United States). In that study, densities of permanent resident and short-distance migrant species tended to be less affected by the site characteristics, or showed responses of the opposite direction to those of long-distance migrants. The findings indicate that different species may respond differently to factors such as patch area and isolation. Partition of the habitat into small, highly isolated patches of forest may adversely affect some species, but other factors may be more important for other species.

While the relationship between biodiversity and fragmentation of natural habitats has been roughly established, the relationship between habitat fragmentation and fragmentation of urban fabric is not as straightforward as might be expected, as Figure 4.9 suggests. An urban area can be highly fragmented with well-connected periurban natural habitats, as the left panel of the figure suggests. In such a context, trying to reduce sprawl by connecting the fragments of urban fabric may have an adverse effect on biodiversity. As the middle panel of Figure 4.9 suggests, such an option will result in high fragmentation of the natural habitats as all major ecological corridors in periurban areas will be disrupted. Finally, the right panel of the same figure suggests that low fragmentation of the urban fabric may coexist with contiguous natural habitats in periurban areas.

Figure 4.9. **Urban fabric versus habitat fragmentation**

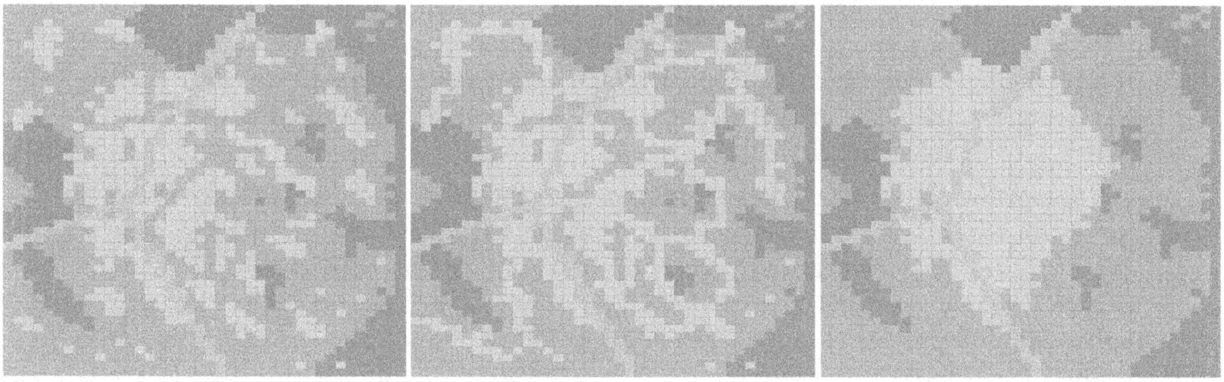

Notes: Left panel: A hypothetical area with highly fragmented urban fabric and minimal habitat fragmentation (three forest islands). Middle panel: Further development that minimises fragmentation of urban fabric results in massive habitat fragmentation (more than fifteen forest islands). Right panel: An alternative pattern with minimal fragmentation of urban fabric and natural habitat. Colour keys: green: natural habitats; blue: water bodies; grey: artificial land; brown: undeveloped areas.

Urban heat islands and resilience to climate change

Prolonged human exposure to high temperatures can be a primary cause of death, for instance by triggering strokes, or a major contributing factor to life-shortening conditions, such as heart and pulmonary disorders. Such health effects are becoming a major issue, as the overall temperature rises and extreme heat events occur more often (Gaffen and Ross, 2008). Robine et al. (2008) estimated that the European heat wave of 2003 caused more than 70 000 excess deaths in the course of a few months. While human exposure to extreme heat events is an overall issue, the problem seems to be more severe in urban contexts. During persistent heat episodes, specific urban areas or entire metropolitan regions known as *urban heat islands* (UHI) have been observed to be significantly warmer than their surrounding rural areas. The critical temperature differential, which can exceed 10°C, can be the result of several factors (Oke, 1982).

Some of these factors that contribute to the emergence of urban heat islands are related to the material composition of built environment. Impervious surfaces such as buildings, roads and other types of infrastructure are more likely to have lower reflectivity (albedo) due to their colour. Such surfaces may have limited capacity to reradiate heat. In addition, the evapotranspiration functions performed by trees and plants in a certain area may be distorted due to the loss of vegetation. In that sense, a low-density development pattern may contribute to exacerbating the phenomenon since it requires a larger uptake of land (not only for buildings, but also for roads and other types of infrastructure) to be covered by material of higher thermal storage capacity.

However, UHIs are far from being homogeneous structures. Instead, Parry (1962) suggested that a UHI can be described as a combination of several smaller areas, each one with its own microclimate that is co-determined by its unique land-use characteristics. Stated differently, the local configuration of the built environment affects microclimate. For instance, it is well-known that the presence of tall buildings gives rise to *urban canyons* that hamper the dispersion of the heat generated by residences and traffic. In that sense, a low-density development pattern characterised by shorter, detached constructs may contribute to the mitigation of the phenomenon.

The various features of development patterns are likely to affect the emergence of UHI in opposing ways. For this reason, current knowledge regarding the urban development pattern that is the least likely to lead to UHIs is scarce (Stone and Norman, 2006). Understanding the mechanisms through which a development pattern may mitigate or exacerbate the phenomenon will be key in promoting urban forms that mitigate climate change and are more resilient to it.

The relationship between urban form and microclimate was recognised early on in the literature, with Clarke (1972) suggesting that the relatively high number of deaths occurring in urban areas during periods of extreme heat can be significantly reduced through appropriate urban land use. Stone and Norman (2006) find that the contribution of individual land parcels to the phenomenon could be reduced by approximately 40% through the adoption of specific land-use planning policies, such as zoning and subdivision regulations, without modifications in the size or albedo of the residential structures. Golany (1996) argues that the thermally desirable configuration of the built environment significantly varies with geographic latitude.

Obesity and other health effects

The incidence of obesity is different across regions and urban areas of different development patterns. For instance, Mokdad et al. (1999) report that during the period between 1991 and 1998 obesity prevalence grew by almost 102% in Georgia but only slightly over 11% in Delaware. The fact that obesity increases relatively faster in geographic areas containing less compact cities has led some researchers to claim that variations in the built environment may have a significant impact on obesity. The rationale is that built environment may impose certain constraints that affect exercise, diet and other lifestyle choices. For instance, as already discussed, low-density areas are costly to be covered by public transport and are harder to become walkable. On the other hand, they may provide better accessibility to open spaces, such as periurban forests, where physical exercise can take place without substantial costs. In line with that, Berrigan and Troiano (2002) find a significant correlation between urban form and physical activity. A conceptual framework that makes explicit the linkages between urban design, car dependency and public health is provided by Frank and Engelke (2001).

A number of studies investigate whether there is a positive relationship between urban sprawl and obesity, but they provide mixed evidence of the existence of such a link (Ewing, Brownson and Berrigan, 2006; Ewing et al., 2003; Frank, Andresen and Schmid, 2004; Giles-Corti et al., 2003; Lopez, 2004; McCann and Ewing, 2003; Saelens et al., 2003; Zhao and Kaestner, 2010). Sturm and Cohen (2004) found that sprawl is associated with physical conditions such as asthma, diabetes, hypertension, arthritis, rheumatism, physical disability, problems in breathing, emphysema or chronic obstructive pulmonary disease (COPD), cancer, neurological conditions, stroke or paralysis, heart failure, coronary artery disease, chronic back problems, abdominal problems (ulcer, colitis, enteritis), chronic liver disease, migraine or chronic severe headaches, chronic bladder problems or problems urinating and other chronic pain conditions. On the other hand, the same study failed to identify a relationship between urban structure and mental health conditions.

While a negative statistical relationship between sprawl and physical health has been identified in the aforementioned studies, none of them managed to establish a causal effect. The most important methodological barrier in most cases is *self-selection*: among others, suburban residents are more likely to have selected suburbs over downtown areas because they favour a less physically-active lifestyle with limited exercise and the vast majority of their trips undertaken by car. Low-density areas accommodate these preferences more cheaply and easily. Overcoming that methodological constraint, Eid et al. (2008) provide one of the best-conducted studies in the potential relationship between sprawl and obesity. They show that previous findings of a positive relationship between sprawl and obesity were most probably due to a failure to properly control for individual characteristics and preferences. The study indicates that trying to curb obesity by changing the built environment may be a poor policy response.

Plantinga and Bernell (2007) find a two-way relationship between sprawl and the body mass index (BMI). In particular, individuals of high BMI are expected to lose weight if they move to denser locations. However, this is not to be attributed to population density *per se*, but to a series of mobility constraints often ceasing when someone moves to a denser area. At the same time, the self-selection effect is confirmed. BMI is an important determinant of the choice: people of high BMI tend to prefer sprawling locations, as they prefer to move by car.

4.4. Concluding remarks

This chapter provided a comprehensive discussion of the main drivers of urban sprawl, as the latter was defined in Chapter 2. Special attention was paid to the preference-driven causes of urban sprawl, as well as to forces that contribute to a growth pattern that may appear to be sprawling in the short run, but constitutes a temporary stage in the long-run development of a compact city. The chapter presented a series of mechanisms through which some policy interventions may give rise to more sprawled urban environments. Furthermore, it provided a review of the multiple impacts of urban sprawl on the environment, economy and society. Abstaining from emotionally-charged indictments of sprawl, the discussion took into explicit account the internal and external validity of numerous studies, some of which provide contradictory evidence. Accounting for the various methodological limitations and assessing the reliability of a voluminous body of literature, it was highlighted that while many of the concerns raised are sensible, many others may lack substantial evidence-based support. Equally important, it was also highlighted that some concerns may refer to effects erroneously attributed to urban sprawl; instead, these effects stem from other forms of urban development, or urbanisation *per se*. Accounting for the critical differences between generic urban expansion and sprawl paves the way for interventions that target urban sprawl, rather than urbanisation. A series of such interventions will be provided in Chapter 5.

Note

1. Groundwater recharge is the hydrological process of water moving from the surface downward to soil pore spaces and fractures of underground rock formations. Evapotranspiration is the process of water moving to the air directly from the soil or through plants.

References

Alberti, M. (2005), "The effects of urban patterns on ecosystem function", *International Regional Science Review*, Vol. 28/2, pp. 168-192.

Alcamo, J. et al. (2005), "Changes in nature's balance sheet: Model-based estimates of future worldwide ecosystem services", *Ecology and Society*, Vol. 10/2, 19.

Alonso, W. (1964), *Location and Land Use*, Harvard University Press, Cambridge, MA.

Anas, A., R. Arnott and K.A. Small (1998), "Urban spatial structure". *Journal of Economic Literature*, Vol. 36/3, pp. 1426-1464.

Arnott, R.J. and J.G. MacKinnon (1977), "The effects of the property tax: A general equilibrium simulation", *Journal of Urban Economics*, Vol. 4/4, pp. 389-407.

Bento, A.M. et al. (2005), "The effects of urban spatial structure on travel demand in the United States", *The Review of Economics and Statistics*, Vol. 87/3, pp. 466-478.

Bento, A.M. et al. (2003), "The impact of urban spatial structure on travel demand in the U.S.", *World Bank Policy Research Working Paper* No. 3007, The World Bank, Washington, DC.

Berke, P.R. et al. (2003), "Greening development to protect watersheds: Does new urbanism make a difference?", *Journal of the American Planning Association*, Vol. 69/4, pp. 397-413.

Berrigan, D. and R.P. Troiano (2002), "The association between urban form and physical activity in U.S. adults", *American Journal of Preventive Medicine*, Vol. 23/2, pp. 74-79.

Bertaud, A. and J.K. Brueckner (2005), "Analyzing building-height restrictions: Predicted impacts and welfare costs", *Regional Science and Urban Economics*, Vol. 35/2, pp. 109-125.

Bhaduri, B. et al. (2001), "Long-term hydrologic impact of urbanization: A tale of two models", *Journal of Water Resources Planning and Management*, Vol. 127/1, pp. 13-19.

Bird, R.M. and E. Slack (2004), "Land and property taxation in 25 countries: A comparative review", in Bird, R.M. and E. Slack (eds), *International Handbook of Land and Property Taxation*, Edward Elgar, Cheltenham, UK, and Northampton, MA, USA.

Braid, R.M. (1991), "Residential spatial growth with perfect foresight and multiple income groups", *Journal of Urban Economics*, Vol. 30/3, pp. 385-407.

Braid, R.M. (1988), "Optimal spatial growth of employment and residences", *Journal of Urban Economics*, Vol. 24/2, pp. 227-240.

Bronstert, A., D. Niehoff and G. Bürger (2002), "Effects of climate and land-use change on storm runoff generation: Present knowledge and modelling capabilities", *Hydrological Processes*, Vol. 16/2, pp. 509-529.

Brueckner, J.K. (2001), "Property taxation and urban sprawl", in Oates, W.E. (ed.), *Property taxation and local government finance*, Lincoln Institute of Land Policy, Cambridge, MA.

Brueckner, J.K. (2000), "Urban sprawl: Diagnosis and remedies", *International Regional Science Review*, Vol. 23/2, pp. 160-171.

Brueckner, J.K. and D. Fansler (1983), "The economics of urban sprawl: Theory and evidence on the spatial sizes of cities", The *Review of Economics and Statistics*, Vol. 65/3, pp. 479-482.

Brueckner, J.K. and H.A. Kim (2003), "Urban sprawl and the property tax", *International Tax and Public Finance*, Vol. 10/1, pp. 5-23.

Brueckner, J.K. and B. von Rabenau (1981), "Dynamics of land-use for a closed city", *Regional Science and Urban Economics*, Vol. 11/1, pp. 1-17.

Burchfield, M. et al. (2006), "Causes of sprawl: A portrait from space", *The Quarterly Journal of Economics*, Vol. 121/2, pp. 587-633.

Carlton, D.W. (1981), "The Spatial Effects of a Tax on Housing and Land", *Regional Science and Urban Economics*, Vol. 11/4: 509-527.

Carruthers, J.I. and G.F. Ulfarsson (2008), "Does smart growth matter to public finance? Evidence from the United States", *Urban Studies*, Vol. 45/9, pp. 1791-1823.

Carruthers, J.I. and G.F. Ulfarsson (2003), "Urban sprawl and the cost of public services", *Environment and Planning B: Planning and Design*, Vol. 30/4, pp. 503-522.

Cavailhès, J. et al. (2004), "The periurban city: Why to live between the suburbs and the countryside", *Regional Science and Urban Economics*, Vol. 34/6, pp. 681-703.

Cervero, R. (2002), "Built environments and mode choice: Toward a normative framework", *Transportation Research Part D: Transport and Environment*, Vol 7/4, pp. 265-284.

Clarke, J.F. (1972), "Some effects of the urban structure on heat mortality", *Environmental Research*, Vol. 5/1, pp. 93-104.

Clawson, M. (1962), "Urban sprawl and speculation in suburban land", *Land Economics*, Vol. 38/2, pp. 99-111.

Coisnon, T., W. Oueslati and J. Salanié (2014), "Urban sprawl occurrence under spatially varying agricultural amenities", *Regional Science and Urban Economics*, Vol. 44, pp. 38-49.

Deng, X. et al. (2008), "Growth, population and industrialization, and urban land expansion of China", *Journal of Urban Economics*, Vol. 63/1, pp. 96-115.

Duncan, J. and Associates (1989), *The search for efficient urban growth patterns: A study of the fiscal impacts of development in Florida*, Florida Department of Community Affairs, Tallahassee, FL.

EEA (2016), *Urban sprawl in Europe – joint EEA-FOEN report*, EEA Report No. 11/2016, Publications Office of the European Union, Luxembourg.

Eid, J. et al. (2008), "Fat city: Questioning the relationship between urban sprawl and obesity", *Journal of Urban Economics*, Vol. 63/2, pp. 385-404.

Eigenbrod, F. et al. (2011), "The impact of projected increases in urbanization on ecosystem services", *Proceedings of the Royal Society of London B: Biological Sciences*, Vol. 278, pp. 3201-3208.

Ewing, R., R.C. Brownson and D. Berrigan (2006), "Relationship between urban sprawl and weight of United States youth", *American Journal of Preventive Medicine*, Vol. 31/6, pp. 464-474.

Ewing, R. et al. (2003), "Relationship between urban sprawl and physical activity, obesity, and morbidity", *American Journal of Health Promotion*, Vol. 18/1, pp. 47-57.

Federal Home Mortgage Association (1994), *National Housing Survey*. Federal Home Mortgage Association, Washington, DC.

Fischel, W.A. (2001), "Why are there NIMBYs?", *Land Economics*, Vol. 77/1, pp. 144-152.

Fischel, W.A. (1985), *The Economics of Zoning Laws: A Property Rights Approach to American Land Use Controls*, The Johns Hopkins University Press, Baltimore, MD.

Foster, S.S.D., B.L. Morris and P.J. Chilton (1999), "Groundwater in urban development – a review of linkages and concerns", in Ellis, B.J. (Ed.), *Impacts of Urban Growth on Surface Water and Groundwater Quality. IAHS Publications*, No. 259, Oxfordshire, UK.

Frank, J.E. (1989), *The Costs of Alternative Development Patterns: A Review of the Literature*, Urban Land Institute, Washington, DC.

Frank, L.D., M.A. Andresen and T.L. Schmid (2004), "Obesity relationships with community design, physical activity, and time spent in cars", *American Journal of Preventive Medicine*, Vol. 27/2, pp. 87-96.

Frank, L.D. and P.O. Engelke (2001), "The built environment and human activity patterns: Exploring the impacts of urban form on public health", *Journal of Planning Literature*, Vol. 16/2, pp. 202-218.

Fujita, M. (1976), "Spatial patterns of urban-growth: Optimum and market", *Journal of Urban Economics*, Vol. 3/3, pp. 209-241.

Gaffen, D.J., and R. Ross (1998), "Increased summertime heat stress in the United States", *Nature*, Vol. 396/6711, pp. 529-530.

Garcia-López, M.-Á., A. Holl and E. Viladecans-Marsal (2015), "Suburbanization and highways in Spain when the Romans and the Bourbons still shape its cities", *Journal of Urban Economics*, Vol. 85, pp. 52-67.

Geniaux, G., J.S. Ay and C. Napoléone (2011), "A spatial hedonic approach on land-use change anticipations", *Journal of Regional Science*, Vol. 51/5, pp. 967-986.

Gibbons, S., S. Mourato and G.M. Resende (2014), "The amenity value of English nature: A hedonic price approach", *Environmental and Resource Economics*, Vol. 57/2, pp. 175-196.

Giles-Corti, B. et al. (2003), "Environmental and lifestyle factors associated with overweight and obesity in Perth, Australia", *American Journal of Health Promotion*, Vol. 18/1, pp. 93-102.

Glaeser, E.L. and M.E. Kahn (2010), "The greenness of cities: Carbon dioxide emissions and urban development", *Journal of Urban Economics*, Vol. 67/3, pp. 404-418.

Glaeser, E.L. and M.E. Kahn (2004), "Sprawl and urban growth", in J.-F. Henderson and J. Vernon Thisse (eds.), *Handbook of Regional and Urban Economics, Vol. 4, Cities and Geography*. Elsevier, Amsterdam.

Golany, G. (1996), "Urban design morphology and thermal performance", *Atmospheric Environment*, Vol. 30/3, pp. 455-465.

Gordon, P. and H.W. Richardson (1997), "Are Compact Cities a Desirable Planning Goal?", *Journal of the American Planning Association*, Vol. 63/1, pp. 89-106.

Haase, D. (2009), "Effects of urbanisation on the water balance – A long-term trajectory", *Environmental Impact Assessment Review*, Vol. 29/4, pp. 211-219.

Haase, D. and H. Nuissl (2007), "Does urban sprawl drive changes in the water balance and policy? The case of Leipzig (Germany) 1870-2003", *Landscape and Urban Planning*, Vol. 80/1, pp. 1-13.

Hankley, S. and J.D. Marshall (2010), "Impacts of urban form on future US passenger-vehicle greenhouse gas emissions", *Energy Policy*, Vol. 38/9, pp. 4880-4888.

Hortas-Rico, M. and A. Albert Solé-Ollé (2010), "Does urban sprawl increase the costs of providing local public services? Evidence from Spanish municipalities", *Urban Studies*, Vol. 47/7, pp. 1513-1540.

Howe, R.W. (1984), "Local dynamics of bird assemblages in small forest habitat islands in Australia and North America", *Ecology*, Vol. 65/5, pp. 1585-1601.

Hundecha, Y. and A. Bardossy (2004), "Modeling of the effect of land use changes on the runoff generation of a river basin through parameter regionalization of a watershed model", *Journal of Hydrology*, Vol. 292/1-4, pp. 281-295.

Ihlanfeldt, K.R. (2007), "The effect of land use regulation on housing and land prices", *Journal of Urban Economics*, Vol. 61/3, pp. 420-435.

Irwin, E.G. and N.E. Bockstael (2004), "Land use externalities, open space preservation, and urban sprawl", *Regional Science and Urban Economics*, Vol. 34/6, pp. 705-725.

Kahn, M. (2000), "The environmental impact of suburbanization". *Journal of Policy Analysis and Management*, Vol. 19/ 4, pp. 569-586.

Karousakis, K. et al. (2012), "Biodiversity", in *OECD Environmental Outlook to 2050: The Consequences of Inaction*, OECD Publishing, Paris, *http://dx.doi.org/10.1787/env_outlook-2012-7-en.*

Kenworthy, J.R. and F.B. Laube (1996), "Automobile dependence in cities: An international comparison of urban transport and land use patterns with implications for sustainability", *Environmental Impact Assessment Review*, Vol. 16/4, pp. 279-308.

Koomey, J.G. et al. (2000), "Buildings sector", in Interlaboratory Working Group, *Scenarios for a Clean Energy Future*, ORNL/CON-476, LBNL-44029, and NREL/TP-620-29379, Oak Ridge National Laboratory, Oak Ridge, TN, Lawrence Berkeley National Laboratory, Berkeley, CA and National Renewable Energy Laboratory, Golden, CO.

Ladd, H.F. (1994), "Fiscal impacts of local population growth: A conceptual and empirical analysis", *Regional Science and Urban Economics*, Vol. 24/6, pp. 661-686.

Ladd, H.F. (1992), "Population growth, density and the costs of providing public services", *Urban Studies*, Vol. 29/2, pp. 273-295.

LeRoy, S.F. (1976), "Urban land rent and the incidence of property taxes", *Journal of Urban Economics*, Vol. 3/2, pp. 167-179.

Lisansky, J. (1986), "Farming in an urbanizing environment: Agricultural land use conflicts and right to farm", *Human Organization*, Vol. 45/4, pp. 363-371.

Liu, Y.B. et al. (2006), "Predicting storm runoff from different land-use classes using a geographical information system based distributed model", *Hydrological Processes*, 20/3, pp. 533-548.

Lopez, R. (2004), "Urban sprawl and risk for being overweight or obese", *American Journal of Public Health*, Vol. 94/9, pp. 1574-1579.

Lynch, L. and J. Carpenter (2003), "Is there evidence of a critical mass in the mid-Atlantic agriculture sector between 1949 and 1997?", *Agricultural and Resource Economics Review*, Vol. 32/1, pp. 116-128.

Lynch, J.F. and D.F. Whigham (1984), "Effects of forest fragmentation on breeding bird communities in Maryland, USA" *Biological Conservation*, Vol. 28/4, pp. 287-324.

MacArthur, R.H. and E.O. Wilson (1967), *The Theory of Island Biogeography*, Princeton University Press, Princeton, NJ.

Mahan, B.L., S. Polasky and R.M. Adams (2000), "Valuing urban wetlands: A property price approach", *Land Economics*, Vol. 76/1, pp. 100-113.

McCann, B.A. and R. Ewing (2003), *Measuring the health effects of sprawl: A national analysis of physical activity, obesity and chronic disease*, Smart Growth America, Surface Transportation Policy Project, Washington, DC.

McColl, C. and G. Aggett (2007), "Land-use forecasting and hydrologic model integration for improved land-use decision support", *Journal of Environmental Management*, Vol. 84/4, pp. 494-512.

McGrath, D.T. (2005), "More evidence on the spatial scale of cities" *Journal of Urban Economics*, Vol. 58/1, pp. 1-10.

McKinney, M.L. (2008), "Effects of urbanization on species richness: A review of plants and animals" *Urban Ecosystems*, Vol. 11/2, pp. 161-176.

McKinney, M.L. (2006), "Urbanization as a major cause of biotic homogenization", *Biological Conservation*, Vol. 127/3, pp. 247-260.

Mills, D.E. (1981), "Growth, speculation and sprawl in a monocentric city", *Journal of Urban Economics*, Vol. 10/2, pp. 201-226.

Mokdad, A.H. et al. (1999), "The spread of the obesity epidemic in the United States, 1991-1998", *Journal of the American Medical Association*, Vol. 282/16, pp. 1519-1522.

Muth, R.F. (1969), *Cities and Housing*. University of Chicago Press, Chicago.

Nechyba, T.J. and R.P. Walsh (2004), "Urban sprawl", *The Journal of Economic Perspectives*, Vol. 18/4, pp. 177-200.

Newman, P. and J. Kenworthy (1989), "Gasoline consumption and cities: A comparison of U.S. cities with a global survey", *Journal of the American Planning Association*, Vol. 55/1, pp. 24-37.

OECD (2009), *Farmland Conversion: The Spatial Dimension of Agricultural and Land Use Policies*, OECD Publishing, Paris, *www.oecd.org/agriculture/44535648.pdf*.

Ohls, J.C. and D. Pines 1(975), "Discontinuous urban development and economic efficiency", *Land Economics*, Vol. 51/3, pp. 224-234.

Oke, T.R. (1982), "The energetic bias of the urban heat island", *Quarterly Journal of the Royal Meteorological Society*, Vol. 108/455, pp. 1-24.

Oueslati, W., S. Alvanides and G. Garrod (2015), "Determinants of urban sprawl in European cities", *Urban Studies*, Vol. 52/9, pp. 1594-1614.

Patacchini, E. and Y. Zenou (2009), "Urban sprawl in Europe", *Brookings-Wharton Papers on Urban* Affairs, Vol. 1, pp. 125-149.

Plantinga, A.J. and S. Bernell (2007), "The association between urban sprawl and obesity: Is it a two-way street?" *Journal of Regional Science*, Vol. 45/3, pp. 473-492.

Poelmans, L., A. van Rompaey and O. Batelaan (2010), "Coupling urban expansion models and hydrological models: How important are spatial patterns?" *Land Use Policy*, Vol. 27/3, pp. 965-975.

Rayne, T.W. and K.R. Bradbury (2011), "Evaluating impacts of subdivision density on shallow groundwater in Southeastern Wisconsin, USA", *Journal of Environmental Planning and Management*, Vol. 54/5, pp. 559-575.

Ready, R.C. and C.W. Abdalla (2005), "The amenity and disamenity impacts of agriculture: Estimates from a hedonic pricing model", *American Journal of Agricultural Economics*, Vol. 87/2, pp. 314-326.

Real Estate Research Corporation (1974), *The Costs of Sprawl: Environmental and Economic Costs of Alternative Residential Development Patterns at the Urban Fringe*, U.S. Government Printing Office, Washington, DC.

Robine, J.M. et al. (2008), "Death toll exceeded 70,000 in Europe during the summer of 2003" *Comptes Rendus Biologies*, Vol. 331/2, pp. 171-178.

Roe, B., E.G. Irwin and H.A. Morrow-Jones (2004), "The effects of farmland, farmland preservation, and other neighborhood amenities on housing values and residential growth", *Land Economics*, Vol. 80/1, pp. 55-75.

Rose, S. and N. Peters (2001), "Effects of urbanization on streamflow in the Atlanta area (Georgia, USA): A comparative hydrological approach", *Hydrological Processes*, Vol. 15/8, pp. 1441-1457.

Saelens, B.E. et al. (2003), "Neighborhood based differences in physical activity: An environment scale evaluation", *American Journal of Public Health*, Vol. 93/9, pp. 1552-1558.

Saiz, A. (2010), "The geographic determinants of housing supply", *The Quarterly Journal of Economics*, Vol. 125/3, pp. 1253-1296.

Savage, I. (2004), "Management objectives and the causes of mass transit deficits", *Transportation Research Part A: Policy and Practice*, 38/3, pp. 181-199.

Savage, I. and A. Schupp (1997), "Evaluating transit subsidies in Chicago", *Journal of Public Transportation*, Vol. 1, pp. 93-117.

Schueler, T. (1994), "Use of cluster development to protect watersheds", *Watershed Protection Techniques*, Vol. 1/1, pp. 137-140.

Schuetz, J. (2009), "No renters in my suburban backyard: Land use regulation and rental housing", *Journal of Policy Analysis and Management*, Vol. 28/2, pp. 296-320.

Semadeni-Davies, A. et al. (2008), "The impacts of climate change and urbanisation on drainage in Helsingborg, Sweden: Suburban stormwater", *Journal of Hydrology*, Vol. 350/1, pp. 114-125.

Shanzi, K., Y. Song and H. Ming (2009), "Determinants of urban spatial scale: Chinese cities in transition", *Urban Studies*, Vol. 46/13, pp. 1-19.

Song, Y. and Y. Zenou (2006), "Property tax and urban sprawl: Theory and implications for US cities", *Journal of Urban Economics*, Vol. 60/3, pp. 519-534.

Soule, M.E. (1991), "Land use planning and wildlife maintenance: Guidelines for conserving wildlife in an urban landscape", *Journal of the American Planning Association*, Vol. 57/3, pp. 313-323.

Speir, C. and K. Stephenson (2002), "Does sprawl cost us all? Isolating the effects of housing patterns on public water and sewer costs", *Journal of the American Planning Association*, Vol. 68/1, pp. 56-70.

Stone, B. and J.M. Norman (2006), "Land use planning and surface heat island formation: A parcel-based radiation flux approach", *Atmospheric Environment*, Vol. 40/19, pp. 3561-3573.

Sturm, R. and D.A. Cohen (2004), "Suburban sprawl and physical and mental health", *Public Health*, Vol. 118/7, pp. 488-496.

Su, Q. and J.S. DeSalvo (2008), "The effect of transportation subsidies on urban sprawl", *Journal of Regional Science*, Vol. 48/3, pp. 567-594.

Sullivan, A.M. (1985), "The general equilibrium effects of the residential property tax: Incidence and excess burden", *Journal of Urban Economics*, Vol. 18/2, pp. 235-250.

Sullivan, A.M. (1984), "The general equilibrium effects of the industrial property tax: Incidence and excess burden", *Regional Science and Urban Economics*, Vol. 14/4, pp. 547-563.

Tang, Z. et al. (2005), "Forecasting land use change and its environmental impact at a watershed scale", *Journal of Environmental Management*, Vol. 76, pp. 35-45.

Taylor, B.D. et al. (2009), "Nature and/or nurture? Analyzing the determinants of transit ridership across U.S. urbanized areas" *Transportation Research Part A: Policy and Practice*, Vol. 43/1, pp. 60-77.

Turnbull, G.K. (1988), "Residential development in an open city", *Regional Science and Urban Economics*, Vol. 18/2, pp. 307-320.

United States Environmental Protection Agency (EPA) (1994), *The Quality of our Nation's Water: 1992*, Report #EPA-841-S-94-002, US EPA Office of Water Quality, Washington, DC.

Ürge-Vorsatz, D. et al. (2007), "Mitigating CO_2 emissions from energy use in the world's buildings", *Building Research and Information*, Vol. 35/4, pp. 379-398.

Wheaton, W.C. (1974), "A comparative static analysis of urban spatial structure", *Journal of Economic Theory*, Vol. 9/2, pp. 223-237.

Wilson, B. and A. Chakraborty (2013), "The environmental impacts of sprawl: Emergent themes from the past decade of planning research", *Sustainability*, Vol. 5/8, pp. 3302-3327.

Wu, J.J., M. Fisher and U. Pascual (2011), "Urbanization and the viability of local agricultural economies", *Land Economics*, Vol. 87/1, pp. 109-125.

Zhao, Z. and R. Kaestner (2010), "Effects of urban sprawl on obesity", *Journal of Health Economics*, 29/6, pp. 779-787.

Rethinking Urban Sprawl
Moving Towards Sustainable Cities

PART II

Chapter 5

Steering urban development to more sustainable pathways

This chapter discusses policies to control urban sprawl and direct urban development to more sustainable pathways. It describes a number of land-use and transport policy instruments that can be used to achieve these objectives and analyses their potential benefits, but also the challenges arising in their implementation. The land-use policy instruments analysed include urban containment policies (e.g. greenbelts, urban growth boundaries), minimum density restrictions, property taxation, development rights and incentives for private provision of public infrastructure. Road pricing, parking policies, motor fuel taxes and investments in sustainable transport infrastructure are the main transport-related policy instruments considered in this chapter. The chapter also highlights the importance of taking into account interactions between different instruments when it comes to the development of urban policy. Finally, it emphasises the need for an integrated approach to make urban development patterns more sustainable.

5.1. Introduction

In many OECD cities, urban development patterns are environmentally, economically and socially unsustainable. Emissions of greenhouse gases and harmful air pollutants are increasing, income inequality is rising and economic growth is hampered by congestion and high costs of providing public services. As discussed in Chapter 4, in many cases, urban sprawl underlies these problems.

Urban sprawl has important private benefits, which should, however, be weighed against their social costs. Urban sprawl is to some extent the result of individual preferences for more space, comfort, safety, privacy, easier access to natural amenities and an aversion to the noise and pollution usually encountered in densely populated areas. It is important to notice, however, that such private benefits of urban sprawl are generally internalised in market prices, and are thus reflected in property values in suburban areas. In sharp contrast, the external costs of urban sprawl, as presented in Chapter 4, are not incurred by property owners in suburban areas. As market forces fail to take external costs into account, policy intervention is in many cases necessary to achieve desirable environmental, economic and social outcomes.

This chapter discusses policies to mitigate the environmental and economic costs of urban sprawl. The chapter describes an array of land-use and transport policy instruments that can be used to this end and discusses their merits and drawbacks. It also provides a word of caution regarding the possible side-effects of policies to control sprawl. In addition, it explains the critical role of policy interactions, both between sectoral policies, e.g. transport and land-use policy, and between policies implemented by different jurisdictions, e.g. by local authorities and national governments. The chapter also emphasises the need for following an integrated approach to direct urban development to more sustainable pathways.

Drawing direct links between specific dimensions of urban sprawl and policy instruments is usually very complex. Most of the policies analysed in this chapter are likely to affect more than one dimension of the phenomenon. For example, the introduction of road pricing would encourage denser and – probably – less fragmented urban forms, as it would increase the private costs of car use, inducing households to move closer to their jobs and their daily activities. However, policies do not always influence different dimensions of urban sprawl in the same way: in fact, a number of policies can affect different dimensions of the phenomenon in opposite ways. For example, while urban containment policies, such as greenbelts, may increase average population density, they can also increase fragmentation and the share of urban population residing in areas of very low density. The reason for this is that, under specific circumstances, greenbelts can cause leapfrog development in remote areas.

The heterogeneity of the impacts of policy instruments on urban sprawl highlights the usefulness of the approach developed in this report. The multidimensional definition and the indicators of sprawl presented in the previous chapters enable a deeper understanding of the impact of each policy on urban form and a more informed assessment of its effectiveness in mitigating the environmental and economic problems caused by urban sprawl. The discussion of specific policy instruments later in the chapter draws to the extent possible on the potential impacts of each instrument on different dimensions of sprawl.

Providing policy recommendations that retain their validity across highly heterogeneous urban settings is particularly challenging. Each city is a unique socioeconomic system, where only a small set of policy mixes can be economically efficient, environmentally effective and socially acceptable. However, different urban areas often face similar environmental and economic challenges. Provided that the behaviour of individuals and firms is guided by the same economic principles in all urban areas, it is possible to identify policy options which are likely to help meeting these challenges in different urban contexts.

Urban sprawl may be manifested at the city level, but its causes and consequences are not contained by the urban limits. Greenhouse gas emissions stemming from sprawling urban forms contribute to climate change and pressures on local finance, which often lead to additional burden for national or regional budgets. Local policy action to address the negative effects of sprawl, e.g. at the municipality or county level, can be undermined by the action of neighbouring local authorities which may engage in policies favouring sprawl or refrain from policy action for their own interests. These challenges call for action from national and regional governments to curb the consequences of urban sprawl.

The policy directions discussed in this chapter are in alignment with the targets of the United Nations' SDG 11, which aims at promoting inclusive, safe, resilient and sustainable cities. Among others, these targets pertain to: i) the reduction of the adverse per capita environmental impact of cities; ii) the support of positive economic, social and environmental links between urban, periurban and rural areas by strengthening national and regional development planning; and iii) access to safe, affordable, accessible and sustainable transport systems for all by 2030 (United Nations, 2015).

The structure of the chapter is as follows. Section 5.2 discusses concrete policy actions to control urban sprawl and mitigate its consequences. Section 5.3 highlights the importance of considering interactions between policy instruments and following an integrated approach to designing and implementing urban policies. Section 5.4 concludes.

5.2. Taking steps to reverse unsustainable urban development patterns

Developing the right policies to reverse the unsustainable trends often observed in urban development is a very challenging task. This section does not attempt to provide city-specific guidance on promoting sustainable urban development. Instead, it discusses a set of policy actions which can help achieve sustainable urban development in the long run in various urban settings. Policy actions are categorised according to the main objectives they aim to achieve: promoting socially desirable levels of population density; or mitigating the adverse environmental and economic effects of sprawl-induced car use. The proposed policy actions are not equally relevant for each urban area: their relevance and potential effectiveness depends *inter alia* on geomorphological factors, population growth and the governance system. Policy instruments which are powerful in specific contexts may have negligible effects or even lead to undesirable consequences in different contexts. The section also puts forward some general directions for the development of policies to control urban sprawl and address its consequences.

Promoting socially desirable levels of urban density and fragmentation

Urban sprawl is manifested in low-density and fragmented development, which may have serious environmental and economic implications. Car dependency and accompanying emissions from car use, loss of open space, and high costs of providing public services, such as waste management, public transport, water supply and wastewater treatment, are some of these implications, which have been discussed in detail in Chapter 4.

High density and contiguity are important characteristics of sustainable urban development, but it is also important to mention some caveats. First, high density should not be considered as a synonym for high average density. Certain cities may be overall dense, while also containing large artificial areas of very low density. Such a development pattern will rarely be sustainable. Thus, policies promoting densification may also be very relevant in the case of these cities. Second, while high-density development can help prevent multiple environmental pressures, it also increases population exposure to a given level of air pollution, noise and natural disaster risks. The external costs of air emissions and noise increase with population density and, thus, corrective policies (e.g. taxes or pollution-control regulation) should be more stringent in high-density areas. At the same time, high-density development in areas vulnerable to natural disasters (e.g. earthquakes, floods, tsunamis) entails higher risks for residents which should be reflected in higher property insurance premiums and/or stricter building codes. Third, infill development policies that incentivise the connection of existing urban fragments should account for the impact such development may have on biodiversity. For example, special care is required when designing policies connecting fragments in suburban areas, as such development may block corridors that are critical for local biodiversity. Infill development should take place in a way that does not induce further natural habitat fragmentation. In case urban development leads to further fragmentation of natural habitats, policy instruments aimed at offsetting or compensating for biodiversity losses need to be considered.

Traditionally, spatial planning and land-use policy has overwhelmingly relied on regulatory instruments to control urban sprawl and mitigate its consequences. Regulatory instruments are used to determine where urban development will take place, where specific land uses will be allowed, and in many cases how urban population will be distributed across space. Regulatory instruments vary *inter alia* in terms of stringency, spatial and temporal control, and links with public infrastructure needs. Despite their widespread use, it is not clear whether, and under what conditions, these instruments eventually result in denser or less fragmented cities.

Land-use policy has leveraged market-based instruments, including taxes on immovable property, and purchase and transfer of development rights, to a much lesser extent to promote socially desirable levels of density and fragmentation. Immovable property taxes are ubiquitous in OECD countries, but they are mostly viewed only as a revenue raising mechanism. By contrast, their potential to encourage more sustainable land-use patterns largely remains to be explored.

Reform urban containment policies

Urban containment policies are perhaps the most direct form of policy intervention to control urban expansion. They essentially set boundaries to urban development, motivated by intentions to protect surrounding forestland and farmland, reduce the costs of public service provision and induce development in vacant land within the contained area (infill development). *Greenbelts* and *urban growth boundaries* are the most popular urban containment policies. Box 5.1 defines these two types of policies and describes their main characteristics.

Box 5.1. **Greenbelts and urban growth boundaries**

A *greenbelt* is a band of natural open space surrounding an urban area, which is designated to function as a permanent boundary to the expansion of the city. In contrast to other land-use policies which are introduced by local authorities, greenbelt policies are often developed at the national or regional level. They are created through public acquisition of open space, purchase of development rights, or through regulation of private property (Bengston, Fletcher, and Nelson, 2004; Bengston and Youn, 2006). Greenbelts are common in the UK, Germany and Korea, while they have also been implemented in urban areas of other OECD countries, including Australia, Canada and the US (Amati, 2016; Bae and Jun, 2003; Lee and Linneman, 1998; Siedentop, Fina, and Krehl, 2016; Taylor, Paine, and FitzGibbon, 1995; Vyn, 2012).

Urban growth boundaries are limits to urban expansion set around the urban area, with the purpose of protecting its surroundings from urban encroachment. In contrast to greenbelts, urban growth boundaries are not intended to be permanent; instead, they are periodically evaluated and, if necessary, expanded. Urban growth boundaries are generally implemented by the use of regulatory policy instruments. Likewise, *urban service boundaries* designate the area within which public services, such as water supply and sewerage, are offered. Provision of these services outside of the boundaries is not permitted. Urban service boundaries are sometimes used in combination with adequate public facilities ordinances to prevent urban expansion beyond the designated area (Bengston, Fletcher, and Nelson, 2004).

Sources: Amati, 2016; Bae and Jun, 2003; Bengston, Fletcher, and Nelson, 2004; Bengston and Youn, 2006; Lee and Linneman, 1998; Siedentop, Fina, and Krehl, 2016; Taylor, Paine, and FitzGibbon, 1995; Vyn, 2012.

Urban containment policies are generally very effective in achieving their objectives, i.e. protecting designated open space and inducing infill development. Infill development results in a denser and possibly less fragmented *contained area*. However, these features do not extend to the rest of the urban area (Bengston and Youn, 2006; Gennaio, Hersperger, and Bürgi, 2009). That is, urban containment policies are known to give rise to leapfrog development beyond the contained area, which often implies an overall more fragmented, and probably less dense, urban area. In turn, these characteristics induce longer commuting distances (Amati and Yokohari, 2006; Bae and Jun, 2003; Bengston and Youn, 2006; Jun, 2004; Vyn, 2012), increase emissions from mobile sources and raise the costs of public transport provision (see also Chapter 4). The above effects are further fuelled by the fact that the modal split depends on the commuting distance. Thus, not only does leapfrog development increase distances between key points of economic activity, but it also affects positively the probability that these will be covered with private vehicles. Thus, the magnitude of the side-effects associated with urban containment policies should be carefully evaluated.

A key determinant of the magnitude of the side-effects of urban containment policies is the amount of developable land remaining in the inbound area, i.e. the area between existing developments and the greenbelt or the growth boundary (see e.g. Siedentop, Fina and Krehl, 2016). A low potential for new urban development in the inbound area may lead to a significant reduction in the elasticity of housing supply, which will, in turn, trigger increases in housing prices (see also Blöchliger et al., 2017; Caldera Sánchez and Johansson, 2011). The higher the increase in housing prices is, the stronger the incentives for leapfrog development are. In contrast, when the containment policy leaves sufficient space for urban development in the inbound area, the extent of leapfrog development is likely to be limited. In that case, however, urban development in the contained area might not be as dense as desired (Siedentop, Fina and Krehl, 2016).

An important determinant of the effectiveness of urban containment policies is their flexibility, especially in terms of allowing for periodic reviews and, if necessary, reforms. For example, a major criticism of greenbelts concerns their permanent character. This lack of flexibility may undermine the effectiveness of the policy, especially when it is implemented in urban areas facing rapid population and economic growth. Increases in housing prices, and leapfrog development in areas beyond the greenbelt are reinforced by the stringency of the policy and significant population pressures that may be present (Amati and Yokohari, 2006; Bae and Jun, 2003; Lee and Linneman, 1998).[1]

The effectiveness of urban containment policies is also influenced by the governance system. In a decentralised system, where the various jurisdictions have the power to administer their own spatial planning and land-use policies, leapfrogging can be intense. This is because the jurisdictions whose fiscal dominion lies beyond the contained area may attempt to attract residents and businesses by implementing laxer policy frameworks than jurisdictions within the contained area. In centralised systems, it is much easier to ensure that individuals are not provided any perverse incentives to reside beyond the contained area. This practice, however, may reduce the price elasticity of housing supply (as developers will be allowed to build in very few locations) and result in higher housing prices and lower housing affordability (Ball et al., 2014; Bengston and Youn, 2006; Blöchliger et al., 2017).

Leapfrogging would be much less of an environmental concern if firms were closely following the movement of their labour pool. In that case, leapfrog developments would eventually be transformed to new urban centres, a polycentric urban structure would emerge and commuting would be largely limited within each centre. However, real-world examples of urban containment policies, such as Seoul's greenbelt, show that in the absence of strong relocation incentives, firms may not be willing to forego the benefits of agglomeration economies in the contained area (see e.g. Bae and Jun, 2003).

Apart from their potential side-effects on urban expansion, external environmental and congestion costs, and housing prices, urban containment policies have also been heavily criticised for creating winners and losers, who see the values of their properties change (in some cases, dramatically). Losers are frequently not compensated for the fall in their property values.[2] In the absence of mechanisms to compensate the losers, the policy will be perceived as unjust and pressures for policy change may be triggered. It is, thus, important to accompany urban containment policies with instruments providing some form of compensation to the losers from the policy intervention.

In summary, urban containment policies are likely to have side-effects, manifested in leapfrog development, excessive commuting and increased housing prices, which can jeopardise their effectiveness in controlling urban sprawl and tackling environmental problems. The magnitude of these side-effects depends *inter alia* on: i) the level of centralisation of the governance system, ii) the stringency of the policy (amount of developable land in the contained area), and iii) the stringency of other land-use and transport policies implemented in the urban area. To some extent, such side-effects can be prevented by introducing a small level of flexibility in stringent urban containment policies, and, most important, by coupling them with laxer density limits.

Relax maximum density restrictions

Maximum density restrictions are common in urban areas of OECD countries and beyond. Most often taking the form of building height restrictions, i.e. limits on building floor-to-area ratios, these policies inevitably hamper densification (Bertaud and Brueckner, 2005; Brueckner and Sridhar, 2012). Despite being relevant in specific locations, such as close to airports, historic buildings or other elements of cultural heritage, stringent maximum density regulations are in many cases unwarranted. Such regulations may lead to low average density levels and, when being overly stringent, are likely to increase the share of urban footprint hosting very low density levels, with important environmental implications (e.g. in emissions) presented in detail in Chapter 4.

Policy makers should be aware of the negative interactions between maximum density regulations and urban containment policies. When the restrictions imposed by these regulatory instruments are too stringent, leapfrog development in remote areas and soaring housing prices in the contained area are very likely outcomes. One of the few cases that this combination of stringent instruments may not have undesirable consequences is when areas in the vicinity of the contained area are zoned for high-density development. Otherwise, actions to relax policy stringency are warranted in order to direct urban development to a more sustainable pathway with lower levels of fragmentation, a more elastic supply of residential floor space and more affordable housing. Such actions may be justified even in the absence of urban containment policies. Further to upzoning (i.e. allowing higher densities than the ones permitted before), it may also be worth considering introducing minimum density restrictions in areas where densification is mostly needed (see also Bengston, Fletcher, and Nelson, 2004; Silva and Acheampong, 2015). It should be noted that relaxing quantity restrictions in housing markets may prove to be a policy challenge *per se*. Current homeowners often have strong incentives to lobby in favour of building height restrictions, as well as other types of regulatory mechanisms that reduce the supply of floor space (Fischel, 2001; Schuetz, 2009), as such regulations may increase the housing prices of the existing dwelling stock (e.g. Ihlanfeldt, 2007).

Reform property taxation to better reflect the social cost of certain urban development patterns

Property taxes are the most commonly used market-based instrument applied to land use. A property tax is a recurrent *ad valorem* tax on immovable property, usually levied by the local authority of the jurisdiction where the property is located. In practice, the primary objective of property taxation has been to raise public revenues for the financing of local services (see e.g. Brandt, 2014), rather than to address the negative externalities of urban development. For example, in Italy, property taxes accounted for about 48% of total municipal revenue in 2010 (Ermini and Santolini, 2017).

In most countries, property taxes are levied on both land and land improvements, i.e. buildings and other structures (Bird and Slack, 2004). This form of taxing property has been argued to be a combination of one of the least distortionary taxes – the tax on land value – and one of the most distortionary ones, the tax on land improvements (Vickrey, 1996). Box 5.2 discusses the merits of land value taxes, but also the possible challenges in their implementation.

Box 5.2. **Land value taxes**

A land value tax is essentially a tax on an economic rent and, thus, it does not discourage any desirable economic activity, such as labour supply or investment. The amount of land is fixed and land supply is fully inelastic – at least in the absence of regulatory land-use policy. This entails that after-tax prices of land would be equal to pre-tax prices and the tax burden would be fully incurred by landowners. The tax burden on landowners does not distort economic efficiency and has long been advocated as a fair outcome (Mirrlees et al., 2011). Land rents reflect windfall gains made by landowners as a result of community efforts (e.g. construction of public infrastructure) and land-use regulation; they do not stem from effortful activity from their side (George, 1879).

Land value taxes incentivise the allocation of land to its most valuable use, which will often be residential or commercial development. They will have desirable effects when it comes to unused land located close to existing infrastructure or in urban cores, as they will induce development where it is most needed. However, land value taxes could also induce development in other areas of high value, such as the ones close to ecologically sensitive areas, including forests and coastlines (Brandt, 2014). Thus, land value taxes would not necessarily lead to less sprawled cities or lower environmental pressures from development. This is why they should be used in combination with some form of regulatory or market-based policy instrument, which would discourage development in ecologically sensitive areas (e.g. zoning, or preferential tax treatment of agricultural and forestry use).

Despite their appeal on economic efficiency and equity grounds, land value taxes have rarely been used in reality. Administrative complexity in assessing land values and political economy reasons explain to a large extent the lack of real-world applications. One of the most important challenges in their implementation is the difficulty in disentangling the value of the land from the value of the improvements made on it (Mirrlees et al., 2011). However, obstacles to the implementation of land value taxes are not always insurmountable and economic arguments for their implementation are strong. Hence, it is important that they are not left completely unconsidered by policy makers.

Sources: Brandt, 2014; George, 1879; Mirrlees et al., 2011.

The direction of the effect of property taxes on urban density is highly uncertain, even on theoretical grounds. Most property tax systems apply the same rates to the value of land and buildings. As discussed in Chapter 4, higher property taxes may result, *ceteris paribus*, in lower land prices, especially when land supply tends to be inelastic. In that case, an increase in the property tax rate may induce development with a lower floor-to-area ratio and a larger footprint, resulting in a less dense urban structure. On the other hand, higher property taxes increase house prices and, therefore, reduce the demand for residential space. Smaller properties imply a smaller urban footprint, more densely developed areas and less land being devoted to urban use. The direction of the effect of single-rate property taxes on urban density is, therefore, theoretically unclear (Brueckner and Kim, 2003).[3] The relatively thin empirical literature investigating the effect of property taxation on urban sprawl does not lead to conclusive evidence either.[4]

Urban areas usually encompass multiple jurisdictions (e.g. municipalities or counties), which set different property tax rates for the same type of land use. Jurisdictions in the hinterlands often set lower rates than jurisdictions at the core of the urban area to attract more residents and firms. However, lower tax rates in the suburban fringe are very likely to act as levers for different manifestations of urban sprawl, especially decentralisation and low density. Empirical evidence from the US and Italy provides support to this argument (Ermini and Santolini, 2017; Song and Zenou, 2009). It is, thus, worth considering removing such incentives for decentralised and low-density development.

Consider using split-rate property taxes

A more targeted fiscal instrument to promote denser development is a *split-rate*, or two-rate, *property tax*, whereby higher tax rates are set on the value of land than on the value of buildings and other property improvements. Higher rates on land values in urban centres would discourage keeping land undeveloped (or underdeveloped) therein and, thus, reduce pressures on development at the rural-urban fringe.[5] Such higher rates would also incentivise the redevelopment of urban brownfields, i.e. unused or underutilised commercial, industrial or residential sites where redevelopment is obstructed by contamination (see e.g. McCarthy, 2002; United States Environmental Protection Agency, 2017). Lower relative tax rates on the value of buildings and other improvements would further incentivise owners to build more intensively or renovate their properties to increase their value. That would enhance the base for property taxation in urban centres and reduce pressures on local finance (Gihring, 1999).

The location where split-rate taxes are implemented is a key determinant of their contribution to the control of urban sprawl (Banzhaf and Lavery, 2010; Gihring, 1999). For example, a combination of a (relatively) high tax on developed land and a (relatively) low tax on buildings at the urban fringe may incentivise the construction of higher buildings and be effective in decelerating the expansion of urban footprint. Such a split-rate tax could increase local density at the fringe, reducing this way the share of population residing in low-density areas and the portion of developed land hosting low density levels. On the other hand, the effect of a split-rate tax on fragmentation is unknown, as a substantial divergence of the two taxes may slow down any local infill development between existing fragments of urban fabric.

Despite their potential effectiveness in increasing urban density, the design and implementation of split-rate taxes is a challenging exercise. This is why they have seen very few applications thus far, and those are almost entirely concentrated in the United States. A major challenge in their application in policy practice is the separation of the value of land from the value of the improvements constructed on it. The implementation of split-rate taxes may also be deterred for political economy reasons (Cohen and Coughlin, 2005).

Develop incentive-based mechanisms to prevent the conversion of farmland and forestland

In many cities, the assessment of property values or the property tax rate varies according to land use. For example, *preferential*, or *use-value*, *tax assessment* is a commonly used instrument in the United States (Anderson, 1993). It provides tax incentives to owners of farmland, forestland and other types of undeveloped land to keep it in its current use, rather than sell it for urban development. This is achieved by taxing land at a *lower value* when it is used for e.g. agriculture or forestry than when it is allocated to residential or commercial uses (Bengston et al., 2004).

In other urban areas, the preservation of farmland and forestland is encouraged through *lower tax rates* on land used for agricultural or forestry purposes (Brandt, 2014). This instrument entails a direct link between the value of the property and the tax benefit that can be obtained from the preservation in its current use. Owners of properties of higher values, such as those close to urban centres or those near environmentally sensitive areas, will have stronger incentives to keep land in its current use. While this might be desirable for the latter, it may not be desirable for properties close to urban cores.

Similarly to the market-based instruments discussed above, spatial targeting is key for the success of policies aiming to prevent the conversion of farmland and forestland. Limiting the use of such incentive mechanisms to relatively undeveloped areas at the outskirts of the city, or close to environmentally sensitive areas (providing that current uses are sustainable and contribute to – rather than harm – the surrounding ecosystem) can prevent further fragmentation of urban development and decentralisation.

Consider developing policies based on development rights

Policies based on development rights are grounded in the idea that land ownership is equivalent to the ownership of a bundle of separable rights, such as mineral rights and development rights (Mills, 1980). *Purchase of development rights* is an instrument frequently used for the protection of open space. The land-owner sells the development rights to the government (or alternatively to a private non-profit organisation) and the land is permanently set aside for conservation purposes. From the government's perspective, purchase of development rights can be much less expensive than public acquisition of land in areas where development pressures are low (Bengston et al., 2004).

A more relevant instrument to promote densification and reduce the fragmentation of urban fabric is, however, the transfer of development rights. *Transferable*, or *tradable, development rights* (TDRs) allow the transfer of density between properties. Almost all TDR schemes developed thus far have been set up in areas where some form of zoning policy had already been in place. More stringent development restrictions apply to the property selling the development rights, whereas the property purchasing the rights is allowed to be more densely developed than what is permitted under baseline zoning.[6] Sending and receiving properties are usually located in different areas, but there are also cases where they are located in the same area (McConnell and Walls, 2009).[7]

TDR programmes are advocated for their potential to achieve the desired level of development – and therefore of open space conservation – in a cost-effective manner, and for their distributional benefits. For TDR schemes to have these desirable properties, key is the establishment of the correct cap, i.e. the total amount of development allowed by the scheme, and the allocation of a sufficient number of development rights to achieve that level of development.[8] Trade of development rights then ensures that each land parcel is devoted to its most efficient use, provided that the market is sufficiently large and competitive (i.e. no participant has market power), and market participants have complete information (Levinson, 1997; McConnell and Walls, 2009; Mills, 1980). Benefits of TDR schemes are not limited to economic efficiency gains. In comparison with policies based on land-use regulation only (e.g. zoning), TDRs can also help address equity concerns. This is because they can lend themselves to compensation mechanisms for landowners whose properties are located in sending areas – areas where development is constrained for conservation or other purposes (Mills, 1980). What is more, compensation is not provided by scarce public funds, but instead through market forces. This attribute of development rights is clearly manifested in cases where they were provided in response to the re-zoning of specific areas. For example, they have been used to compensate landowners in areas which have been downzoned (McConnell and Walls, 2009).

TDR schemes can be particularly useful as a complement to other policies promoting densification, such as upzoning or minimum density restrictions. Nevertheless, the success of TDR programmes heavily relies on the level of activity in the TDR market. Market activity is generally higher when: (a) baseline zoning in sending areas is relatively stringent; and (b) demand for additional density in receiving areas – determined by both the discrepancy between desired and current density and the willingness of existing residents to accept higher density developments in their vicinity – is high.[9] On the other hand, activity in the TDR market can be hampered by: (a) high transaction costs (e.g. pecuniary and time costs incurred in search of information about TDR prices);[10] (b) additional requirements imposed on developers; and (c) the presence of other instruments allowing increased density in receiving areas (McConnell and Walls, 2009; Pruetz and Standridge, 2008).

Incentivise developers to provide public infrastructure for new constructions

More contiguous and centralised development can also be promoted through instruments requiring developers to cover – at least to some extent – the costs of providing public infrastructure to new constructions. *Development impact fees* are fees levied on developers to help pay for the capital costs of providing public infrastructure to new developments (Bengston et al., 2004; Juergensmeyer and Roberts, 2013, p. 319). Even though an instrument primarily used to finance the development of public infrastructure, development impact fees can act as powerful levers to direct urban expansion to areas closer to existing infrastructure (Bengston et al., 2004). As costs of constructing new infrastructure are lower in these areas, developers are indirectly incentivised to build in contiguous land.

Mitigating the environmental and economic consequences of sprawl-induced car use

Sustainable urban development cannot be achieved without greening urban transport systems and shifting travel demand towards other modes, such as public and non-motorised transport. Several dimensions of urban sprawl, such as low density, fragmentation and decentralisation, are strongly interlinked with car use, as it has been highlighted in Chapter 4. Travel distances are longer and the provision of public transport is significantly more costly in sprawling cities. This way, car becomes the most attractive, and for specific trip purposes, the only sensible transport alternative. Car dependency translates to immediate external effects, such as congestion and environmental externalities, which have to be mitigated. It also has long-run implications, as households and firms adjust their long-term decisions accordingly. That is, households will choose residences far from their workplace and shopping malls will be located far from their clients. This pattern creates a vicious circle where car dependency leads to even higher car use and additional needs for extensions of the road network and expansions of its capacity. This has important consequences for the environment and economic growth, manifested in significant increases in emissions, losses of open space and productive and valuable time lost in congestion.

The policies discussed here can lead to more sustainable urban transport patterns and mitigate some of the environmental and economic consequences of urban sprawl. Through changing the paradigm of urban mobility, they may also have significant long-term effects on the evolution of urban form itself. The discussion that follows focuses on a range of policies, including road pricing, parking policies, subsidies for public transport and motor fuel taxes. It also touches upon the potential effects of infrastructure investments, such as investments in road capacity expansion, on urban sprawl.

Introduce road pricing mechanisms

Motorists are rarely charged for the externalities they cause: congestion that implies time losses incurred by other road users; air pollution, with health consequences for the urban population; emissions of greenhouse gases, with global implications for climate.

Congestion leads to notable losses of productive time and, therefore, to significant economic costs. Schrank et al. (2012) show that congestion caused 5.5 billion hours of delay in the United States in 2011, a number that roughly corresponds to a total time cost close to 0.9% of the GDP. In the same year, congestion caused a fuel waste of USD 121 billion, i.e. an additional 0.78% of the country's GDP (not taking into account the associated external costs of fuel combustion). Regarding air pollution, it is well known that a substantial part of the emissions in urban areas originates from the use of private vehicles. The economic consequences of air pollution have been examined at the global scale in OECD (2016).

Efficient road pricing requires that the above costs are well reflected in road charges. As the aforementioned externality costs vary across road segments, charges should be higher in more congested and more densely populated parts of urban space, and *vice versa*. In addition, an ideal pricing scheme should also be time-variant, as traffic levels vary across time intervals of a given day and across days of the week. This ultimately entails that congestion charges should vary across routes and time intervals (Anas and Lindsey, 2011). As air emissions largely depend on fuel type, pollution control technologies, the weight and vintage of the car, optimal charges should also vary by car model and vintage.

Apart from mitigating the direct consequences of unsustainable urban patterns, road pricing mechanisms may provide long-run incentives for denser, more contiguous development, as they could shorten distances between residential locations and key points of economic activity. On top of the spatial configuration of a given area, the long-run effect of road pricing on urban form depends on two important parameters. First, the technical features of the implemented scheme determine who is going to be affected by it. That is, the extent to which the scheme obliges drivers to internalise the external effects of car use determines the size of the population groups for which *short-run responses* to it (e.g. switching to public transport, shorter shopping and leisure trips with car) and *long-run adjustments* (e.g. household relocation, change of employment location) are relevant. A pricing scheme is therefore more likely to affect urban form (in the long run) when it affects the behaviour of a relatively larger population group, i.e. when it leaves a relatively smaller portion of traffic unpriced. Second, the effect of a road pricing policy on urban form depends on its potential to induce long-run adjustments to the behaviour of the affected groups. In that sense, permanent road pricing schemes may induce higher density levels around major employment locations, especially if the regulatory mechanisms in land and housing markets are laxer.[11]

Optimal road pricing instruments are very effective in mitigating traffic externalities and in greening urban transport. In addition, they may play an auxiliary role in inducing desirable changes in urban form in the long run. However, time- and space-variant optimal road charges are costly to implement in practice, mainly due to the large costs of installing the required infrastructure. Therefore, road pricing schemes that are simpler in administrative terms may currently be more feasible to implement. The following analysis focuses on two such types of second-best road pricing schemes, i.e. cordon tolls and flat kilometre taxes, their potential to mitigate the external effects of car use (mainly air pollution and congestion) and the extent to which they could influence the evolution of urban form, as the latter was presented in Chapter 2 and measured in Chapter 3.

Cordon tolls

Cordon tolls charge all inbound (and sometimes also outbound) trips to a certain bounded area, which usually encompasses a central business district. These charges are distance-invariant, in the sense that a given driver pays the same fee when entering or exiting the bounded area, regardless of the total length of the trip. In general, cordon tolls are more effective in reducing congestion in urban settings resembling monocentric cities, in which the vast majority of peak-hour car trips are destined to locations inside the cordon (Mun et al., 2003, 2005; Verhoef, 2005). The measure has been shown to reduce car traffic considerably. For example, a fee on cars entering or exiting Stockholm's inner city has been shown to reduce car traffic around charging points by 22% (Eliasson et al., 2009). Because congestion is a non-linear phenomenon, i.e. small reductions in traffic levels may give rise to substantial time savings, travel times in parts of the network fell by more than 22%. From an environmental point of view, the cordon toll reduces aggregate emissions by inducing changes in the modal split, i.e. by inducing some car users to switch to public transport or other modes. It also increases urban travel speeds to levels where fuel consumption per kilometre is lower. Because in many cases the time savings are associated with fewer traffic jams occurring in network bottlenecks, the scheme may help reduce the non-exhaust emissions arising from queuing (e.g. wear and tear in brakes and tyres, which is more intense with start-and-stop driving). In Stockholm, the reduction in air pollutant concentrations inside the cordon was estimated to lie between 10% and 14% (depending on the pollutant), although it was found to be substantially smaller for nitrogen oxides (8.5%).

Policy makers should also keep in mind that a cordon toll increases the accessibility of locations lying within the bounded area, as all trips with origin and destination within that area go uncharged. Therefore, the measure creates a long run centripetal force which increases demand for land and housing (and, in turn, their respective prices) within the cordon. Therefore, the *ceteris paribus* effect of that force on average population density could be significantly positive, provided that housing supply within the cordon is elastic. The effect on the allocation indicators presented in Chapter 2 is more perplexed. That is, cordon tolls are expected to increase the average population density in locations within the cordon and reduce it in locations outside of it, but the overall effect on the two indicators depends on the relative change between the two areas. Finally, with such a policy all traffic in locations outside the cordoned area goes unpriced. Thus the policy *per se* should not be expected to affect fragmentation levels in periurban areas significantly.

Flat kilometre taxes

The drawbacks of a cordon toll scheme call for a distance-based charge that accounts for the strong positive correlation between the external costs of a trip and its length. The recent technological advances made the use of Global Positioning Systems (GPS) with tracking devices cheaper and easier to implement. These technologies have made the introduction of a flat kilometre tax in an urban area a meaningful alternative to a cordon toll. Under this scheme, the use of private vehicles is charged on a distance basis, but only within the predetermined boundaries of the implementation zone. The tax is flat in the sense that it does not vary across space or over time. From an environmental point of view, the measure complements motor fuel taxes: it increases the kilometre costs of car use in areas where the external costs of it (congestion, pollution) are particularly high and allows motor fuel taxes to be used for pricing carbon emissions and possibly other policy purposes.

The long-run effect of a flat kilometre tax on urban form is very different from that of a cordon toll. *Ceteris paribus*, the former scheme contributes to more compact development, in which jobs, residences and key points of economic activity lie closer to each other. In monocentric settings, this translates to an overall densification (higher average population density) and a decrease in the share of population residing in areas of very low density (below 1 500 inhabitants per km^2) Furthermore, distance-based charging in monocentric settings is expected to decrease fragmentation, because leapfrog development, which is usually occurring in remote areas, becomes more expensive. In polycentric cities, distance-based charges may have significantly different effects.

Possible distributional effects of road pricing schemes, as well as interactions between road pricing and the fiscal system should be taken into consideration prior to implementation. Specific types of road pricing, such as cordon tolls, are likely to create winners and losers or distribute their welfare gains unequally. In these cases, recycling revenue in a way that favours the affected areas and population groups, such as earmarking revenues to subsidise public transport, may be warranted. Furthermore, labour supply from areas with limited accessibility to public transport is likely to be affected, especially if the toll levels are set high enough to reflect the social costs of generalised private vehicle use in these areas. The erosion of the labour income tax base due to a road toll in the commuting hours may at first appear as small. However, numerical simulations show that in a highly-distortionary fiscal framework it may be large enough to neutralise the welfare gains from the mitigation of the traffic-related externalities (Parry and Bento, 2001; Tikoudis, Verhoef and van Ommeren, 2015). To circumvent this issue, the aforementioned groups should be identified prior to the implementation of the scheme and offered a lower toll during the peak commuting hours.

In summary, policy makers should consider the introduction of road pricing as a meaningful alternative to massive investments in roads and highways, which have characterised public policy during the last decades. Urban congestion management is a meaningful alternative which, as demonstrated by the steadily increasing number of cities adopting it (e.g. London, Milan, Oslo, Singapore, Stockholm), is gaining momentum around the world. Road pricing, i.e. charges reflecting the costs of congestion, air pollution and other externalities of private vehicle use, is a very powerful policy instrument to influence travel behaviour and location choices. In the long run, road pricing is likely to incentivise infill development, encourage more polycentric structures and promote densification of urban areas. Those effects will be significantly stronger when road pricing is combined with efficient motor fuel taxes.

Increase motor fuel taxes to account for the marginal external costs of fuel consumption

Motor fuel consumption has significant environmental costs, caused by emissions of greenhouse gases and air pollutants. Despite the widespread use of motor fuel taxes in OECD countries and beyond, they are in many cases set at relatively low levels, which do not fully cover the marginal external costs of fuel consumption.[12] This is especially the case in countries where road pricing does not exist and motor fuel taxes are supposed to also reflect other externalities of car use (e.g. congestion). In most countries, taxes on diesel fuel are lower than those on gasoline, inducing more travel in (usually more polluting) diesel cars (Harding, 2014). Setting motor fuel taxes at lower than desirable levels has similar effects on car use and urban form as leaving congestion unpriced. It leads to excessive car use and in the long-run to more sprawling city structures, characterised by sparser and more decentralised development. It is thus important that motor fuel taxes are set at levels fully accounting for the environmental costs of fuel consumption and, in combination with road pricing, incentivise more sustainable urban development patterns.

Reform parking policy

Urban areas allocate enormous amounts of land to car parking. Parking spaces are provided on street, in residential and commercial buildings, in car parks and elsewhere. High parking supply not only induces expansion of the urban fabric because it consumes land that could be allocated to other – potentially more productive – uses, but also because it encourages car ownership and use. Households with easy access to parking spaces close to their residence and workplace are likely to own more cars than households who do not (De Groote, van Ommeren and Koster, 2016; Guo, 2013). In addition, the availability of a parking space at the origin and/or destination is an important determinant of one's decision to make a trip by car rather than by another transport mode (Weinberger, 2012).

Parking policy does not only influence households' modal choice: it also affects their choice of residence location. Widespread availability of low-priced parking spaces may well induce households to move further away from business centres as they can conveniently rely on their cars to cover their everyday needs.

Consider removing minimum parking requirements and replacing them with maximum ones

Policies aimed at regulating the supply of parking spaces have important effects on how an urban area is shaped and how car-dependent it becomes. *Minimum parking requirements* for residential and commercial buildings are widespread in OECD countries and beyond. In practice, this regulatory instrument usually requires developers to provide a sufficient number of parking spaces to cover peak demand for free parking (Shoup, 1999a). In most cases, minimum parking requirements were established to provide low-priced off-street parking to motorists, so that local congestion (caused by cars cruising to find a parking space) is prevented and local business is stimulated (Shoup, 1999a, 1999b). However, minimum parking requirements result in more parking spaces per parcel than what would have been provided if developers were free to decide how many spaces they would offer (Cutter and Franco, 2012). They drive building costs up and, therefore, discourage new development (Shoup, 1999a). They also encourage car use, as the oversupply of parking spaces decreases the total costs of urban trips by car (Manville, 2013). In sum, minimum parking requirements are very likely to lead eventually to less dense and more decentralised cities and unsustainable urban development (Willson, 1995). Therefore, it is worth considering the removal of minimum parking requirements for new developments.

The unintended consequences of minimum off-street parking requirements have induced policy makers to seek alternative instruments to regulate parking. Several major cities in the OECD, including London, New York City and Paris, have applied some form of *maximum parking requirements* for particular land uses. Evidence from London's major parking policy reform in 2004 shows that the replacement of minimum parking requirements with maximum ones led to a notable 49% reduction of parking spaces in new developments. The largest part of that change was due to the removal of the minimum parking requirements, which particularly affected developments in Inner London. In contrast, maximum parking requirements mainly affected new developments in London's suburbs (Li and Guo, 2014).

Price on-street parking appropriately

Parking policy is mainly based on the use of regulatory instruments. If on-street parking were priced at its marginal social cost, i.e. the sum of the costs of providing a parking space and the external costs of that space, the need for regulatory policies on off-street parking would be almost completely eliminated. The external costs of parking provision comprise the external costs of cruising for parking, stemming from the time losses caused by searching for a space, and the external costs of open space lost to convert land to parking space (see also Inci, 2015). External costs of congestion and air emissions vary across space and over time and, hence, parking tariffs should ideally be space- and time-variant (Vickrey, 1954, cited in Inci, 2015). Perhaps the most well-known real-world application of space- and time-varying parking tariffs is San Francisco's *SFpark* programme (see Pierce and Shoup, 2013).

In reality, however, on-street parking is significantly underpriced, and prices of parking spaces rarely cover the costs of provision – let alone external costs. The underpricing of on-street parking is well manifested in the important price differences existing in most cities between on-street and garage parking. If prices were equal, cruising for parking would, at least in theory, be eliminated (Inci, 2015). The underpricing of on-street parking can have important implications for urban sprawl, as it reduces the monetary costs of car trips, and therefore encourages car dependency.[13] Car dependency encourages lower density and more decentralised development, as households are anyway used to cover virtually all their travel needs by car. On-street parking prices reflecting the full costs of parking provision – including external costs – is an important instrument in policy makers' hands to control urban sprawl, raise public revenues and promote sustainable urban development.

Shift investments to more sustainable forms of transport infrastructure

Excessive investment in road transport infrastructure is responsible for more car use, higher emissions from road transport and urban sprawl. For example, it has been shown that the construction of highways induces urban areas to sprawl to remote locations and become more fragmented and decentralised (Garcia-López, Holl, and Viladecans-Marsal, 2015; Garcia-López, Solé-Ollé, and Viladecans-Marsal, 2015; Su and DeSalvo, 2008).

Shifting investments from new road transport infrastructure to public transport or to infrastructure for non-motorised modes (e.g. bikeways and sidewalks) is likely to lead in the long run to substantially less car use, deter further urban sprawl and induce infill development. It may also lead to more polycentric urban structures. The effects of this shift of investments will be reinforced when it is accompanied by efficient pricing of congestion, on-street parking and motor fuel consumption.

Increasing effectiveness and public acceptance of policies to mitigate urban sprawl's consequences

Regardless of the policy instrument used to control urban sprawl or mitigate its consequences, a number of actions can help design better policies and increase their public acceptance. For example, policy makers should take care to design policies which can control sprawl without impeding urbanisation, consider the long-term effects of proposed policies, ensure that they have well understood their possible distributional consequences and how they will be addressed, and be aware of their fiscal implications.

Control urban sprawl without hampering urbanisation

To address concerns over urban sprawl, it is important to understand the differences between that phenomenon and the phenomenon of urbanisation and identify whether urban development patterns are following an unsustainable path in a particular city context. This report can contribute to such efforts, as it indicates urban areas where development patterns may need increased attention from policy makers (see Chapter 3). In general, policies should focus on mitigating the consequences of urban sprawl without hampering urbanisation. Policies discouraging urbanisation may be detrimental for economic growth, as the latter has been shown to be fostered by the positive externalities arising from the clustering of people and firms in space, i.e. from the formation and growth of urban areas. By treating urban sprawl as a problem of city growth, policy makers may end up favouring interventions, such as restrictions in housing supply, that attempt to curtail the latter without offering a remedy to the environmental and economic consequences of urban sprawl.

Consider carefully the future social costs and benefits of land-use policy decisions

Policies implemented today will determine social costs and benefits in the medium and long run. Spatial planning and land-use policies have persistent long-term effects: land-use decisions taken today will lock cities in specific development patterns for many years to come. For example, postponing densification policies implies a higher future social cost of public transport provision and a lower frequency of service in a larger part of the urban area. In turn, that increases the likelihood of future adoption of policies favouring the use of private vehicles, such as investments in new roads. It is, thus, of primary importance that the long-term social benefits and costs of alternative urban policies are well understood before relevant decisions are made.

Share positive and negative experiences with policies to control urban sprawl

The environmental, economic and social effects of urban policies are highly context-specific. Although the same principles may apply to different urban settings, policies which are proven to be effective in one urban context will not necessarily be effective in other contexts. However, there are important lessons to be learnt from other cities' experiences with specific urban policies. A city may be similar to others in a number of aspects and, thus, policies which work in that city could also work in cities which are relatively similar to it. It is important that city authorities engage in further sharing of their urban policy experiences and highlight the policies that have been effective in achieving their objectives, as well as the ones that failed to do so.

Engage the public and relevant stakeholders

Communicating clearly the long-term benefits of green urban policies to the public and relevant stakeholders can increase support for these policies. In most cases, the public and other stakeholders may not be aware of the various environmental and economic consequences of rapid, uncontrolled expansion of the urban fabric. Furthermore, the vast majority of the population is not aware of the fiscal challenges related to providing low-density areas with public services. Therefore, public support of many of the seemingly unpopular policies aiming to control urban sprawl could be increased once their net social benefits are clearly conveyed to the public and other stakeholders. At the same time, consultation of the public and relevant stakeholders at an early stage of decision-making ensures that their voices and concerns are heard and facilitates the identification of possible complementary measures needed to compensate the losers from the policy intervention.[14]

Ensure that potential distributional consequences of green urban policies are minimised

Policies to control urban sprawl or mitigate its negative effects are sometimes abandoned due to concerns over their possible distributional consequences. However, these concerns are not always well-founded and in many cases distributional effects are overplayed. More importantly, even when green urban policies are anticipated to place a disproportionate burden on more vulnerable population groups, this burden can be removed by targeted compensatory mechanisms. For example, part of the revenues raised from tax-based instruments could be used to provide direct financial support to vulnerable households, e.g. in the form of tax credits. Another mechanism could involve earmarking a part of the revenues to develop policies that promote environmental quality in the areas where more vulnerable groups reside or to finance improvements in the function of the public transport system.

Consider whether policy instruments can contribute to fiscal consolidation

Green urban policies can also help governments at all levels consolidate their budgets. Unsustainable urban development patterns are often responsible for significant pressures on public finance. For example, providing public services to low-density or remote areas can be especially challenging from a financial perspective, and can even lead to large deficits. In many cities, the social cost of providing services in such areas should be internalised in development costs and housing prices to a greater extent. National and local governments should reconsider the substantial subsidies required to maintain the provision of public transport, water, sewerage and other goods and services, and seek alternative financing mechanisms that reflect better the external costs of urban sprawl (e.g. development impact fees).

Be committed to implemented policies

For urban policies to be successful, it is necessary that they are not perceived as short-term remedies which will be discontinued in the longer term. Governments should show commitment to implemented policies, so that all stakeholders are convinced to take them into account when making longer-term decisions. Given the time required by most urban land-use and transport policies for their long-run effects to kick in, it is important that government support of them extends beyond one or more terms of office.

5.3. Following an integrated approach to make urban development more sustainable

Urban development is heavily influenced by policy interactions, both between sectoral policies and between policies implemented by different jurisdictions. Taking these interactions into account before policy action is a key determinant of arriving at the right policy mix for sustainable urban development. This section discusses two types of policy interactions affecting urban development: i) interactions between policies developed by different jurisdictions; and ii) interactions between sectoral policies, e.g. between land-use and transport policies. It then highlights the need for an integrated approach to policy-making to control urban sprawl and mitigate its consequences.

Interactions between policies developed by different jurisdictions

The consequences of urban sprawl would ideally be tackled with policies at the urban area level. However, this is rarely the case in practice for two reasons. First, urban areas are seldom defined within the boundaries of a single jurisdiction. They usually encompass multiple jurisdictions which have the authority to develop and implement policies within their own administrative boundaries. Despite their good intentions, unilateral policies to control urban sprawl by a certain jurisdiction are likely to be ineffective as population growth and development may shift to neighbouring jurisdictions in the same urban area. Second, urban areas are not static structures; they are dynamic organisms whose boundaries evolve over time. The boundaries of administrative powers, on the other hand, do not usually change in a timely manner with the evolution of urban development.

Decentralised governance systems – where local governments have the power to set land-use policies within their own jurisdiction – have been shown to provide implicit incentives for urban sprawl. In contrast, more centralised governance systems – where land-use policy is set at the national, regional or state level – are more likely to lead to more compact urban development, but also to insufficient supply of housing (Blöchliger et al., 2017).

Two main reasons can explain the influence of decentralised systems on urban sprawl. First, developers can circumvent stringent local land-use policies by shifting to nearby jurisdictions with laxer policy frameworks. This induces leapfrog development, which can result in a more sprawled urban area (Blöchliger et al., 2017; Glaeser and Kahn, 2004). Second, in more decentralised settings, homeowners may have the power to influence local land-use policies for their benefit. For example, homeowners have incentives to lobby for more stringent zoning rules which will attract high-income households in their neighbourhood and increase the prices of their dwellings (a process which is also known as fiscal zoning). Such ordinances are likely to induce low-density urban development and social segregation (Blöchliger et al., 2017; Hilber and Robert-Nicoud, 2013).

In general, the alignment of policies implemented by neighbouring local authorities can be key for controlling urban sprawl and tackling its consequences. Each urban area has a unique spatial and institutional configuration, but it is important that governments at higher levels, such as national and regional/state governments, have a complete understanding of the environmental and economic implications of that configuration. In some urban areas, national and/or regional authorities have endorsed the establishment of formal clusters of neighbouring local governments, who have the overall responsibility for spatial planning and the provision of public services in the urban area. This could also be something worth considering in the case of other cities. Under specific circumstances, it may also be meaningful for higher-tier governments to consider the compilation of national or regional *urban policy frameworks* with clear environmental and economic objectives. Regardless of the governance system, guidance from national or regional authorities can significantly contribute to the development of more sustainable urban policies.

At the same time, it is important that national, regional and local policies to control urban sprawl and mitigate its effects are better aligned. Several policy instruments controlled by national or regional governments often trigger similar behavioural responses to those induced by instruments controlled by local authorities. Even worse, the efficacy of policies developed by an authority may be undermined by policies implemented by authorities at other levels of government. Policies designed by different government levels usually serve very diverse objectives, but their design could be reconsidered to discourage undesirable urban development patterns.

Interactions between sectoral policies

The incentives provided by land-use, transport and environmental policies may reinforce or offset each other. Effective long-term urban planning implies that interactions between sectoral policies are clearly understood and taken into account, but sectoral policy often considers instruments in isolation from the others. For example, the role of massive investments in urban highways in generating incentives for low-density development has, in many cases, been persistently neglected by policy makers in OECD countries. Similarly, urban planning policies have neglected the pressures they may impose on the transport system. These pressures should be reflected in appropriate urban planning policy instruments.

An integrated approach towards more sustainable urban development

It is important that policy makers undertake the challenging task of developing integrated solutions to control the various manifestations of urban sprawl and mitigate its effects. An integrated approach should be followed at all stages of policy-making: identification of the problem that needs to be tackled by policy intervention, policy design, implementation and evaluation. This integrated approach is at the heart of concepts which have often been used as paradigms for future urban development, such as the *compact city* or the *smart city*. A relatively more concrete integrated approach that cities could be inspired from is *transit-oriented development*.

Compact, high-density, mixed-use development around major transport nodes may be an answer to multiple economic and environmental challenges emerging in urban areas. Transit-oriented development, hereafter TOD, can significantly reduce car dependency, make the public transport system and other key points of interest accessible to everyone, sharply decrease the costs of the provision of public services, protect natural amenities and periurban ecosystems, increase proximity to open spaces, reduce population exposure to air pollution and mitigate the problem of affordable housing.

Instruments that can be used to promote TOD, and are critical for its effectiveness in achieving the objectives above, include minimum height restrictions in undeveloped periurban areas to be conceded for future development, appropriate pricing of car use (including pricing for congestion, parking and the environmental costs of car use), measures to prioritise densification around key nodes of the existing public transport network, and a shift of investments from roads to urban public transport infrastructure.

5.4. Conclusions

Sprawling urban development patterns have multiple *private* benefits, which should, however, be weighed against their *social* costs. Market forces fail to take these social costs into account and, thus, policy intervention is in many cases necessary to direct urban development to more sustainable patterns. Acknowledging that developing policies to this end is very challenging and highly context-specific, the chapter discussed a number of land-use, transport and fiscal policy reforms that can be relevant in certain urban settings.

The chapter also highlighted the need for an integrated policy approach to understanding the issues at stake and developing solutions to address them. This integrated approach would also involve identifying and taking into account relevant policy interactions, both between sectoral policies and between policies implemented by different jurisdictions, before making relevant decisions. In any case, policy development should be based on a mix of instruments which would provide both immediate remedies to the consequences of harmful development patterns and long-term solutions to unsustainable urban expansion. Policy instruments targeted to greening urban transport can be particularly effective in the short run, while land-use policy reforms can pay off in the longer run.

Notes

1. Periodical reviews of greenbelts may also be useful for another reason. As congestible local public goods, the total value of the amenity they provide increases with the total number of people enjoying it. However, many of the ecosystem and recreational services provided by greenbelts are prone to congestion, and accessibility to the greenbelt itself will decrease with an increased number of users. Thus, even though the greenbelt might have been able to provide a close to optimal level of ecosystem and recreational services at its inception, it is unlikely that it will keep doing so following significant population and economic growth (Lee and Linneman, 1998).
2. For example, landowners in German and Korean urban areas were not compensated for the loss of their development rights when their properties were included in a greenbelt (Lee, 1999; Siedentop et al., 2016). In 1998, however, about 21 years after the establishment of the first greenbelt in Korea, a Constitutional Court decision ruled that those who lost development rights due to the greenbelt regulation should be compensated (Bengston and Youn, 2006; Cho, 2002).
3. Brueckner and Kim's (2003) analysis of stylised monocentric city models shows that the direction of the effect of property taxes on urban density *inter alia* depends on the magnitude of the elasticity of substitution between housing and other goods. A higher elasticity implies a lower likelihood of property taxes encouraging low-density development.
4. Empirical work in this area has been limited to the context of the United States and is inconclusive. On the one hand, the cross-sectional analysis of Song and Zenou (2006) shows that the average *statutory* property tax rate has a negative effect on the size of the urban area, for a given population size. On the other hand, the panel data analysis of *effective* property tax rates of Wassmer (2016) reveals an effect in the opposite direction.
5. The effectiveness of split-rate property taxes in increasing density is also supported by empirical evidence on the United States. In their study of urban areas in Pennsylvania, Banzhaf and Lavery (2010) show that split-rate property taxation leads to higher urban densities, both in terms of structures and (to a lesser and more uncertain extent) population.
6. The majority of TDR programmes are established in areas with maximum density limits.
7. TDR programmes have been popular in the United States but have recently been implemented also in other OECD countries, including Australia, Italy and, although in a different context, the Netherlands (Harman, Pruetz, and Houston, 2015; Janssen-Jansen, 2008; Micelli, 2002).
8. In practice, this might be a challenging task, as it implies that policymakers have complete information about the external benefits of open space conservation and the external costs of development (Mills, 1980).
9. The demand for TDRs is in the majority of cases lower than that anticipated by planning agencies (McConnell and Walls, 2009).
10. Market activity can be facilitated and transaction costs can be reduced with the help of TDR banks, i.e. entities officially accredited by local authorities to purchase and resell TDRs. TDR banks can further stabilise the market and alleviate sellers' concerns over finding purchasers for their TDRs in the short term (Pruetz and Standridge, 2008).
11. Empirical evidence of the effects of road pricing schemes or parking policy reforms (see relevant section below) on urban form are generally absent from the literature. An important reason for this is probably that the majority of road pricing schemes and parking policy reforms were introduced rather recently, therefore not allowing an empirical investigation of their effects on long-term changes in urban development patterns.
12. As already discussed, road pricing is a more efficient instrument to price the external costs of air emissions from car use.
13. The impact of on-street parking underpricing on the total private costs of trips is uncertain, as it depends on the time and other costs incurred in cruising to find a parking space.
14. This is also in line with the three pillars of the Aarhus convention on access to information, public participation in decision-making and justice in environmental matters (UNECE, 1998).

References

Amati, M. (2016), "Green Belts: A Twentieth-century Planning Experiment", in Amati M. (Ed.), *Urban Green Belts in the Twenty-first Century*, Routledge, Abingdon, UK.

Amati, M. and M. Yokohari (2006), "Temporal changes and local variations in the functions of London's green belt", *Landscape and Urban Planning*, Vol. 75/1, pp. 125-142.

Anas, A. and R. Lindsey (2011), "Reducing Urban Road Transportation Externalities: Road Pricing in Theory and in Practice", *Review of Environmental Economics and Policy*, Vol. 5/1, pp. 66-88.

Anderson, J.E. (1993), "Use-Value Property Tax Assessment: Effects on Land Development", *Land Economics*, Vol. 69/3, pp. 263-269.

Bae, C.-H.C. and M.-J. Jun (2003), "Counterfactual Planning", *Journal of Planning Education and Research*, Vol. 22/4, pp. 374-383.

Ball, M. et al. (2014), "Urban growth boundaries and their impact on land prices", *Environment and Planning A*, Vol. 46/12, pp. 3010-3026.

Banzhaf, H.S. and N. Lavery (2010), "Can the land tax help curb urban sprawl? Evidence from growth patterns in Pennsylvania", *Journal of Urban Economics*, Vol. 67/2, 169-179.

Bengston, D.N., J.O. Fletcher and K.C. Nelson (2004), "Public policies for managing urban growth and protecting open space: policy instruments and lessons learned in the United States", *Landscape and Urban Planning*, Vol. 69/2, pp. 271-286.

Bengston, D.N. and Y.-C. Youn (2006), "Urban containment policies and the protection of natural areas: The case of Seoul's greenbelt", *Ecology and Society*, Vol. 11/1, pp. 3.

Bertaud, A. and J.K. Brueckner (2005), "Analyzing building-height restrictions: Predicted impacts and welfare costs", *Regional Science and Urban Economics*, Vol. 35/2, pp. 109-125.

Bird, R.M. and E. Slack (2004), "Land and property taxation in 25 countries: A comparative review", in Bird, R.M. and E. Slack (eds), *International Handbook of Land and Property Taxation*, Edward Elgar, Cheltenham, UK, and Northampton, MA, USA.

Blöchliger, H., et al. (2017), "Local taxation, land use regulation, and land use: A survey of the evidence", *OECD Economics Department Working Papers*, No. 1375, OECD Publishing, Paris, *http://dx.doi.org/10.1787/52da7c6a-en*.

Brandt, N. (2014), "Greening the Property Tax", *OECD Working Papers on Fiscal Federalism*, No. 17, OECD Publishing, Paris, *http://dx.doi.org/10.1787/5jz5pzw9mwzn-en*.

Brueckner, J.K. and H.-A. Kim (2003), "Urban Sprawl and the Property Tax", *International Tax and Public Finance*, Vol. 10/1, pp. 5-23.

Brueckner, J.K. and K.S. Sridhar (2012), "Measuring welfare gains from relaxation of land-use restrictions: The case of India's building-height limits", *Regional Science and Urban Economics*, Vol. 42/6, pp. 1061-1067.

Caldera Sánchez, A. and Å. Johansson (2011), "The Price Responsiveness of Housing Supply in OECD Countries", *OECD Economics Department Working Papers*, No. 837, OECD Publishing, Paris, *http://dx.doi.org/10.1787/5kgk9qhrnn33-en*.

Cho, C.-J. (2002), "The Korean growth-management programs: Issues, problems and possible reforms", *Land Use Policy*, Vol. 19/1, pp. 13-27.

Cohen, J.P. and C.C. Coughlin (2005), "An Introduction to Two-Rate Taxation of Land and Buildings", *Federal Reserve Bank of St. Louis Review*, Vol. 87/3, pp. 359-374.

Cutter, W.B. and S.F. Franco (2012), "Do parking requirements significantly increase the area dedicated to parking? A test of the effect of parking requirements values in Los Angeles County", *Transportation Research Part A: Policy and Practice*, Vol. 46/6, pp. 901-925.

De Groote, J., J.N. van Ommeren and H.R.A. Koster, (2016), "Car ownership and residential parking subsidies: Evidence from Amsterdam", *Economics of Transportation*, Vol. 6, pp. 25-37.

Eliasson, J. et al. (2009), "The Stockholm congestion-charging trial 2006: Overview of effects", *Transportation Research Part A: Policy and Practice*, Vol. 43/3, pp. 240-250.

Ermini, B. and R. Santolini (2016), "Urban sprawl and property tax of a city's core and suburbs: Evidence from Italy", *Regional Studies*, Vol. 51/9, pp. 1374-1386.

Fischel, W.A. (2001), "Why are there NIMBYs?", *Land Economics*, Vol. 77/1, pp. 144-152.

Garcia-López, M.-Á., A. Holl and E. Viladecans-Marsal (2015), "Suburbanization and highways in Spain when the Romans and the Bourbons still shape its cities", *Journal of Urban Economics*, Vol. 85, pp. 52-67.

Garcia-López, M.-Á., A. Solé-Ollé and E. Viladecans-Marsal (2015), "Does zoning follow highways?", *Regional Science and Urban Economics*, Vol. 53, pp. 148-155.

Gennaio, M.-P., A.M. Hersperger and M. Bürgi (2009), "Containing urban sprawl – Evaluating effectiveness of urban growth boundaries set by the Swiss Land Use Plan", *Land Use Policy*, Vol. 26/2, pp. 224-232.

George, H. (1879), *Progress and Poverty: An Inquiry into the Cause of Industrial Depressions and of Increase of Want with Increase of Wealth: The Remedy*, Doubleday, Page & Co, Garden City, NY.

Gihring, T.A. (1999), "Incentive property taxation: A potential tool for urban growth management", *Journal of the American Planning Association*, Vol. 65/1, pp. 62-79.

Glaeser, E.L. and M.E. Kahn (2004), "Sprawl and urban growth", in Henderson, V. and J.-F. Thisse (Eds.), *Handbook of Regional and Urban Economics, Vol. 4, Cities and Geography*, Elsevier, Amsterdam, pp. 2481-2527.

Guo, Z. (2013), "Does residential parking supply affect household car ownership? The case of New York City", *Journal of Transport Geography*, Vol. 26, pp. 18-28.

Harding, M. (2014), "The Diesel Differential: Differences in the Tax Treatment of Gasoline and Diesel for Road Use", *OECD Taxation Working Papers*, No. 21, OECD Publishing, Paris, *http://dx.doi.org/10.1787/5jz14cd7hk6b-en*.

Harman, B.P., R. Pruetz and P. Houston (2015), "Tradeable development rights to protect peri-urban areas: Lessons from the United States and observations on Australian practice", *Journal of Environmental Planning and Management*, Vol. 58/2, pp. 357-381.

Hilber, C.A.L. and F. Robert-Nicoud (2013), "On the origins of land use regulations: Theory and evidence from US metro areas", *Journal of Urban Economics*, Vol. 75, pp. 29-43.

Ihlanfeldt, K.R. (2007), "The effect of land use regulation on housing and land prices", *Journal of Urban Economics*, Vol. 61/3, pp. 420-435.

Inci, E. (2015), "A review of the economics of parking", *Economics of Transportation*, Vol. 4/1-2, pp. 50-63.

Janssen-Jansen, L.B. (2008), "Space for Space, a transferable development rights initiative for changing the Dutch landscape", *Landscape and Urban Planning*, Vol. 87/3, pp. 192-200.

Juergensmeyer, J.C. and T. Roberts (2013), *Land Use Planning and Development Regulation Law*, Third Edition, Hornbook Series, West Academic, St. Paul, MN.

Jun, M.-J. (2004), "The effects of Portland's urban growth boundary on urban development patterns and commuting", *Urban Studies*, Vol. 41/7, pp. 1333-1348.

Lee, C.-M. (1999), "An intertemporal efficiency test of a greenbelt: Assessing the economic impacts of Seoul's greenbelt", *Journal of Planning Education and Research*, Vol. 19/1, pp. 41-52.

Lee, C.-M. and P. Linneman (1998), "Dynamics of the greenbelt amenity effect on the land market – The case of Seoul's greenbelt", *Real Estate Economics*, Vol. 26/1, pp. 107-129.

Levinson, A. (1997), "Why oppose TDRs? Transferable development rights can increase overall development", *Regional Science and Urban Economics*, Vol. 27/3, pp. 283-296.

Li, F. and Z. Guo (2014), "Do parking standards matter? Evaluating the London parking reform with a matched-pair approach", *Transportation Research Part A: Policy and Practice*, Vol. 67, pp. 352-365.

Manville, M. (2013), "Parking requirements and housing development: Regulation and reform in Los Angeles", *Journal of the American Planning Association*, Vol. 79/1, pp. 49-66.

McCarthy, L. (2002), "The brownfield dual land-use policy challenge: Reducing barriers to private redevelopment while connecting reuse to broader community goals", *Land Use Policy*, Vol. 19/4, pp. 287-296.

McConnell, V. and M. Walls (2009), "Policy Monitor: U.S. Experience with Transferable Development Rights", *Review of Environmental Economics and Policy*, Vol. 3/2, pp. 288-303.

Micelli, E. (2002), "Development rights markets to manage urban plans in Italy", *Urban Studies*, Vol. 39/1, pp. 141-154.

Mills, D.E. (1980), "Transferable development rights markets", *Journal of Urban Economics*, Vol. 7/1, pp. 63-74.

Mirrlees et al. (2011), "The Taxation of Land and Property", in Mirrlees et al. (ed), *Tax by Design: The Mirrlees Review*, Oxford University Press, Oxford.

Mun, S.I., K.J. Konishi and K. Yoshikawa (2005), "Optimal cordon pricing in a non-monocentric city", *Transportation Research Part A: Policy and Practice*, Vol. 39/7, pp. 723-736.

Mun, S.I., K.J. Konishi and K. Yoshikawa (2003), "Optimal cordon pricing", *Journal of Urban Economics*, Vol. 54/1, pp. 21-38.

Parry, I.W. and A. Bento (2001), "Revenue recycling and the welfare effects of road pricing", *The Scandinavian Journal of Economics*, Vol. 103/4, pp. 645-671.

Pierce, G. and D.C. Shoup (2013), "Getting the prices right: An evaluation of pricing parking by demand in San Francisco", *Journal of the American Planning Association*, Vol. 79/1, pp. 67-81.

Pruetz, R. and N. Standridge (2008), "What makes transfer of development rights work? Success factors from research and practice", *Journal of the American Planning Association*, Vol. 75/1, pp. 78-87.

Schrank, D., B. Eisele and T. Lomax (2012), *TTI's 2012 Urban Mobility Report*, Texas A&M Transportation Institute, The Texas A&M University System, College Station, TX.

Schuetz, J. (2009), "No renters in my suburban backyard: Land use regulation and rental housing", *Journal of Policy Analysis and Management*, Vol. 28/2, pp. 296-320.

Shoup, D.C. (1999a), "The trouble with minimum parking requirements", *Transportation Research Part A: Policy and Practice*, Vol. 33/7, pp. 549-574.

Shoup, D.C. (1999b), "In Lieu of Required Parking", *Journal of Planning Education and Research*, Vol. 18/4, pp. 307-320.

Siedentop, S., S. Fina and A. Krehl (2016), "Greenbelts in Germany's regional plans – An effective growth management policy?", *Landscape and Urban Planning*, Vol. 145, pp. 71-82.

Silva, E. and R. Acheampong (2015), "Developing an Inventory and Typology of Land-Use Planning Systems and Policy Instruments in OECD Countries", *OECD Environment Working Papers*, No. 94, OECD Publishing, Paris, *http://dx.doi.org/10.1787/5jrp6wgxp09s-en*.

Small, K.A. and S. Song (1994), "Population and employment densities: Structure and change", *Journal of Urban Economics*, Vol. 36/3, pp. 292-313.

Song, Y. and Y. Zenou (2009), "How do differences in property taxes within cities affect urban sprawl?", *Journal of Regional Science*, Vol. 49/5, pp. 801-831.

Song, Y. and Y. Zenou (2006), "Property tax and urban sprawl: Theory and implications for US cities", *Journal of Urban Economics*, Vol. 60/3, pp. 519-534.

Su, Q. and J.S. DeSalvo (2008), "The effect of transportation subsidies on urban sprawl", *Journal of Regional Science*, Vol. 48/3, pp. 567-594.

Taylor, J., C. Paine and J. FitzGibbon (1995), "From greenbelt to greenways: Four Canadian case studies", *Landscape and Urban Planning*, Vol. 33/1-3, pp. 47-64.

Tikoudis, I., E.T. Verhoef and J.N. van Ommeren (2015), "On revenue recycling and the welfare effects of second-best congestion pricing in a monocentric city", *Journal of Urban Economics*, Vol. 89, pp. 32-47.

United Nations (2015), *Transforming our World: The 2030 Agenda for Sustainable Development*, Resolution adopted by the General Assembly on 25 September 2015. A/RES/70/1.

UNECE (1998), *Convention on Access to Information, Public Participation in Decision-making and Access to Justice in Environmental Matters*, Aarhus, Denmark, 25 June.

United States Environmental Protection Agency (2017), Brownfield Overview and Definition. Retrieved from: www.epa.gov/brownfields/brownfield-overview-and-definition (accessed 3 March 2017),

Verhoef, E.T. (2005), "Second-best congestion pricing schemes in the monocentric city", *Journal of Urban Economics*, Vol. 58/3, pp. 367-388.

Vickrey, W.S. (1996), "Simplification, Progression and a Level Playing Field", *Columbia University Discussion Paper Series*, No. 9596-5, New York, NY.

Vickrey, W.S. (1954), "The economizing of curb parking space", *Traffic Engineering*, Vol. 25/2, pp. 62-67.

Vyn, R.J. (2012), "Examining for Evidence of the Leapfrog Effect in the Context of Strict Agricultural Zoning", *Land Economics*, Vol. 88/3, pp. 457-477.

Wassmer, R.W. (2016), "Further empirical evidence on residential property taxation and the occurrence of urban sprawl", *Regional Science and Urban Economics*, Vol. 61, pp. 73-85.

Weinberger, R. (2012), "Death by a thousand curb-cuts: Evidence on the effect of minimum parking requirements on the choice to drive", *Transport Policy*, Vol. 20, pp. 93-102.

Willson, R.W. (1995), "Suburban parking requirements: A tacit policy for automobile use and sprawl", *Journal of the American Planning Association*, Vol. 61/1, pp. 29-42.

ORGANISATION FOR ECONOMIC CO-OPERATION AND DEVELOPMENT

The OECD is a unique forum where governments work together to address the economic, social and environmental challenges of globalisation. The OECD is also at the forefront of efforts to understand and to help governments respond to new developments and concerns, such as corporate governance, the information economy and the challenges of an ageing population. The Organisation provides a setting where governments can compare policy experiences, seek answers to common problems, identify good practice and work to co-ordinate domestic and international policies.

The OECD member countries are: Australia, Austria, Belgium, Canada, Chile, the Czech Republic, Denmark, Estonia, Finland, France, Germany, Greece, Hungary, Iceland, Ireland, Israel, Italy, Japan, Korea, Latvia, Luxembourg, Mexico, the Netherlands, New Zealand, Norway, Poland, Portugal, the Slovak Republic, Slovenia, Spain, Sweden, Switzerland, Turkey, the United Kingdom and the United States. The European Union takes part in the work of the OECD.

OECD Publishing disseminates widely the results of the Organisation's statistics gathering and research on economic, social and environmental issues, as well as the conventions, guidelines and standards agreed by its members.

OECD PUBLISHING, 2, rue André-Pascal, 75775 PARIS CEDEX 16
(97 2017 73 1 P) ISBN 978-92-64-18982-9 – 2018

www.ingramcontent.com/pod-product-compliance
Lightning Source LLC
Chambersburg PA
CBHW061215240926
51846CB00006B/1236